Working with India

Wolfgang Messner

Working with India

The Softer Aspects of a
Successful Collaboration with the
Indian IT & BPO Industry

 Springer

Dr. Wolfgang Messner
wolfgang.messner@capgemini.com
wolfgang.messner@gmail.com

ISBN: 978-3-642-10033-8   e-ISBN: 978-3-540-89078-2

ACM Computing Classification (1998): K.6, K.4

© Coverphoto by Wolfgang Messner

Cover design: KünkelLopka, Heidelberg

Printed on acid-free paper

5 4 3 2 1 0

springer.com

Foreword from Capgemini

Offshoring to India creates the opportunity to allocate resources in more cost-effective ways, achieve performance and quality improvements through industrialization, and thus realize a number of competitive advantages.

Enhancing the level of quality delivered depends on the way collaboration is organized as well as on the level of expertise in setting-up and running the project, in preparing and transforming the organization, and in factoring in cultural differences. The impact of culture is less measurable than differences in cost rates or effort estimations. Consequently, the cultural impact is often underestimated and it does not stay on the leadership radar.

India is a mature nation for offering offshore services. Its IT and BPO industry directly employs more than 2.0 million people with a growing trend. However, many people in the Western world still see India as a country where people live in extreme poverty and the oriental magic of the unknown prevails. This contrast does not really promote confidence and faith in an economically successful collaboration with India.

This book complements offshoring as a strategic instrument and is a great start on the journey of cultural appreciation. We are confident that it will provide important insights for people involved in offshoring IT development, maintenance, and BPO business to India.

Salil Parekh
CEO
Capgemini India SBU

Baru Rao
Deputy CEO
Capgemini India SBU

Foreword from SIETAR India

I have the pleasure of watching this book emerge; not just from the wings. As a part of Capgemini's Rightshore® program, Wolfgang Messner and I have been engaged in a series of trainings across Europe and India. This book was born out of a need that became evident during those trainings for a researched 'ready reckoner' on collaborating with India.

As a professional body of intercultural trainers, educationists, and researchers, SIETAR India welcomes all efforts that help to consolidate the collective learning in this field, raise awareness for the importance of this learning and emphasize the need for a systematic approach to imparting this abstract learning.

Readers have been long missing a single book on India that describes the merits of being a good offshore destination, sheds light on possible challenges in collaborating with the country, and also provides solutions for the same. I am pleased to note that this book far exceeds being just the much awaited comprehensive reference primer on doing business with India.

Given Wolfgang Messner's experience at work coupled with the insider's view that he has gained through his marriage to an Indian, his approach to handling the communication gaps with Indians are hands-on and facilitate collaboration.

This book will be an excellent resource for a guided and systematic journey in to the Indian offshoring landscape.

On behalf of SIETAR India, I thank Wolfgang Messner for his efforts to facilitate a better understanding of Indian work culture and wish him all success.

Sreemathi Ramnath
President
SIETAR India
Society for Intercultural Education
Training and Research

Preface

Most wealthy countries in the Western hemisphere are moving away from mass manufacturing and specialize in the services and knowledge industry while leaving the low-skill industries to the poorer countries in the developing world. However, India does not fall into this plan.

Today, the country is one of the fastest growing economies in the world and a leading force in the global services revolution. Its importance in the world of information technology (IT) and business process outsourcing (BPO) is growing; few people can afford to ignore the contribution of Indian software engineers, researchers, and service center agents in their projects and companies.

To be able to comprehend the scale of opportunities, it is necessary to experience India, understand the dramatic transformation of its IT and BPO industry in recent years, and get a hold of the current situation in order to shape the future. However, there is also a revolution taking place at other levels, namely in terms of attitudes and understanding. Here, we are still at a very early stage. From an intercultural perspective, we need to understand how things really work in India to benefit from the numerous business advantages the country has to offer.

Target Audience

This book is designed for managers, project leaders, and offshore coordinators who work together with Indians, either while in an office somewhere in the Western world, on a business trip to India, or on a long-term expatriate delegation to India. It is also a resource for business mangers and company strategists seeking to understand what is behind the headlines that the India IT & BPO business so frequently creates.

Content and Structure of this Book

The book opens with a description of cultural dimensions that help to break down culturally driven matters. It provides background information about India as a country and a social system. Examining the development and current status of India's IT and BPO industry, it moves on to describe the dynamics of its work-force. The book then provides practical information on how to communicate, negotiate, and interact with Indian employees and intelligently utilize expatriates. It closes by formulating recommendations for a more effective collaboration.

The chapters of this book build on each other but do not demand reading in a linear fashion. The book allows you to browse, jump, or hunt for the chapters that are most relevant to you. It is academically well researched, yet also represents an account of my personal India experience.

- *Chapter 1, Why Intercultural Competency?* reasons that in the flat world of globalization, culture plays a particularly prominent role. It breaks down the matters that are primarily driven by culture into cultural dimensions and thereby sensitizes readers for working and communicating outside their comfort zones, i.e. outside their own familiar and trusted cultures. It shows how individuals and organizations can master the path to a better understanding of their Indian IT and BPO partners.

- *Chapter 2, India – the Country* is about the Indian subcontinent, its geography, history, government, and economy.
- *Chapter 3, The Society and Culture in India* highlights the multiple influences that form the Indian society and the cultural framework of India's IT engineers and service center agents.
- *Chapter 4, India's IT & BPO Industry* provides an overview of the development and current state of India's IT and BPO industry, scrutinizes the phenomena of overheating, examines country risk factors, and looks at the implications for managing the business continuity of companies in India.
- *Chapter 5, Human Resources* describes the dynamics of human resource management in India and concentrates on combating attrition. The chapter further focuses on the aspects of organizational hierarchy, leadership, management, and provides a three-dimensional typology of employees.
- *Chapter 6, Interactions with India* highlights the peculiarities of Indian English and illustrates the culture shock Westerners experience when they work together with Indians or travel to India for the first time. This is followed by practical advice on intercultural interaction and communication in meetings, negotiations, via emails, and on the telephone; a short overview on business and social etiquette rounds off the chapter.
- *Chapter 7, Conducting Offshore Projects* is about managing from a distance, initiating offshore projects, monitoring work progress, and transitioning from IT development to maintenance.
- *Chapter 8, Use of Expatriates* is a note on intelligent ways of utilizing expatriates, both from the Western world in India and vice versa.
- *Chapter 9, Recommendations for Effective Collaboration* closes the book by proposing five behavior changes that facilitate a more effective collaboration with the Indian IT & BPO industry.

Many intercultural challenges and hurdles lie in the way of a successful partnership with India. However, the opportunities for effectively utilizing global delivery models are great. I sincerely hope this book and my experience narrated herein will help you in your collaboration with the Indian IT and BPO industries.

Enjoy the book!

Wolfgang Messner

Acknowledgements

I got to know the life and the business culture in India over a number of years. Some I spent as an expatriate project manager with Deutsche Software India Pvt. Ltd., a then fully owned subsidiary of Deutsche Bank AG, some as a visiting faculty at the Indian Institute of Management Bangalore (IIM-B), and I am now on deputation to Capgemini India as director. I would like to thank all unnamed friends, colleagues, and business partners who have helped me to gain a deep insight into the Indian mentality and drivers of its industry. Most of my experience comes from directly interacting with employees in India across all hierarchical levels.

I have met my wife Pratibha in India and I thank her, her family, and friends for a great reception in this country. She started her career as a software engineer in the Indian IT industry; she then moved on to international assignments in Germany, Switzerland, and the USA. After an MBA degree in the UK, she changed to the risk function and now heads operational risk management for an international bank in India. I had many discussions with her and I appreciate her most valuable feedback from a native Indian point of view, as it has truly enriched the book. Without her support, this book would not have been possible.

At Capgemini my special gratitude goes to Holger Martens for providing both the necessary management support for our India Rightshore® initiative as well as for being a great mentor and coach. Anja Hendel (now with Celesio AG) and Frank Thun are wonderful colleagues; together we edited the earlier *Rightshore!* handbook on Capgemini's mature concept for a global delivery strategy.

With Sreemathi Ramnath, President of SIETAR India, I have conducted many intercultural communication skill workshops for Capgemini in Europe – and also at the other end for our Indian colleagues at Capgemini India; interacting with her has very much enriched my view on India.

Oliver Franiel of Capgemini has once more done a great job at proof-reading the book and enhancing the linguistic quality. A special thanks goes to Ralf Gerstner at Springer for accompanying the editing and production process of this book.

Table of Contents

1 Why Intercultural Competency?

Does culture still matter in a 'flat' world? In a world where the computer and the Internet are omnipresent, where far apart continents are interlinked through secure VPN connections, where colleagues in India, Australia, the USA, and in several countries in Europe look at the same computer screen at the same time and discuss issues over IP telephony? The world has become "a global Web-enabled playing field that allows for multiple forms of collaboration – the sharing of knowledge and work – in real time, without regard to geography, distance, or in the near future, even language".[1] This is what the American columnist Thomas Friedman connotes when he talks about a 'flat' world. But is it a reality that the global Web is seamlessly bringing together colleagues from far apart nations who then collaborate easily and without disturbance?

1.1 Definition of Culture

A book on intercultural communication should first begin with a definition of culture. However, there is a seemingly endless number of definitions by learned researchers to choose from.[2]

Let us start with a quote from anthropologist Edward T. Hall's well-known book on 'Beyond Culture' dating back to 1976: "Culture is man's medium; there is not one aspect of human life that is not touched and altered by culture. This means personality, how people express themselves [...], the way they think, how they move, how problems are solved, how their cities are planned and laid out, how transportation systems function and are organized, as well as how economic and government systems are put together and function."[3]

Various anthropologists highlight different aspects of culture in their definitions; three characteristics are common:

- Culture is not innate but learned
- The various facets of culture are interrelated
- Culture is shared and thus defines the boundaries of different groups.

Culture consists of various levels. Only a small part of observational behavior (the 'doing') is visible. However, most of it is invisible and below the surface. This view of culture is embodied in the popular *iceberg model* (Figure 1-1). The parts below the waterline encompass the cognitive level (the 'thinking') and the emotional level ('the feeling'). When one first arrives in a foreign culture, one starts at the tip of the iceberg (see chapter 6.2).

---

[1]   [Friedman 2005, p. 176]
[2]   Cf. [Jones 2007, p. 2]
[3]   [Hall 1976, p. 16-17]

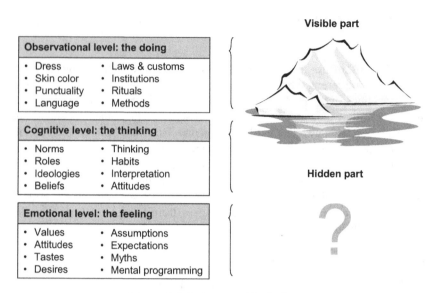

Figure 1-1. Iceberg model of culture

The ingredients of culture are acquired from birth and later influenced by family, school, religion, workplace, friends, television, written media, and many other sources:[4]

- Learning of values (dominant beliefs and attitudes)
- Partaking in rituals (collective activities)
- Modeling against heroes (role models)
- Understanding of symbols (myths, legends, dress, jargon, lingo, etc.).

However, the personalities of individuals sit on top of culture and are just as important. It is no good trying to explain all behaviors with cultural differences alone.

1.2   Research on Intercultural Dimensions

Early Works

Already in 1954 two Americans, the sociologist Alex Inkeles and the psychologist Daniel Levinson, published a broad survey of the literature on national culture. They suggested issues that qualify as common basic problems worldwide. In 1967, Bartels related the importance of culture, illustrating the concept in decision-making and business ethics; he identified several criteria for the identification of cultural differences.[5]

---

[4] Cf. [Jones 2007, p. 3]
[5] Cf. [Bartels 1967; Jones 2007, p. 2]

Hofstede's Cultural Dimensions

In the 1980s, Geert Hofstede studied a large body of survey data about the values of people in more than fifty countries around the world working in the local subsidiaries of a multi-national corporation.[6] He stresses that "Culture is more often a source of conflict than of synergy. Cultural differences are a nuisance at best and often a disaster."[7] Edward T. Hall had even gone further by highlighting that "... denying culture and obscuring the effects that it can have on human talents can be as destructive and potentially dangerous as denying evil."[8]

Hofstede's research provided valuable insight into the dynamics of cross-cultural relationships. He devised four dimensions to characterize cross-cultural differences, and later introduced a fifth element.

However, his groundbreaking work did not escape criticism on a number of accounts. It is an attitude-survey which is highly efficient but contended to be not appropriate for studying cultures. It also draws data from a single company only, and the question is how a multi-national corporation may have influenced its employees so that their values no longer reflect aspects of national local cultures. Subsequent research has identified anomalies to Hofstede's findings, e.g. on the level of hierarchy in some societies.[9]

GLOBE Study

Between 1994 and 2004, a team of 170 scholars teamed up to study societal culture, organizational culture, and attributes of effective leadership in 62 cultures. The Global Leadership and Organizational Behavior Effectiveness (GLOBE) study surveyed more than 17,000 middle managers from 950 organizations in the financial services, food processing, and telecommunications industries. It involved 170 co-investigators from the participating countries; the results were published in two books in 2004 and 2007.[10] Based on prior studies and theorizing, a 735 questionnaire item was developed and tested in two pilot studies. These analyses identified eight[11] attributes of cultures.[12] Taken the risk of generalization, they can be considered as cultural dimensions having an effect on the functioning of societies, groups, and individuals:

---

[6]   Cf. [Hofstede/Hofstede 2005, p. 22-25; Jones 2007, p. 3]. The study took place within IBM world-wide during the years 1967 to 1978 and comprised 110,000 questionnaires, from which over 60,000 people responded.

[7]   [Hofstede ---]

[8]   [Hall 1976, p. 7]

[9]   Cf. [Jones 2007, p. 5-6]

[10]   Cf. [House et al. 2004; Chhokar/Brodbeck/House 2007]. For a comparative review of GLOBE and Hofstede see e.g. [Javidan et al. 2006]

[11]   Nine attributes as per [House 2004, p. 11] considering the split of collectivism into institutional and in-group collectivism; this book clubs both dimensions and considers in-group collectivism more relevant for working together with the IT industry in India.

[12]   Cf. [House/Javidan 2004, p. 11]

- Power distance. The degree to which members of an organization or society expect and agree that power should be shared unequally.
- Collectivism. The relationship between the individual and the group described by the degree to which societal and institutional practices encourage and reward collective action.
- Assertiveness. The reflection of beliefs as to whether people should be assertive, aggressive, confrontational, and tough in social relationships.
- Uncertainty avoidance. The extent to which ambiguous situations are threatening to individuals, to which rules and order are preferred, and to which uncertainty is tolerated in society.
- Future orientation. Describes the orientation towards planning and sacrificing instant individual or collective gratification for long-term future rewards.
- Performance orientation. The degree to which an organization or a society encourages and rewards its members for high standards, excellence, and performance improvement.
- Gender egalitarianism. The extent to which an organization or a society minimizes gender role differences while promoting gender equality.
- Humane orientation. Describes if individuals in organizations or societies are encouraged or rewarded for being fair, altruistic, friendly, generous, caring, and generally kind to others.

This chapter details these dimensions and looks at them from an Indian vs. Western cultural viewpoint. The GLOBE study provides indices for these dimensions on a scale of 1 to 7 to compare current perceptions (as-is, practices) of different societies. Another index assesses the societies' perceptions of the ideal (should-be, values). This chapter compares India on both indices, firstly against a sample of offshoring countries (Australia, Austria, Canada,[13] Denmark, Finland, France, Germany,[14] Great Britain, Italy, Japan, Netherlands, Sweden, Switzerland, USA), and secondly against a sample of typical nearshoring or offshoring destinations (Argentina, China, Hungary, Ireland, Israel, Mexico, Philippines, Poland, Portugal, Russia, Slovenia, Spain, Taiwan, Thailand). In addition, major connotations and variations of these constructs are listed at a societal and organizational level; these tables are intended to be used as a guide, showing cultural attributes that tend to form clusters; but societies will always have a mixture of the two extreme sets of attributes.

---

[13] English-speaking part of Canada

[14] The GLOBE study has collected separate indices for the Western and Eastern part of the country, i.e. the former Federal Republic of Germany and the German Democratic Republic (GDR). Eighteen years after reunification, Germany's industry remains concentrated in the Western part of the country, many people have relocated from the East to the West and pursued their professional carrer in the West. Hence the index for Germany (West) appears to be more relevant to the purpose of this book.

Personality vs. Culture – A Word of Caution

Research on cultural dimensions and intercultural communication noticeably encouraged a propensity towards national stereotyping that is very common in international teams involving India.[15] While cultural differences captured by these dimensions explain one part of our way of operating and the impact of culture is still very pronounced, it is also important to understand the unique personality underneath. There are universal values which everyone in the IT industry world-wide expects to get from their work and projects:

- The opportunity for learning, achievement, and career advancement, i.e. to succeed personally.
- To succeed collectively as a team.
- To be treated with respect.

In many situations it is helpful not to think about intercultural differences but to acknowledge a common humanity. The answer to a simple question – 'If I were in the shoes of the Indian programmer or BPO employee, how would I like to be treated?' – will resolve many issues in daily project interaction.

Many national differences are not really cultural at all but reflect economic and political history.[16] A high proportion of people in the so-called developing regions of the world are ambitious, whereas a good set of people in the developed world are a little laid-back and professionally relaxed, simply because they have already accumulated enough wealth to support their retirement.

1.2.1 Power Distance

Definition

Inequality exists in any society; communities accept and endorse authority, difference in power, and status privileges.[17] Societies can be distinguished by the way in which they deal with these inequalities; this can e.g. be measured with the power distance index[18]. The power distance index expresses the extent to which the less powerful members of a society accept that power is distributed unequally.

In high power distance cultures some individuals are perceived to have a higher overall rank, enjoying power that is unquestionable and virtually unattainable by those of lower ranks. In low power distance countries each individual is respected and appreciated for what that person has to offer.[19]

---

[15] Cf. [Bloch/Whiteley 2007, p. xxiv]
[16] Cf. [Bloch/Whitley 2007, p. 59]
[17] Cf. [Carl/Gupta/Javidan 2004, p. 513]
[18] Cf. [Hofstede/Hofstede 2005, p. 39-72]
[19] Cf. [Carl/Gupta/Javidan 2004, p. 518]

There are various sources of power, i.e. answers to the question what gives an individual power or influence over others:[20]

- Coercive power depends on the fear of punishment for non-compliance.
- Reward power is based on positive motivation; rewards are obtained from a powerful person on the basis of good deeds.
- Legitimate power is vested in a person based on the position in a formal hierarchy.
- Expert power is the ability to influence on the basis of expertise.
- Referent power refers to the feeling of oneness with leaders and the desire to identify with them.
- Structural holes arise if subgroups in a society are not fully connected and someone comes to fill the gap in power.

Cultural Characteristics

The root of power distances lies in the upbringing of individuals within the framework of parents and families. This is where the mental software is modeled after the examples set by the elders.

Figure 1-2 shows key differences between small and large power distance societies. In large power distance societies, children are expected to be obedient toward their parents. Respect towards elders is seen as a virtue, and there is also a strong need for dependence and guidance. The educational process at school is teacher-centered; instructors outline the path to be followed. This is continued at the workplace; superiors and subordinates consider themselves as existentially unequal in a hierarchical system: subordinates expect to be told what to do.

In small power distance situations, the goal of education is to let children take control of their own affairs as soon as possible and implant a need for independence in the mental software. Schools are student-centered, and students are expected to find their own path, make uninvited interventions, and ask questions whenever they do not understand or agree with something. The hierarchical system at the workplace is a system of roles established for mere convenience, where roles may be changed as required

Scores and Observations

The left column in Figure 1-3 shows that compared to offshoring countries, India ranks highest in terms of unequal power distribution. Italy and France come closest to India but still show less power distance. The Netherlands and Denmark are on the opposite end of the scale.

---

[20] Cf. [Carl/Gupta/Javidan 2004, p. 514-515] for a classification of power sources with reference to original research

	Small power distance	Large power distance
Society	• Inequalities among people should be minimized • Social relationship should be handled with care • There is interdependence between less and more powerful people • High upward social mobility	• Inequalities among people are expected and desired • Status should be balanced with restraint • Less powerful people should be dependent • Limited upward social mobility
Learning	• Parents treat children as equal and vice versa • Teachers are experts; they expect initiative from students in class • Learning is a two-way communication	• Parents teach children obedience; respect for parents and older relatives is a basic and lifelong virtue • Teachers are gurus who project personal wisdom; they are expected to take initiative in class • Quality of learning depends on teacher's excellence
Organization	• Decentralization of power in companies is popular • Fewer hierarchy levels • Narrow salary range between top and bottom of the organization • Managers rely on their own experience and on subordinates; subordinates expect to be consulted • Subordinate-superior relations are pragmatic • Privileges and status symbols are frowned upon • Information in the company is shared; skill and knowledge are transient and sharable power bases	• Centralization of power in companies is popular • Many hierarchical levels; people expect to be guided and to become managers at an early career stage • Wide salary range between the top and bottom of the organization • Managers rely on their own experience and formal rules; they are unlikely to consult subordinates • Subordinates expect to be told what to do • Subordinate-superior relationships are emotional; there is a strong bonding • Privileges and status symbols are normal and popular • Information in the company is localized

Figure 1-2. Key differences between small and large power distance[21]

Country	Practice (as-is score)	Value (should-be score)	Country	Practice (as-is score)	Value (should-be score)
India	**5.47**	**2.64**	Argentina	5.64	2.33
Italy	5.43	2.47	Thailand	5.63	2.86
France	5.28	2.76	Hungary	5.56	2.49
Germany (West)	5.25	2.54	Russia	5.52	2.62
Great Britain	5.15	2.80	Spain	5.52	2.26
Japan	5.11	2.86	**India**	**5.47**	**2.64**
Austria	4.95	2.44	Philippines	5.44	2.72
Switzerland (GE)	4.90	2.44	Portugal	5.44	2.38
Finland	4.89	2.19	Slovenia	5.33	2.57
USA	4.88	2.85	Mexico	5.22	2.85
Sweden	4.85	2.70	Taiwan	5.18	3.09
Canada (EN)	4.82	2.70	Ireland	5.15	2.71
Australia	4.74	2.78	Poland	5.10	3.12
Netherlands	4.11	2.45	China	5.04	3.10
Denmark	3.89	2.76	Israel	4.73	2.72

Figure 1-3. Power distance index (GLOBE study)[22]

---

[21] Compiled and adapted to IT industry from [Carl/Gupta/Javidan 2004, p. 536; Hofstede/Hofstede 2005, p. 48-70]

[22] Extract from [Carl/Gupta/Javidan 2004, p. 539-540]; higher scores indicate greater power distance on a scale of 1 to 7

Weighing the power distance in India against other offshoring destinations (Figure 1-3, right column), a different picture emerges: Argentina, Thailand, Hungary, Russian, and Spain score higher than India. Ireland, Poland, China, and Israel are at the lower end of the spectrum.

There is a strong negative correlation between the index of societal practice (as-is scores) and value (should-be scores). Societies with a high power distance prefer a more equitable distribution of power compared to societies with low power distance which prefer a less equitable distribution of power. However, in all societies the power distance value index is lower than the as-is score, thus making power distance worldwide the least desirable feature of social practices.[23]

The Indian society and businesses are rather structured and stratified because of three factors:

- The century-old caste system (see chapter 3.1) had laid the basis for the social and economic structuring of the Indian society and has influenced the practice of leadership in India (see chapters 5.2 and 5.3).
- During colonial times the British had used the Indian Civil Service, which was a very hierarchical and formal structure, as an important instrument of governance; an 'Indianized' version of it still exists today.[24]
- Religions and philosophies also influence the acceptance of a higher or lower degree of power distance. Experience and tradition in Confucian and Hindu societies, and the emphasis on hereditary class roles and spiritual leaders in the Hindu, Islamic, and Roman Catholic societies, predispose their members to accept strong power distance. Protestant societies emphasize individual initiatives to realize individual aspirations; their members are more reluctant to acceptant power distance. Buddhist societies aim to bridge social dividers and emphasize a community spirit; they endorse low levels of power distance.[25]

These factors have a widespread impact on the society and the organization of businesses. Seating arrangements and especially the allocation of separate cabins tend to reflect the status of individuals in the organization, but they do not necessarily follow operational requirements. In most organizations the HR and payroll department, which processes confidential information, has to cope with cramped and shared offices due to the low hierarchical status of its employees in the organization. Especially in government offices, work titles are frequently displayed on doors; in the IT industry this is not very common, but employees make a note of mentioning the work title when introducing themselves or other colleagues, e.g. 'This is Ashok Kumar, he is an associate director and heads our testing center of excellence.'

Wealthy families employ full-time domestic help and refer to their household employees as maids or servants. In every village or sector of a city there are

---

[23] [Carl/Gupta/Javidan 2004, p. 539-541]

[24] Cf. [Chhokar 2007, p. 991]

[25] Cf. [Carl/Gupta/Javidan 2004, p. 518]

influential families whose power in various social and business functions is generally understood, accepted, and sought after.

Correlation Between Power Distance and Corruption

Power distance adds to the frequency of corruption. Power corrupts, and excessive power frequently results in the abuse of power[26] as there are less preventive checks and processes in place. One speaks of corruption when people use the power of their position to illegally enrich themselves, buy the collaboration of authorities for private purposes or to get something done. Countries are ranked using the corruption perception index (CPI) that describes the degree to which corruption is perceived to exist among public officials and politicians.[27] Figure 1-4 shows the correlation between the CPI and the power distance index.

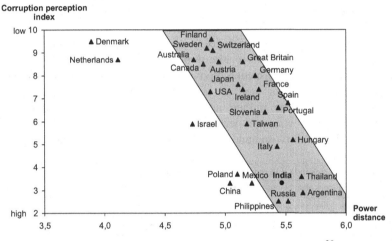

Figure 1-4. Correlation of power distance with corruption[28]

1.2.2   Individualism and Collectivism

Definition

Collectivism relates to societies in which people are integrated into strong groups that protect them in exchange for unquestioned loyalty. Institutional practices at the society level encourage and reward collective action. Individuals express pride, loyalty, and interdependence in their families.

---

[26] Cf. [Carl/Gupta/Javidan 2004, p. 518]

[27] Cf. [Lambsdorff 2007, p. 324]

[28] Power distance index based on Figure 1-3 and corruption perception index based on [Lambsdorff 2007, p. 324-330]

Individualism is the opposite and characterizes societies with loose ties between individuals. Everyone is expected to look after themselves and their immediate family.

Cultural Characteristics

The degree of individualism or collectivism in a society has numerous implications on the structure and processes in organizations; Figure 1-5 offers an overview.

In organizations in collectivist cultures, members view themselves as highly interdependent with the organization, they share the same values, and the organization becomes part of its employees' identity; relationships, duties, and obligations are central in employment decisions. Managers assume their employees to make personal sacrifices in order to fulfill obligations toward the company; in turn, employees would expect the organization to stand by them in hard economic times.[29]

In individualist societies, employees of an organization consider themselves as largely independent;[30] the relationship between employer and employee is conceived as a business transaction. Poor performance on the part of the employee is an accepted reason for contract termination. Employees would be willing to leave the organization if their needs or goals are better served elsewhere. An individual's hard work and performance is instrumental in attaining a bonus payment and there will be an underlying notion of fairness in its calculation.

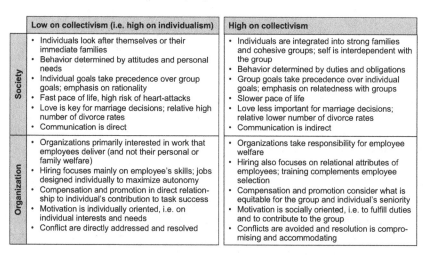

	Low on collectivism (i.e. high on individualism)	High on collectivism
Society	• Individuals look after themselves or their immediate families • Behavior determined by attitudes and personal needs • Individual goals take precedence over group goals; emphasis on rationality • Fast pace of life, high risk of heart-attacks • Love is key for marriage decisions; relative high number of divorce rates • Communication is direct	• Individuals are integrated into strong families and cohesive groups; self is interdependent with the group • Behavior determined by duties and obligations • Group goals take precedence over individual goals; emphasis on relatedness with groups • Slower pace of life • Love less important for marriage decisions; relative lower number of divorce rates • Communication is indirect
Organization	• Organizations primarily interested in work that employees deliver (and not their personal or family welfare) • Hiring focuses mainly on employee's skills; jobs designed individually to maximize autonomy • Compensation and promotion in direct relationship to individual's contribution to task success • Motivation is individually oriented, i.e. on individual interests and needs • Conflict are directly addressed and resolved	• Organizations take responsibility for employee welfare • Hiring also focuses on relational attributes of employees; training complements employee selection • Compensation and promotion consider what is equitable for the group and individual's seniority • Motivation is socially oriented, i.e. to fulfill duties and to contribute to the group • Conflicts are avoided and resolution is compromising and accommodating

Figure 1-5. Key differences between individualism and collectivism[31]

---

[29] Cf. [Gelfand et al. 2004, p. 446-447]

[30] Cf. [Gelfand et al. 2004, p. 446]

[31] Collected from [Gelfand et al. 2004, p. 453-461] and adapted to IT industry.

Scores and Observations

Figure 1-6 shows that India ranks second highest in terms of collectivism on the organizational level compared to other offshoring destinations; the distance to all offshoring countries is very significant. Italy, Austria and Japan rank highest on collectivism among the offshoring countries. But Canada, USA, Australia, England, Finland, Germany, Switzerland, Netherlands, Sweden, and Denmark have very individualistic corporate cultures. As an overall observation, wealthy countries usually score high on individualism.

In all countries with a high individualism index, the general notion is that these countries should practice significantly more collectivism. Interestingly, the should-be score of India then falls into the range of the should-be score of these countries. This downward trend in India is caused by a focus on materialism among the managerial middle classes, which experience competition at an individual level in the workplace on a daily basis.[32] In their values, Indians and Westerners are not so far apart but both are captured in the operational boundaries of their respective organizational practices.

The ideas of collectivism are anchored in the Indian mindset at a very early stage. The family continues to be one of the basic units of Indian society, its members first and foremost depend on support from the family – and later in life, start providing support to family members in need (see chapter 3.2). In dealing with problems and personal crises, the help of family and friends is often sought.[33] In Indian restaurants, starters and dishes are always shared; the concept of

Country	Practice (as-is score)	Value (should-be score)	Country	Practice (as-is score)	Value (should-be score)
India	**5.92**	**5.32**	Philippines	6.36	6.18
Italy	4.94	5.72	**India**	**5.92**	**5.32**
Austria	4.85	5.27	China	5.80	5.09
Japan	4.63	5.26	Mexico	5.71	5.95
France	4.37	5.42	Thailand	5.70	5.76
Canada (EN)	4.26	5.97	Russia	5.63	5.79
USA	4.25	5.77	Taiwan	5.59	5.45
Australia	4.17	5.75	Poland	5.52	5.74
England	4.08	5.55	Portugal	5.51	5.94
Finland	4.07	5.42	Argentina	5.51	6.15
Germany (West)	4.02	5.18	Spain	5.45	5.79
Switzerland (GE)	3.97	4.94	Slovenia	5.43	5.71
Netherlands	3.70	5.17	Hungary	5.25	5.54
Sweden	3.66	6.04	Ireland	5.14	5.74
Denmark	3.53	5.50	Israel	4.70	5.75

Figure 1-6. Collectivism index (GLOBE study)[34]

---

[32] Cf. [Brodbeck/Chhokar/House 2007, p. 1032]

[33] Cf. [Chhokar 2007, p. 991]

[34] Extract from societal in-group collectivism scores [Gelfand et al. 2004, p. 469/471]; higher scores indicate greater collectivism on a scale of 1 to 7.

ordering a dish for oneself is simply unheard of; it is only introduced by Western style restaurants.

Correlation of Collectivism and Power Distance

Many countries with a high collectivism index score also high on power distance and thus show a positive correlation. The relationship is plotted in Figure 1-7.

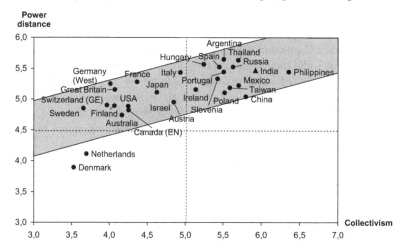

Figure 1-7. Correlation between collectivism and power distance

1.2.3   Assertiveness

Definition

Cultural assertiveness reflects beliefs as to whether people should be assertive, aggressive,[35] and tough or modest, non-aggressive, and tender in social relation-ships.[36]

   Assertiveness is a behavior typically more associated with men than with women – but this is a gender-related stereotype that reflects beliefs rather than actual behavior. Besides gender, assertiveness is also associated with the stereo-type of a successful manager.[37]

Cultural Characteristics

Figure 1-8 provides a summary of what it means to be a member of a modest or assertive society.

---

[35] In this context aggressiveness is understood within the boundaries of social acceptability.
[36] Cf. [Hartog 2004, p. 395]
[37] Cf. [Hartog 2004, p. 400]

	Low on assertiveness (i.e. high on modesty)	High on assertiveness
Society	• Have sympathy for the weak • Relationship and quality of life are important drivers • People from other cultures should integrate • Value harmony with the environment • Believe that the world is unjust	• Have sympathy for the strong • Challenge, earnings, recognition, and advancement are important • People from other cultures should assimilate • Try to have control over the environment • Have a just-world belief • Believe that anyone can succeed if he tries hard enough
Organization	• Value cooperation; humanization of work by building warm relationships • People underrate their own performance (ego-effacement) • Discuss issues indirectly and emphasize 'face-saving'; value ambiguity and subtlety in language • Emphasize tradition, seniority, and years of experience • Value integrity, loyalty, and cooperative spirit • Build trust on basis of predictability through good relationship	• Value competition, success, and progress • People overrate their own performance (ego-boosting) • Communicate directly and unambiguously; be explicit and to the point • Emphasize results over relationships • Value taking initiative, reward performance • Expect demanding and challenging targets • Build trust on basis of capabilities

Figure 1-8. Key differences between assertiveness and modesty[38]

Index and Observations

India scores with a low assertiveness index (Figure 1-9); but people indicate that they want much more assertiveness than they currently have. For India, the should-be score of the countries listed in Figure 1-9 is second highest after China.

Indians feel that they could do well with more assertiveness and dominance to survive in the very competitive environment[39] that they have created.

Implications for Intercultural Communication

In assertive societies people tend to communicate directly, clearly, and explicitly. This is referred to as *low-context communication*. More modest cultures use *high-context language*, which is less direct, more subtle, and sometimes sounds ambiguous for people from assertive societies. In high-context language, messages are implied 'in between the lines' rather than explicitly stated; the meaning of words is inextricably bound to the context of communication. Most of the information is implicit and thus hidden in the context.[40]

Both communication styles and their repercussion on cross-cultural email communication are compared in Figure 1-10; chapter 6.5 discusses the implications of high-context Indian communications, its importance for face management, and the challenges of deciphering the real information in greater detail.

---

[38] Collected from [Hartog 2004, p. 405; Hofstede/Hofstede 2005, p. 128-160] and adapted to IT industry.

[39] Cf. [Hartog 2004, p. 409,412]; also see chapter 3.3 on the competitiveness of the Indian education system.

[40] Cf. [Hall 1976, p. 85-101; Messner 2008c, p. 112]

In the medium-level assertive culture of France, there is occasionally a lot of verbal insult between managers and subordinates. But behind this apparent conflict there is a sense of understanding that enables both parties to continue working together. In high assertiveness societies, like Austria, Germany, USA, and Switzerland, there is a general feeling that conflicts should be battled out.[41]

Country	Practice (as-is score)	Value (should-be score)	Country	Practice (as-is score)	Value (should-be score)
Austria	4.62	2.81	Hungary	4.79	3.35
Germany (West)	4.73	3.09	Mexico	4.45	3.79
USA	4.55	4.32	Spain	4.42	4.00
Switzerland	4.51	3.21	Israel	4.23	3.76
Netherlands	4.32	3.02	Argentina	4.22	3.25
Australia	4.28	3.81	Poland	4.06	3.90
Great Britain	4.15	3.70	Philippines	4.01	5.14
France	4.13	3.38	Slovenia	4.00	4.59
Italy	4.07	3.82	Ireland	3.92	3.99
Canada (EN)	4.05	4.15	Taiwan	3.92	3.28
Finland	3.81	3.68	China	3.76	5.44
Denmark	3.80	3.39	**India**	**3.73**	**4.76**
India	**3.73**	**4.76**	Russia	3.68	2.83
Japan	3.59	5.56	Portugal	3.65	3.58
Sweden	3.38	3.21	Thailand	3.64	3.48

Figure 1-9. Assertiveness index (GLOBE study)[42]

Low context email communication	High context email communication
• Short email • Focuses on task or problem at hand • Approaches task or problem directly without mincing matters • Gives commands	• Relatively long email • Soft entry into the subject • Exchange of pleasantries • Creates harmony and focuses on relationship between individuals • Asks for help, advise, and support • Use of smiley ☺, ☹, and multiple question or exclamation marks (???, !!!)
Low context communication as perceived from a high context culture:	**High context communication as perceived from a low context culture:**
• Impolite, harsh, rude • Lacking the human touch • Demotivating, frustrating • Not interested in the individual	• Not to the point • Confusing ('what do they want?') • Wasting time • Not business-like

Figure 1-10. Low vs. high-context language in email communication

---

[41] Cf. [Hofstede/Hofstede 2005, p. 143]
[42] Extract from [Hartog 2004, p. 410-411]; higher scores indicate greater ascertiveness on a scale of 1 to 7

1.2.4   Uncertainty Avoidance

Definition

Ways of handling uncertainty are part of any culture around the world. All human beings have to face the fact that they do not know what will happen tomorrow. Uncertainty avoidance[43] is the extent to which members of a culture feel threatened by ambiguous or unknown situations, to which rules and order are preferred, and to which uncertainty is tolerated in a society.[44] This is expressed through the level of nervous stress and the need for rules, formalized procedures, and laws to cover situations in daily private or professional lives.

Cultural Characteristics

Rules, policies, technology, and religion or rituals are means used by societies to cope with uncertainty. Airbags for cars, security systems for intrusion detection, heartbeat monitors and other medical devices are technologies invented to control uncertainty; insurance policies, product warranties, and investment or retirement plans are techniques developed to reduce uncertainty. Laws provide formal rules to guide individual behavior and keep others informed on what to expect. When humans cannot control through technological or legal resolutions, uncertainty is often attempted to be coped with through religion, rites, and rituals.[45]

In countries with high uncertainty avoidance, employees and managers alike typically look for long-term employment; a job is considered a long lasting relationship. In strong uncertainty avoidance countries, life is hectic and people are driven by an inner urge to be constantly active. In low uncertainty avoidance countries, people only work hard if there is a need for it, but they also like to relax. Time is not an ever-present concern for them.[46]

Figure 1-11 summarizes the key differences between low and high uncertainty avoidance.

Index and Observations

India scores with a medium uncertainty avoidance index (Figure 1-12) and people indicate that they want much higher uncertainty avoidance. However, the data also shows that Indians have a much higher risk taking tendency than most Western offshoring countries.

---

[43] Uncertainty avoidance should not be confused with risk avoidance. Risk is focused on something specific, whereas uncertainty is a diffuse feeling.

[44] Cf. [de Luque/Javidan 2004, p. 602-603]

[45] Cf. [de Luque/Javidan 2004, p. 607]

[46] Cf. [Hofstede/Hofstede 2005, p. 183]

	Low uncertainty avoidance	High uncertainty avoidance
Society	• Uncertainty is a normal 'feature' of life • Low stress and low anxiety • People generally have less worries and feel happier • There should be no more rules than absolutely necessary • Tolerance for ambiguity and chaos • Tendency to informal interactions with others • Show more tolerance for breaking rules	• Uncertainty is considered a threat and needs to be fought continuously • High stress and anxiety • People have many worries and feel less happy • Emotional need for rules & regulations to allow predictability of behavior • Need for precision and formalization • Tendency to formalize interactions with others • Show less tolerance for breaking rules
Organization	• Rely on the word of (trustworthy) others rather than contractual agreements • Be less concerned with maintenance of records and documentation • Rely on informal interactions • Facilitate the initiation phase of a project through high risk taking; minimal planning or controls during implementation • Show less resistance to change • Frequent job changes and shorter durations in one job	• Tendency to document everything in carefully crafted contracts • Keep meticulous records, document meetings • Rely on formalized policies and procedures; verify communications in writing • Facilitate projects through risk aversion and tight controls • Show strong resistance to change • Longer service in one job; frequent job changes are considered as unstable

Figure 1-11. Key differences between low and high uncertainty avoidance[47]

Country	Practice (as-is score)	Value (should-be score)	Country	Practice (as-is score)	Value (should-be score)
Switzerland	5.37	3.16	China	4.94	5.28
Sweden	5.32	3.60	Taiwan	4.34	5.31
Denmark	5.22	3.82	Ireland	4.30	4.02
Germany (West)	5.22	3.32	Mexico	4.18	5.26
Austria	5.16	3.66	**India**	**4.15**	**4.73**
Finland	5.06	3.85	Israel	4.01	4.38
Netherlands	4.70	3.24	Spain	3.97	4.76
Great Britain	4.65	4.11	Thailand	3.93	5.61
Canada (EN)	4.58	3.75	Portugal	3.91	4.43
France	4.43	4.26	Philippines	3.89	5.14
Australia	4.39	3.98	Slovenia	3.78	4.99
India	**4.15**	**4.73**	Argentina	3.65	4.66
USA	4.15	4.00	Poland	3.62	4.71
Japan	4.07	4.33	Hungary	3.12	4.66
Italy	3.79	4.47	Russia	2.88	5.07

Figure 1-12. Uncertainty avoidance index (GLOBE study)[48]

---

[47] Collected from [de Luque/Javidan 2004, p. 618; Hofstede/Hofstede 2005, p. 128-160] and adapted to IT industry.

[48] Extract from [de Luque/Javidan 2004, p. 622-623]; higher scores indicate greater uncertainty avoidance on a scale of 1 to 7

In India, attempts to reduce uncertainty and unpredictability are quite common. There is an established legal system (see chapters 2.3 and 4.5.5); social customs and norms for major life events such as birth, marriage, and death differ depending on religion and social groups, but they are well established within the various jatis (see chapter 3.1) and widely followed. Religious beliefs and practices are important attempts to reduce and positively influence uncertainty in the present and next life (see chapter 3.4). The middle classes emphasize good performance in school as a stepping stone for a successful business career.[49]

The IT industry has established quality norms and process controls in order to govern the outcome of deliverables (see chapter 4.1.4). While this could be seen as an outcome of the medium uncertainty avoidance score, it is more likely to be introduced in order to match the quality expectations of Western offshoring countries which score even higher on the uncertainty avoidance scale and sometimes feel threatened by the – in their eyes – high risk taking mentality of Indians.

1.2.5 Future Orientation

Definition

Time orientation relates to the subjective experience of time. Future orientation is a dimension of time orientation; it means planning and looking for long-term (future) rewards.

Cultural Characteristics

Future orientation is developed during childhood and adolescence; but socio-economic and political conditions, education, gender roles, religion, society, culture, and geographic factors determine adult attitudes. Good socio-economic conditions and political stability influence greater future orientation because they allow people to confidently look beyond the immediate future. A better education allows them to think abstractly in order to structure the future. Spirituality in religion is oriented towards the future and can significantly contribute towards a society's future orientation. These societal effects carry over to organizations.[50]

Figure 1-13 summarizes the key differences between low and high future orientation societies.

---

[49] Cf. [Chhokar 2007, p. 991]
[50] Cf. [Ashkanasy et al. 2004, p. 301]

	Low future orientation	High future orientation
Society	• Society has less economic success • Social pressure and propensity to spend now rather than save for the future • View materialistic success and spiritual fulfillments as dualities which require trade-off • Respect for traditions • Concern with social status, obligations, and face-saving	• Society has achieved economic success • Propensity to save for the future • View materialistic success and spiritual fulfillment as an integrated whole • Respect for circumstances (instead of traditions)
Organization	• Organizations have shorter strategic orientation • Leadership focuses on repetition of reproducible and routine sequences • Less intrinsic motivation of individuals • Value instant gratification; place higher priorities on immediate rewards	• Organizations have longer strategic orientation • Leadership is capable of seeing patterns in the face of chaos and uncertainty • More intrinsic motivation of individuals • Value the deferment of gratification, placing a higher priority on long-term success; willingness to subordinate oneself for a business purpose

Figure 1-13. Key differences between lower and higher future orientation[51]

Index and Observations

On future orientation, India scores with an upper medium index (Figure 1-14) and people indicate that they would still like to see a higher future orientation. Switzerland, Netherlands, Austria, Denmark, and Canada are in the top band.

Sweden, Japan, Great Britain, Germany, Finland, USA, and Australia fall into the same band of future orientation as India. France and Italy have significantly lower values.

Country	Practice (as-is score)	Value (should-be score)	Country	Practice (as-is score)	Value (should-be score)
Switzerland	4.73	4.79	India	**4.19**	**5.60**
Netherlands	4.61	5.07	Philippines	4.15	5.93
Austria	4.46	5.11	Ireland	3.98	5.22
Denmark	4.44	4.33	Taiwan	3.96	5.20
Canada (EN)	4.44	5.35	Mexico	3.87	5.86
Sweden	4.39	4.89	Israel	3.85	5.25
Japan	4.29	5.25	China	3.75	4.73
Great Britain	4.28	5.06	Portugal	3.71	543
Germany (West)	4.27	4.85	Slovenia	3.59	5.42
Finland	4.24	5.07	Spain	3.51	5.63
India	**4.19**	**5.60**	Thailand	3.43	6.20
USA	4.15	5.31	Hungary	3.21	5.70
Australia	4.09	5.15	Poland	3.11	5.20
France	3.48	4.96	Argentina	3.08	5.78
Italy	3.25	5.91	Russia	2.88	5.48

Figure 1-14. Future orientation index (GLOBE study)[52]

---

[51] Collected from [Ashkanasy et al. 2004, p. 300-302; Hofstede/Hofstede 2005, p. 212] and adapted to IT industry.

[52] Extract from [Ashkanasy et al. 2004, p. 304,306]; higher scores indicate greater future orientation on a scale of 1 to 7

Historically the Indian society has always emphasized the 'hereafter' in preference to the 'here and now', and has generally been very future oriented. The government supports future orientation by providing tax breaks on savings, tax benefits for housing mortgages, and supporting the provident fund scheme to provide post-retirement benefits. Following the doctrine of karma (see chapter 3.4), people engage in ceremonies and rituals to improve their chance for a better lot in the next life.[53]

1.2.6 Performance Orientation

Definition

Performance orientation reflects the degree to which an organization or a society encourages and rewards its members for high standards, excellence, and performance improvement.[54]

Cultural Characteristics

All societies accept job-related accomplishment as an important work goal, but they measure performance differently. For instance, career success can be defined as achieving results, delivering content, having high potential, or showing good management, interpersonal, or communication skills.

Regarding the performance orientation index, most cultures do not fit neatly into stereotyped descriptions. Hence, a useful picture of key differences cannot be provided.

Index and Observations

India scores in the upper medium band on performance orientation (Figure 1-15).

The Indian society recognizes individual achievement; parents are very proud of the scholastic performance of their kids, admission to leading colleges and business schools is almost always based on academic performance, and finally universities award medals to their top graduates (see chapter 3.3). Organizations operate performance appraisal systems, and promotions take into account a combination of achievement (performance rating, accomplishments), ascription (seniority, education, alma mater, connections), and suitability for the job at the next higher level. However, it is not uncommon to avoid poor performance ratings in order to avoid attrition (see chapter 5.1.3) and provide a possibility for saving face when conveying negative news (see chapter 6.5.4).

---

[53] Cf. [Chhokar 2007, p. 990]
[54] Cf. [Javidan 2004, p. 239]

Country	Practice (as-is score)	Value (should-be score)	Country	Practice (as-is score)	Value (should-be score)
Switzerland	4.94	5.82	Taiwan	4.56	5.74
Canada (EN)	4.49	6.15	Philippines	4.47	6.31
USA	4.49	6.14	China	4.45	5.67
Austria	4.44	6.10	Ireland	4.36	5.98
Australia	4.36	5.89	India	4.25	6.05
Netherlands	4.32	5.49	Mexico	4.10	6.16
Germany (West)	4.25	6.01	Israel	4.08	5.75
India	4.25	6.05	Spain	4.01	5.80
Denmark	4.22	5.61	Thailand	3.93	5.74
Japan	4.22	5.17	Poland	3.89	6.12
France	4.11	5.65	Slovenia	3.66	6.41
Great Britain	4.08	5.90	Argentina	3.65	6.35
Finland	3.81	6.11	Portugal	3.60	6.40
Sweden	3.72	5.80	Hungary	3.43	5.96
Italy	3.58	6.07	Russia	3.39	5.54

Figure 1-15. Performance orientation index (GLOBE study)[55]

1.2.7   Gender Egalitarianism

Definition

One of the most fundamental ways in which societies differ is how they prescribe and proscribe different roles for women and men. The extent to which an organization or a society minimizes gender role differences while promoting gender equality is mapped in the gender egalitarianism index.

Gender egalitarianism has both an attitudinal domain and behavioral manifestations. The attitudinal domain relates to the fundamental values, beliefs, and attitudes held by the society with regard to gender stereotypes and gender role ideology; the behavioral manifestations are actions and observed behaviors in a society in relation to gender egalitarianism, e.g. gender discrimination and gender equality.[56]

There are several potential causes for cross-cultural differences in gender egalitarianism:[57]

- Parental investment in child rearing. Greater involvement of men in child rearing may give women more time to pursue non-traditional social or professional roles, which in turn exposes more and more children to women and men in non-traditional roles.
- Climate or geographical latitude. A higher level of cultural masculinity can be found in warmer than in colder climates; it is more demanding to raise

---

[55] Extract from [Javidan 2004, p. 250-251]; higher scores indicate greater performance orientation on a scale of 1 to 7

[56] Cf. [Enrich/Denmark/Hartog 2004, p. 348]

[57] Cf. [Enrich/Denmark/Hartog 2004, p. 351-359]

offspring in cold climates (food, shelter, safety) and this requires closer co-operation between men and women. This kind of cross-gender exchange can result in more egalitarian behavior – of course moderated today by a country's wealth and social security system.

- Religion. Virtually all monotheistic religions worship a male god, which has been observed to be linked to a lower status of women in a society. However, this relationship becomes complicated by the fact that a society's gender norm affects its religious mentality.
- Economic development. The impact of a nation's wealth on gender egalitarianism is dubious because economic development does not necessarily create new roles for women.
- Social structure and resource control. In societies where women have greater control over economical, social, and psychological resources, men pay greater deference to women, and women are allowed greater decision-making authority.
- Mode of production. As the mode of production in historical or tribal societies moves away from agriculture and becomes more sophisticated, women's power and prestige tends to decline. Similar to religion as a driver for gender equality, the causal role of the relationship is open for discussion.
- Political systems. The nature and openness of a country's political system may be a causal factor for women's success in attaining leadership roles which were traditionally reserved for men.

Cultural Characteristics

As described above, the drivers for gender equality are complex and the cause-effect relationship is often unclear. Figure 1-16 portraits societies of low and high gender egalitarianism.

Low gender egalitarianism (male domination)	High gender egalitarianism
• Generally accord women a lower status in society • Lower percentage of women in positions of authority and participating in labor force • Lower level of education and literacy among females • Occupational sex segregation • Give women a smaller role in family or community decision making	• Generally accord women an equal status in society • Percentage of women and men in positions of authority and participation in labor force roughly equal • Similar levels of education and literacy rates of females and males • Less occupational sex segregation • Women have an equal role in family or community decision making

Figure 1-16. Key differences between lower and higher gender egalitarianism[58]

Index and Observations

India scores very low on gender egalitarianism, i.e. very high on male domination (Figure 1-17). The Germanic cluster of Europe (Austria, Germany, Switzerland)

---

[58] Adapted from [Enrich/Denmark/Hartog 2004, p. 359]

comes next to India. The Scandinavian countries Denmark, Sweden, and Finland with some distance score very high on gender equality; some research attributes this to the time of the Vikings (800–1,000 AD) where the men would go on long journeys and the women had no choice but to take responsibility for managing the villages.[59]

There are no professions that Indian women are legally prevented from entering,[60] but still India continues to be a male-dominated society and business culture. The role of the family and women is elucidated in chapter 3.2.

Country	Practice (as-is score)	Value (should-be score)	Country	Practice (as-is score)	Value (should-be score)
Denmark	3.93	5.08	Hungary	4.08	4.63
Sweden	3.84	5.15	Russia	4.07	4.18
Canada (EN)	3.70	5.11	Poland	4.02	4.52
Great Britain	3.67	5.17	Slovenia	3.96	4.83
France	3.64	4.40	Portugal	3.66	5.13
Netherlands	3.50	4.99	Philippines	3.64	4.58
Australia	3.40	5.02	Mexico	3.64	4.73
Finland	3.35	4.24	Argentina	3.49	4.98
USA	3.34	5.06	Thailand	3.35	4.16
Italy	3.24	4.88	Ireland	3.21	5.14
Japan	3.19	4.33	Israel	3.19	4.71
Germany (West)	3.10	4.89	Taiwan	3.18	4.06
Austria	3.09	4.83	China	3.05	3.68
Switzerland	2.97	4.92	Spain	3.01	4.82
India	2.90	4.51	India	2.90	4.51

Figure 1-17. Gender egalitarianism index (GLOBE study)[61]

1.2.8   Humane Orientation

Definition

The ideas and values of humane orientation have existed since ancient times and are reflected in the way people treat each other and in social programs institutionalized within each society. The humane orientation index describes if individuals in organizations or societies are encouraged or rewarded for being fair, altruistic, friendly, generous, caring, and in general kind to others.

Cultural Characteristics

A number of aspects determine whether a society has a low or high humane orientation:[62]

---

[59] Cf. [Hofstede/Hofstede 2005, p. 158-159]

[60] Cf. [Chhokar 2007, p. 990]

[61] Extract from [Emrich/Denmark/Hartog 2004, p. 365-366]; higher scores indicate greater gender egalitarianism on a scale of 1 to 7, i.e. lower scores signify greater male domination

- Religious conviction. Religion is one of the major means of understanding people's behavior. In Judaism, Christianity, and Islam, God is associated with goodness, and his orders include duties and prohibitions which lead to good and humanitarian behavior. In Asian religions, such as Buddhism, Hinduism, and Taoism, there is no monotheistic God pointing in the direction of goodness.
- Social and family practices. Central norms in every society govern the behavior of their people. In different societies, children are attributed with either economic value or psychological value. Economic value refers to a child physically helping the family and guaranteeing old age treatment of the parents; psychological value attributes friendship, companionship, and generally sources of pleasure with the offspring. Therefore, in developing economies, children are taught obedience rather than autonomy to ensure the purpose of economic value. In most developed Western societies and Japan, children are more viewed as a source of psychological satisfaction.
- Human rights and discrimination. These are standards that are considered the minimum condition for a dignified life.
- Economics and role of government. In many industrialized nations of the developed world, a welfare state has replaced informal and family relationships; members of the society can rely on the state to take care of their survival and well-being. In the developing world, individuals are expected to seek and offer moral and material support amongst each other.

Figure 1-18 summarizes major forms of humane orientation.

	Low humane orientation	High humane orientation
Society	• Self-interest is most important • Values: pleasure, comfort, self-enjoyment, power, self-enhancement, material possessions • Welfare state guarantees social and economic protection; lack of support for others • People are expected to solve personal problems on their own • Children should be autonomous; all family members are independent • In more developed societies, children are not expected to provide material support to their parents in old age	• Others (family, friends, community, strangers, colleagues) are important • Values: altruism, benevolence, kindness, love, generosity, affiliation • Family and other personal relationships induce protection • Children should be obedient; parents closely control their kids • In less developed societies, children are expected to provide material support to their parents in old age
Organization	• Formal relationships • Supervisory support • Organizations are controlled by legislation and unionization • Greater influence of the state and the trade unions on the business system • Employees prefer to be left alone to get jobs done	• Informal relationships • Managers provide mentoring and patronage support • Organizations are trusted and autonomous in their HR practices • Less influence of the state and the trade unions on the business system • Employees prefer to team up with others to get jobs done

Figure 1-18. Key differences between lower and higher humane orientation[63]

---

[62] Cf. [Kabasakal/Bodur 2004, p. 565-569]

[63] Adapted from [Kabasakal/Bodur 2004, p. 570]

Index and Observations

India scores very high on humane orientation compared to offshoring countries and most other offshoring destinations (Figure 1-19); Germany, France, Switzerland, and Italy are at the low end of the spectrum.

Country	Practice (as-is score)	Value (should-be score)	Country	Practice (as-is score)	Value (should-be score)
India	4.57	5.28	Philippines	5.12	5.36
Canada (EN)	4.49	5.64	Ireland	4.96	5.47
Denmark	4.44	5.45	Thailand	4.81	5.01
Japan	4.30	5.41	India	4.57	5.28
Australia	4.28	5.58	China	4.36	5.32
USA	4.17	5.53	Taiwan	4.11	5.26
Sweden	4.10	5.65	Israel	4.10	5.62
Finland	3.96	5.81	Argentina	3.99	5.58
Netherlands	3.86	5.20	Mexico	3.98	5.10
Austria	3.72	5.76	Russia	3.94	5.59
Great Britain	3.72	5.43	Portugal	3.91	5.31
Italy	3.63	5.58	Slovenia	3.79	5.25
Switzerland	3.60	5.54	Poland	3.61	5.30
France	3.40	5.67	Hungary	3.35	5.48
Germany (West)	3.18	5.46	Spain	3.32	5.69

Figure 1-19. Humane orientation index (GLOBE study)[64]

In India, being altruistic and charitable is considered to help improve one's lot in the next life (see chapter 3.4 for the *karma* doctrine). Whenever someone suffers a personal or family tragedy, relatives, neighbors, friends, acquaintances, and colleagues offer and also do provide help. Hence, on the subcontinent, humane orientation partially overlaps with future orientation (see chapter 1.2.5).[65] India demonstrates high paternalistic values, i.e. people in authority are expected to act like a benevolent parent and take care of subordinates and their families.[66] This leads to employees being selected, evaluated, and promoted on the basis of their relationship to the superior rather than the organization's requirements or the skills of the individual (see chapter 5.3).

Even though India is a developing country, there are laws and regulations around reporting and investigating work-related accidents with mandatory compensations for the victims. Special schools have been established to cater for the needs of the handicapped, and some institutions provide food for the homeless and the poor – although only a small percentage of people in need have access to such

---

[64] Extract from [Kabasakal/Bodur 2004, p. 573-574]; higher scores indicate greater humane orientation on a scale of 1 to 7

[65] Cf. [Chhokar 2007, p. 990-991]

[66] Cf. [Kabasakal/Bodur 2004, p. 566]

support. Personal disputes are mostly settled through conciliation or arbitration –
partly due to a reputation of the police for not helping and of the judicial system
for being overburdened. [67]

1.3   Intercultural View against India

How the attributes of cultural dimensions affect collaboration across countries can
be best visualized by comparing the index values in one diagram. Figure 1.3
compares India against three typical offshoring countries (France, Germany, USA).

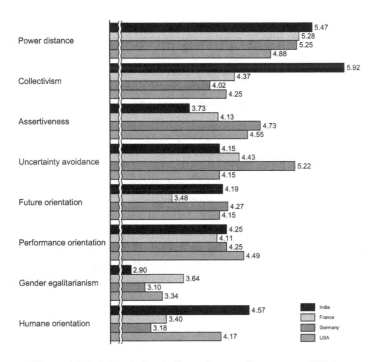

Figure 1-20. Cultural view India vs. France, Germany, and USA

When analyzing this chart, it is less important to look at absolute values but at
the differences between two countries, e.g. does India score higher on power
distance than France? Is there more power distance in Germany than in the USA?

1.4   Soft Skills Key to Success

Many companies rush into offshore deals in order to improve their market
positions through better cost structures. Hastily entered offshore deals are prone
to failure. Looking at the root causes, five key failures have been identified by

---

[67] Cf. [Chhokar 2007, p. 990]

Gartner, the research company – and all five of them have something or other to do with a lack of intercultural soft skills:[68]

- The business case and promised cost savings could not be realized. The company is fixated on saving money which today remains the most common driver for offshore deals. Some organizations calculate the business case solely on wage disparities rather than identifying the right function or project to move offshore; they forget to include expenses associated with planning and startup, infrastructure, due diligence, communication, governance, travel from and to India, and cultural training.
- Productivity has gone down after offshoring. Many offshore engagements are launched with misguided productivity assumptions, i.e. it is assumed that offshore resources will match the productivity levels of internal and onsite resources. Reasons for the loss of productivity are confusions due to process maturity, high attrition rates, less development, domain or country experience, low morale in the retained onsite team, and the need for more detailed specifications.
- Senior leadership is perceived as poorly committed. Often senior level governance on both sides of the offshoring deal is not secured and the deal is not kept on track.
- Cultural differences between two national cultures and also between two companies have lead to communication problems. Challenges associated with distance and time zones are usually factored into the business plan but those raised by cultural mismatches are sometimes overlooked. Different communication styles, decision making habits, codes of conduct, and hierarchy levels are examples of such hurdles. "Not everything that works is intuitive – and not everything that seems intuitively obvious in a local setting will work in a global delivery model."[69]
- Lack of offshore expertise and organizational readiness. Many companies embark on the offshore adventure without previous internal preparations. Business and IT stakeholders need to be on board, country-specific risks for business continuity management have to be examined, outsourcing skills and governance models have to be established, and – last but not least – employees have to be prepared for working together with colleagues from another culture.

On the other hand, expert intercultural competencies can help to avoid these five pitfalls. Of course, soft skills alone never make projects work but they are a key ingredient to success. This book helps to develop this talent and thus aids in preparing Western organizations in their offshore journey to India.

---

[68] Cf. [Huntley 2005]; adapted

[69] [Huntley 2005, p. 5]

1.5   Phases of Intercultural Encounters

Intercultural encounters are often accompanied by a shift of feelings over time following the acculturation curve shown in Figure 1-21; feelings towards working together with India are plotted on the vertical axis and time on the horizontal one.

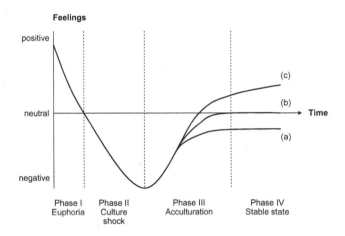

Figure 1-21. Acculturation curve for intercultural encounters[70]

Phase I is usually a rather short period of *euphoria*, it is about the excitement of job enrichment and maybe even getting a travel opportunity to India for the project kick-off. Phase II is the period *of culture shock* when the project actually starts in the new distributed and international environment. Phase III, *acculturation*, begins when the project members have slowly learned how to collaborate with India and the project is up to speed under the new conditions. Phase IV is the *stable state* of the project. The feelings in phase IV can (a) remain negative, if a smooth project communication has not been established and there are problems with project deliverables. If it is (b) neutral, then working together with India is just about as good as getting the job done back at home. If it is (c), the feeling about working together with India can be positive. This can only be achieved by acquiring intercultural abilities on the personal front and following a mature model for distributed delivery with established processes.

1.6   Learning Intercultural Communication

The acquisition of intercultural skills follows three phases:

- Awareness brings along the recognition that everyone carries particular mental software because of the way one was brought up, together with an ability to appreciate the motives actuating other persons from different cultures.

---

[70] Cf. [Hofstede/Hofstede 2005, p. 324]

- Knowledge follows awareness. One has learnt about the particularities of another culture, its symbols, heroes, rituals, and where they differ from one's own culture.
- Skills come along with practice. Symbols of the other culture are no longer only understood but recognized and applied. One experiences a certain satisfaction from getting along in the other culture's environment and being able to resolve some of the problems.

Intercultural communication can to some extent be taught and learnt. Some participants in intercultural trainings easily adopt the training messages while others do not. Among the latter, one can frequently find people with inflated egos, a low uncertainty tolerance, with political sympathies for extreme parties or racism, and who cannot distance themselves from their own cherished environment.

Two types of courses are offered.[71] Traditional courses or briefings for expatriates convey specific knowledge of the other culture, inform about the other country's geography, history, customs, food, and dos and don'ts. However, their content could as easily be conveyed by books. Cultural awareness trainings are a different story altogether. They focus on the cultural and mental software of individuals. They can be conducted culture-independent or having a target culture in mind. Such courses focus on how to get things done effectively in another culture rather than on how to live there. While this book features elements of both courses, it cannot replace the guidance of a gifted intercultural trainer.

Intercultural trainings should not only be attended by the people working together with the other culture, but also by their management in order to get an understanding and support for the issues people are facing when working together with a different culture such as India.

---

[71] For a full classification of intercultural training courses see e.g. the overview in [Holtbrügge/ Schillo 2008, p. 137-139]

2 India – the Country

2.1 Geography

Looking at the world map, the Indian subcontinent can be best described as a "… triangular shaped appendage hanging off the bottom of Asia, just below the Himalayas."[72] It is the seventh largest country in the world, its land mass about one third of the USA, half the size of Australia, and roughly comparable with Western Europe. It spans 3,200 kilometers from North to South, and 3,000 kilometers from West to East covering around 3.2 million square kilometers.

India has six borders with Bangladesh, Bhutan, China, Myanmar, Nepal, and Pakistan. Stretches of the borders are still disputed, especially along the line of control in Kashmir with Pakistan and parts of the border with China. There are two sets of islands belonging to India, the Lakshadweep islands in the Arabian Sea, and the group of Andaman and Nicobar Islands in the Indian Ocean.

India is made up of 28 federal states and seven union territories (see Figure 2-1); regional nationalism and separatism are the reason for the not so rare carving out of new ones.

India boasts of enormous rivers like the Ganges and Brahmaputra in the East, the Indus in the West, and the Cauvery in the South. In the North-West towards the border to Pakistan, there are deserts, in the North-East one will find tea gardens at the bottom of the Himalayan range. India's highest mountain is the Kanchenjunga, its 8,586 meters (28,169 feet) making it the world's third highest after Mount Everest and K2. Going down south, there are mountain ranges (the Western and Eastern Ghats) with peaks between 600 and 2500 meters; high plains, coffee plantations, coconut groves, and rice fields follow each other. Tropical rainforests and bamboo jungles fall down to either stony or stunning sandy beaches.

India can be very hot in summer; maximum temperatures are reached in and around New Delhi, where the Himalayan Mountains to the North act as a natural barrier and re-circulate the hot air back into the country. During monsoon time between June and September, Mumbai, the West, and the East coast receive heavy rainfalls with many villages and roads flooded. Hot temperatures and high humidity turn the place into a steam pot. It is a tropical climate, but because of the different topography, regional climates can be very different. Climatically, the best places to be are the cities at higher elevation inside the country, such as Bangalore or Pune. Hill stations like Ooty, Munnar, or Kodaikanal have an even more relaxed climate; the British had made good use of them as summer residences during colonial times.

---

[72] [Davies 2004, p. 11]

Figure 2-1. The Indian subcontinent

India is rich in minerals; with an estimated 200 billion tons, coal is India's most important natural resource. While there are also some supplies in iron ore, manganese, chrome, magnesium, bauxite, copper, lead, and zinc, India is a net importer for most resources. Crude oil is very rare which poses a big challenge for India's future economic development.

Agriculture has been around in India for ages. Even today, 60% of the country's population works in this sector.[73] One third of the world's rice harvest comes from India; tea, coffee, cotton, sesame, mustard, pepper are important export goods.

2.2   Brief History

"India's story is one of the grand epics of world history".[74] Throughout thousands of years it had seen great civilizations, invasions, cataclysms, and the birth of several religions. Indian history has always been 'work-in-progress', it has never

---

[73] Cf. [CIA Worldbook], data for 2003
[74] [Singh et al. 2005, p. 38]

reached a final state but has always been a constant process of development. From this stream of change, today, a modern nation has emerged.

2.2.1 Ancient Times[75]

Stone age rock shelters with paintings at Bhimbetka in the state of Madhya Pradesh are among the earliest known traces of human life in India. They date back to 10,000 BC, but there are absolutely no archaeological findings older than 500,000 years, leading to the assumption that homo sapiens did not settle south of the Himalayas. Permanent settlements appeared around 7,000 BC. In the Indus and Ghaggar-Hakra river valleys, in what is today Pakistan and western India, it developed around 2,500 BC into the Harappa or Indus Valley Civilization, representing the cradle of civilization on the Indian subcontinent. This phase is contemporary to the Early to Middle Bronze Age, to Mesopotamian Ur III, pre-palatial Minoan Cretem, and the First Intermediate Egyptian Period. The people of the Indus Valley Civilization achieved great mastery in measuring length, mass, and time. Engineers already followed the decimal division of measurement. In the coastal city of Harappa, remarkable docks were built after studying the effects of tides, waves, and currents. The first worldwide evidence of dentistry and in vivo drilling of human teeth was discovered in Mehrgarh and dates 7,500 to 9,000 years back.[76] The yearly flooding of the Indus river was used to irrigate the fields of wheat, barley, sesame, pulses, mustard, dates, vegetables, and most likely also rice. Cities were also of remarkable size; estimates put the population of Moenjodaro as high as 40,000 to 50,000. Many elements of this culture would later find their way into Hinduism. Clay figurines suggest worship of a Mother goddess (later personified as Kali) and a male three-faced god (the prehistoric Shiva).

This great civilization started to fall into decline from around 2,000 BC. The reason is not quite clear; some historians attribute it to floods or decreased rainfall which threatened the agricultural base, but others claim that Aryan tribes from Afghanistan and Central Asia began to invade the northwest of India.

During this period of transition (1,500–1,200 BC), the Vedas were composed which laid the foundations of Hinduism. The canonical division of the Vedas is fourfold. The Rig-Veda are verses of praise in meter, and intended for loud recitation; the Yajur-Veda are in prose and intended for recitation in a lower tone at sacrifices; the Sama-Veda are again in meter and intended for chanting at the Soma ceremonies; the Atharva-Veda is a later addition and the recitation of its hymns is supposed to prolong life, cure diseases, or effect the ruin of enemies.

During the so-called Vedic Civilization various kingdoms were formed. From around 550 BC, sixteen independent kingdoms and republics known as the Maha-janapadas were established across the subcontinent.

---

[75] Cf. [Singh et al. 2005, p. 38-40; Johnson 1995, p. 58-71

[76] Cf. [Coppa et al. 2006]

India narrowly avoided two major invasions from the West. The Persian king Darius had managed to annex Punjab and Sindh along today's India-Pakistan border. Alexander the Great made his way to India from Greece in 326 BC, but his troops refused to cross the Beas River in Himachal Pradesh; he had to return home without putting a part of India under his control.

Around 500 BC two important religions arose in India: Buddhism and Jainism. Both condemned the caste system and questioned the Vedas. But the Jains, unlike the Buddhists, did not deny their Hindu heritage.

In the third century BC, after a number of military conquests, emperor Ashoka united most of South Asia. His empire stretched from present-day Afghanistan and parts of Persia in the West, to the present-day Indian states of Bengal and Assam in the east, and as far south as the city of Mysore in Karnataka. Most relics of the emperor Ashoka have been inscribed with the Ashoka Chakra, a wheel with 24 spokes. Today, it is used in the center of the national flag of India in a navy-blue color replacing the symbol of the spinning wheel (charkha) which was used in the pre-independence versions. During Ashoka's reign, arts and philosophy flourished; Buddhism was declared the state religion in 262 BC.

After the death of Ashoka in 233 BC, the empire slowly disintegrated and totally collapsed fifty years later in 184 BC. Despite this instability, this period was one of intense development. Trade with the Roman Empire through overland routes and by sea through India's southern ports was substantial, and there was also an overland exchange of goods with China.

From 180 BC, a number of invasions from Central Asia followed; the most successful one was lead by nomads from north-west China, the Kushanas.

2.2.2   Modern History[77]

It is believed that St Thomas the Apostle arrived in Kerala in 52 AD, which accounts for the large number of Christians in this state even today.

From the third century AD, the Gupta dynasty oversaw a period known as India's Golden Age. Science, engineering, art, literature, astronomy, and philosophy flourished. Some of the finest work was done at the caves of Ajanta and Ellora. Towards the end of the Gupta period, Hinduism became once again the dominant religious force in India. Devotion and iconolatry date back to these days; the gods Shiva and Vishnu are heading the Hindu-pantheon.

The invasion of the Huns signaled the end of the Gupta period, and in 510 the Gupta army was defeated by the Hun leader Toramana.

Between the 10th and 12th century, invasions from Central Asia took place once again. In the center point of Muslim expansion was Mahmud of Ghazni, who had turned Ghazni, a city between Kabul and Kandahar in today's Afghanistan, into a glorious capital. He funded its glory through 17 raids into India, the most infamous of which was the raid on the Shiva temple at Somnath in Gujarat where a Hindu force of 70,000 died trying to defend the temple. In a single raid he stole

---

[77]   Cf. [Singh et al. 2005, p. 41-45; Johnson 1995, p. 73-127]

6.5 tons of gold. After Mahmud's death in 1033, Ghazni was first seized by the Seljuys and afterwards by the Ghurs from western Afghanistan, who also advanced into India in 1191. Their general Qutb-ud-din captured Delhi, was awarded the position of governor, and subsequently first sultan of Delhi; it was he who built the Qutb Minar complex, still today a great landmark in Delhi. Wherever he had destroyed a Hindu temple, he asked for a Muslim mosque to be built on top of its ruins. Large parts of North India came under the rule of the Delhi Sultanate, fighting off attacks from the Mongols while pushing the border southwards.

Meanwhile, a separate set of powerful kingdoms had emerged in South India, among them the Shatavahanas, Kalingas, and Vakatakas. However, the greatest empires emerged from the tribal territories on the fertile coastal plains: the Cholas, Pandyas, Chalukyas, Cheras, and Pallavas. Surviving architectural highlights of the Pallava rule can be found in the shore temple and Five Rathas in Mahaballipuram, the temples at Kanchipuram, and the Rock Fort Temple at Tiruchirappalli. Through trade with the Egyptians, Romans, and other Southeast Asian civilizations, the south of India became prosperous. The Cholas followed the Pallavas and under king Raja Raja (985–1014) they then controlled almost the whole of South India, the Deccan plateau, Sri Lanka, parts of the Malay peninsula, and the Sumatran-based Srivijaya kingdom. Throughout Hinduism remained the source of the South Indian culture.

In the North, Mohammed Tughlaq came to power in 1320 after murdering his father; he went on successful military campaigns in the South, moved his capital from Delhi 1,100 km south to Daulatabad near Aurangabad in Maharashtra. Missing inhabitants for his new capital, he sought to force-march the entire population of Delhi to Daulatabad resulting in heavy losses of life. But soon he realized that this left Delhi defenseless, and so he moved the entire capital back again – leaving behind a huge hilltop fortress which is a tourist sight in Daulatabad today.

Delhi's fate was sealed when in 1398 Tamerlane of Samarkand in Central Asia invaded India; his soldiers are said to have slaughtered every single Hindu inhabitant. Meanwhile, several small kingdoms arose in the south: the Muslim Bahmani sultanate 1345 in Gulbarga and later in Bidar, the Hindu Vijayanagar empire in 1336 in Hampi (see Figure 2-2). Both kingdoms engaged in several fierce battles.

Simultaneously, in Kabul the Mughal dynasty came into power; its founder Babur was a descendent of both Genghis Khan and Tamerlane. His army was technologically superior and the Mughals expanded their kingdom to gradually cover most of the subcontinent. Also the arts and literature flourished presenting India with another golden age.

However, Babur's son Humayun was defeated by Sher Shah from eastern India in 1539 and had to withdraw into Iran. After Sher Shah's death, he returned and re-conquered Delhi. His successor Akbar finally managed to consolidate the empire and brought relative peace to the country during his 49-year reign. As a Muslim ruler, he understood that the influence of Hinduism could not be neglected and

Figure 2-2. Remains of the Vijayanagar empire at Hampi[78]

tried to integrate Hindus into his state apparatus. He abolished the pilgrimage tax Hindus had to pay in order to assemble for religious ceremonies; also Hindus were now allowed to renovate their old temples and build new ones. He even formulated a new religion, Deen Ilahi, which combined his favorite parts of all religions he had encountered and studied. His new capital Fatehpur Sikri, close to Agra, is an example of great architecture. However, it was only inhabited for 15 years after which he moved the capital to Lahore to be closer to some insurgence in Afghanistan.

Akbar was followed by Jehangir and then by Shah Jahan, who had built the Red Fort in Delhi, converted the Agra Fort into a palace, and constructed the Taj Mahal (see Figure 2-3) which today ranks as one of the wonders of the world. Ironically, the Agra Fort later became his jail when his son Aurangzeb imprisoned him. He got greedy again and tried to expand his empire further. The Hindu population became irritated by rising tax burdens and newly erupted religious intolerance. In addition, the empire faced challenges from the Marathas in central India and the British in Bengal. In 1739, the Persian ruler Nadir Shah invaded Delhi.

---

[78] Photo by author

Figure 2-3. Taj Mahal[79]

In Rajasthan, the Rajputs remained strong Hindu powers but eventually became vassal states of the Mughal empire. In central India, the Marathas gathered Hindu support under their leader Shivaji. Between 1646 and 1680, he did many heroic acts against the Mughals, was even taken prisoner by the Mughals but managed to escape from Agra Fort again. In the long run, they managed to undermine the Mughal empire by supplying troops and then actually taking control of the land. The expansion of the Marathas to the west was halted by Ahmad Shah Durani from Afghanistan in 1761, but at least they managed to consolidate their power in central India. Nonetheless, they did not manage to hold up against the British imperial power.

2.2.3   Arrival of the Europeans[80]

"The British were not the first European power to arrive in India, nor were they the last to leave – both of these 'honors' go to the Portuguese".[81]

In 1498, Vasco da Gama landed in Kerala, having sailed around the Cape of Good Hope in Africa. Only a few years later, the Portuguese captured Goa in 1510 and Diu in 1531. They held and controlled both enclaves until 1961.

---

[79] Photo by Sandeep Dhirad (permission granted)
[80] Cf. [Singh et al. 2005, p. 46-47; Johnson 1995, p. 128-140]
[81] [Singh et al. 2005, p. 46]; spelling adapted

Looking at the Indian history, there were already long lasting economical connections with the countries of the Mediterranean. But it was only the Portuguese with their ships who started trading in big terms. Initially, European merchants had to pay for Indian goods in cash, because up to the 19th century Europe did not have much to offer to the Indian customers. Second to trade for the Portuguese came missionary activities. But the European influence was hardly noticeable before the 18th century. Instead, the Europeans were regarded as an oddity and as petitioners for valuable Indian goods.

However, in the long run, Portugal did not have the necessary power to maintain a worldwide empire and had to quickly surrender space to the British and French. In the 16th and 17th century, the Europeans competed for and sometimes also fought over trading rights with India. In 1613, representatives of the East India Company established first trading posts in Gujarat, later in Chennai, Bengal, and Mumbai. For nearly 250 years a commercial trading company – and not the British government – practically ruled over British India.

The French had established themselves in 1672 in Pondicherry on the west coast. Rivalry between British and French control over India began. Initially, the French appeared to hold the upper hand and took Chennai in 1746, but already had to hand it back three years later. In 1750 all French aspirations ended when the directors of the French East India Company decided that their local representatives were playing too much politics and did not focus on trade. A settlement was reached with the British, which in the short term increased the profit of the French but effectively meant the beginning of the decline of French power on the sub-continent.

The Mughals granted the British a license to trade in Bengal. Having established a trading post in Kolkata, their business began to expand rapidly. In 1725, there were already around 30–40 British owned and operated vessels stationed in Kolkata. The growing business and fortification of the British trading posts was eyed suspiciously by the nawabs, the local rulers. Eventually, the nawab decided that British power had become excessive and attacked Kolkata in 1756. Six months later, Kolkata was re-taken under leadership of Robert Clive, an employee in the military service of the East India Company and later Governor of Bengal.

The British took advantage of several quarrels between Indian kingdoms and especially the power vacuum created by the disintegration of the Mughal empire in the north. The Marathas were divided among themselves and so Warren Hastings, governor in Bengal from 1771, was able to expand the company's control by entering a series of treaties with local rulers.

In the South, the situation was less clear due to a strong British-French rivalry. Hyder Ali and his son Tipu Sultan of Mysore started a series of determined campaigns against the British. But in the fourth Mysore war (1789–1799), Tipu Sultan was killed at Srirangapatnam and British power could advance further.

2.2.4   British Colonialism[82]

By 1856, most of India was under the control of the British East India Company. There was still a patchwork of independent states governed by maharajas (Indian princes) or nawabs (local rulers), which administered their own territory. From 1784 onwards, the East India Company had developed a system of central government with increased backing from the British government in London. The British continued to focus on trade and getting profit out of their India engagement. This brought far-reaching changes to India: coal and iron mining were developed, tea, coffee, and cotton became key crops, irrigation projects were started, and first steps were taken in building a vast railway system on the subcontinent. English was imposed as the language of administration which significantly eased the running of the country for the British but also kept them at a good distance from the general populace.

In 1857, the first rebellion – commonly referred to as the First War of Independence or Sepoy Mutiny – challenged British rule. The real underlying causes and triggers for this uprising are still subject of debate amongst historians. Key factors were the dispossession of territories from local rulers, taxes imposed on landowners, and the influx of industrially produced cheap textiles and other goods from Britain, which destroyed the livelihood of the small people in India. But the uprising was sparked by an incident in the army barracks in Meerut in Uttar Pradesh on May 10, 1857. The British had introduced a new type of bullet and there were rumors that the greasing of the bullets was done by either cow or pig fat. Since loading a rifle involved biting off the end of the waxed cartridge, these rumors caused considerable unrest with both Hindus and Muslims; cows are considered sacred by Hindus and pigs unclean by Muslims. The commanding officer in Meerut directly marched Indian soldiers into prison who refused to bite off the ends of their bullets. 47 out of the 74 Indian battalions of the Bengal army mutinied and marched to Delhi and Lucknow. But eventually this uprising failed and India came under direct control of the British Crown as a colony of the British Empire. The British government announced it would support the existing rulers of the princely states and not interfere in local matters as long as they showed their loyalty to the British crown.

But the desire to be free from foreign powers remained among many Indians. Opposition against the British colonial power was spearheaded by the country's oldest political party, the Indian National Congress, also known as the Congress Party, or simply as Congress.

The situation calmed down with the outbreak of the First World War. India contributed heavily, sent more than one million Indian volunteer soldiers overseas, and suffered well over 100,000 casualties. The Congress had supported India's involvement in the war and hoped for a reward – which never came. Disillusion was followed by new disturbances and uprisings. In April 1919, a British army

---

[82] Cf. [Singh et al. 2005, p. 47-48; Johnson 1995, p. 146-172]

contingent fired into a crowd of unarmed protesters in Punjab, killing more than 1,000. Politically, this massacre made many so far apolitical Indians turn to the Congress. At this time, the Congress had found a new leader in Mahatma Gandhi who preached a policy of non-violence. As the movement gained momentum, the Muslim population got concerned about their future in a Hindu dominated free India. In the 1930s they started the discussion about a separate Muslim state. Again, political events in Europe and the outbreak of the Second World War disrupted this movement. Many Congress supporters were preemptively jailed by the British in order to prevent any disruption to the war effort.

British elections in July 1945 brought victory to the Labour Party and for the first time, Indian independence was discussed as a legitimate matter. But the dialogues did not manage to bring together the two Indian parties. While Jawaharlal Nehru, leader of the Congress, campaigned for a united and liberated India, Mohammed Ali Jinnah, leader of the Muslim League, argued for a separate Muslim state. The country was on the edge of civil war. In August 1946, a planned slaughter of Hindus by Muslims in Kolkata called for retaliation. The situation was out of control for the British and they announced Indian independence for June 1948. Despite British led negotiations between Congress and Muslim League about a united India, both parties could not agree and the decision was taken to divide the country in two. Mahatma Gandhi remained the sole opponent to this plan. Increasing civil violence made the British to bring forward the day of independence to August 15, 1947. An independent British referee was tasked in drawing the border line between Hindu and Muslim territories. Some areas were clearly Hindu or Muslim, but others had mixed populations. Even worse, there were islands of communities in areas dominated by the other religion. Muslim Pakistan got a western and eastern part divided by a Hindu India. Even though it was obvious that this split was deemed to fail one day, it took East Pakistan 25 years to become a separate state like Bangladesh.

Why could the unity of India not be saved? Historians offer three explanations:[83]

- The Congress leadership underestimated the Muslim League under Ali Jinnah.
- Ali Jinnah was personally ambitious and pursued a separate state at all costs; the Muslim League did not care about human consequences.
- The British promoted a divide between Hindus and Muslims in an effort to perpetuate their rule. "Most British officials were predisposed to prefer Muslims, for, compared with Hindus, their forms of worship and ways of life were less alien. Overall, policy deepened religious divisions, which helped consolidate the white man's rule".[84]

In October 1947, the Time magazine reported that "In the first six weeks of Independence, about half as many Indians were killed as Americans died during nearly four years of the Second World War. There is still no possible numbering

---

[83] Cf. [Guha 2007, p. 26-27]
[84] [Guha 2007, p. 27]

of the wounded and the mutilated who survived, or of those who must yet die for lack of the simplest medical facilities, or of so much as a roof over their heads. It is unbearable, and unwise as well, to cherish memory of the bestial atrocities which have been perpetrated by Moslem and Sikh and Hindu alike. It is beyond human competence to conceive, far less to endure the thought of, the massiveness of the mania of rage, the munificence of the anguish, the fecundity of hate breeding hate, perhaps for generations to come".[85] Communal violence killed an estimated 1 million Hindus, Muslims, and Sikhs; about 3.5 millions Hindus and Sikhs from the newly created territory of Pakistan migrated to India.

At the initiative of Gandhi and Nehru, the Congress passed a resolution on the rights of religious minorities in India. Whatever the situation was like for Hindus in Pakistan, India was planned to become a secular state where all citizens enjoy equal rights and protection of the state. However, other political and religious streams did not support this viewpoint and wanted to turn India into a Hindu nation. With continued attacks on Muslims, Gandhi resorted to a fast on January 13, 1948. Firstly, he wanted to address the people of India, Hindus and Muslims, to live in peace and brotherhood. Secondly, he pledged the Pakistani government to stop driving out Hindu minorities from their territory. Thirdly, he requested the Indian government to release money owed to the government of Pakistan, which the British had paid for Indian contributions during the Second World War. However, Gandhi stood almost alone in urging religious tolerance. On the evening of January 30, 1948, he was shot dead by a Hindu zealot at his daily prayer meeting.

Gandhi's most powerful followers, Vallabhbhai Patel and Jawaharlal Nehru, were reunited in the course of events, and "[...] told the nation that while their master had gone, his message remained".[86]

2.2.5   Post-Independence[87]

Within India, the British left behind a geopolitical problem far greater than the separation of India and Pakistan. There were more than 500 distinct pieces of territory, chiefdoms, and princely states. These states owed their shape, power – or lack thereof – to the British, who had used them as strategic allies against the French and to ensure the best possible return on investment of their colonial engagement in India. Hardly any of these states had a coastline; few had any modern industry, or a modern form of education.[88] In a speech by Lord Mountbatten, the last British viceroy and governor general of India, these states were now released from their obligations to the British Crown. He persuaded them to integrate with India and come to terms with the Congress, which would now rule India.[89]

---

[85] [Time 1947]

[86] [Guha 2007, p. 23]

[87] Cf. [Guha 2007; Singh et al. 2005, p. 49-54] and various wikipedia sites

[88] An exception were the maharajas of Mysore and Baroda who had founded good universities, worked for dissolving caste differences, and supported modern enterprises.

[89] Cf. [Guha 2007, p. 34-44]

Prior to the British withdrawal from India, the state of Jammu and Kashmir came under pressure from both Muslims and Hindus to join either future Pakistan or India. The maharaja of Jammu and Kashmir wanted to remain independent and delayed a decision. Parallel to the British withdrawal, the state was invaded by tribal and regular Pakistani soldiers. The maharaja then decided to join India, which in turn promptly sent its own troops. The Pakistani offensive ran out of steam towards the end of 1947, fronts solidified, and small-scale battles continued till late 1948. In December 1948, a formal ceasefire was declared; India retained three fifths of Jammu and Kashmir.

On the international front, Jawaharlal Nehru, India's first prime minister, tried a policy of nonalignment, balancing relationships with Britain, being a member of the Commonwealth, and moving closer to the USSR. The latter was due to conflicts with China and support for Pakistan from the US.

In 1949, India faced the next plight of close to 1 million refugees from East Pakistan owing to an outbreak of communal violence against Hindus. The Indian states did not have the resources to absorb so many refugees; hence, the Indian government started talks with Pakistan and signed a treaty pledging both nations to protect their respective minorities. As a result, many Hindus returned to East Pakistan and the relations temporarily thawed.

India's new constitution came into effect on January 26, 1950, the first national elections were held in 1952, and the Congress won with an overwhelming majority, with further election victories in 1957 and 1962. Rajendra Prasad became India's first president and Jawahrlal Nehru began a second term as prime minister.

Extensive internal reforms improved the rights of women in Hindu society and further legislated against caste discrimination and untouchability. A socialist model for the Indian economy was established, farmers did not have to pay taxes, blue-collar workers were guaranteed minimum wages and other benefits; heavy industries were nationalized. At the same time children were encouraged to enroll for primary education, thousands of schools and the Indian Institutes of Technology were founded.

On the western coast, Goa remained a Portuguese colony until 1961, when India, after continual petitions for a peaceful handover, invaded and annexed the territory.

In 1961, China and India engaged in a brief war over the borders in the Himalayas. The war was a disaster for the Indian army which was not used or trained to fighting in high-altitude terrain above 4,250 meters (14,000 feet); as a result, India lost control over both disputed territories. Nehru was faced with a complete disintegration of his armies and appealed to the USA for military help, should China advance further into India. News of the dispatch of an US aircraft carrier to the Bay of Bengal forced China to unilaterally declare a ceasefire and withdraw from lands occupied in the northeast. Till today China continues to occupy Aksai Chin in Kashmir and disputes India's sovereignty over Arunachal Pradesh. The conflict over Sikkim was peacefully resolved in 2003. The disaster of the Sino-Indian war led to increased patriotism in India and to a rebuild of the Indian army.

Jawaharlal Nehru died in 1964, and his daughter Indira Gandhi[90] was elected as prime minister in 1966.

In 1965, Pakistan still sensed a weakened Indian army and its troops tried to infiltrate into Indian Kashmir and hoped for an uprising of the local population. However, the plan backfired as the Kashmiris arrested the infiltrators. Pakistan opened other fronts. In September 1965, the United Nations Security Council passed a resolution calling for an unconditional ceasefire; the war ended the next day, and a formal ceasefire was agreed under brokerage of the Soviet Union. The war claimed casualties of more than 6,500 on both sides.

However, the ceasefire lasted only for six years. After elections in East Pakistan, the state sought independence from Pakistan. In March 1971, a rebellious army in Bangladesh declared independence from Pakistan. Indira Gandhi, prime minister of India, expressed full support of the Bangladeshi independence struggle. As India opened her borders to Bangladesh, more than 10 million refugees fled to India causing financial hardship and instability to the country. The USA promised to support Pakistan with military equipment. As a countermeasure, Indira Gandhi toured Europe and convinced the governments of Great Britain and France to block any pro-Pakistan directives in the United Nations Security Council. She greatly shocked the USA, when in August 1971 she signed a twenty-year treaty with the Soviet Union declaring friendship and cooperation.

By November, the military built-up at the border was immense and the Indian army only waited for winter to start, as the ground would allow easier operations and the Himalayan passes would be blocked by snow to prevent China from intervening. In December, Pakistan was desperate and launched a pre-emptive air strike into India. Pakistani planes went as far as to Agra, around 480 kilometers from the border, and attacked several airbases. This gave India sufficient reason to launch a full-scale attack against Pakistan, both on the Western and Eastern front. India's campaign was a true blitzkrieg, resulting in the surrender of the Pakistani army within two weeks. However, on the brink of defeat, Pakistan started a pogrom against the Hindu minority in Bangladesh killing many intellectuals who were seen as possible rebels. The human cost of the war was high and estimates of casualties range from 300,000 to 3 million. India took 90,000 prisoners of war in the east.[91] In the following year, and as part of the Simla peace agreement, India returned most of the captured territory to Pakistan and wanted to enter a lasting peace agreement.

Within India, economical and social problems combined with high levels of corruption were the reason for increasing political unrest. In 1974, the High Court found prime minister Indira Gandhi guilty of misusing government means for election purposes. The opposition demanded her immediate resignation, and

---

[90] Despite the same name, there is no relationship between Indira Gandhi and Mahatma Gandhi

[91] Cf. [Guha 2007, p. 460]

strikes further paralyzed the economy. President Fakhruddin Ali Ahmed declared a state of national emergency in 1975, which allowed Indira Gandhi to restore law and order; but she also severely cut into civil liberties and postponed elections at various levels. India's economy benefited, but corruption and authoritarian control by the state increased. The police was accused of arresting and torturing innocent people, the Health Ministry carried out forced vasectomies of men and sterilization of women to control population growth, slums were demolished killing thousands and leaving many more displaced. In 1977, Indira Gandhi finally called for elections, only to suffer an electoral defeat against an amalgamation of opposition parties; Morarji Desai became the first non-Congress prime minister. Indira Gandhi and her son were arrested for political power abuse during the emergency era. However, soon the coalition crumbled. In 1979, Charan Singh formed an interim government, and already in January 1980 the Congress and Indira Gandhi were back into power with a large majority.

The eighties saw a rise of insurgency in Punjab, communal violence in Assam, and when military forces raided the militant hideouts in the Golden Temple of Amritsar, the death of many civilians and damage to the temple inflamed many members of the Sikh community across India. On October 31, 1984, the Sikh bodyguards of Indira Gandhi murdered her. Further communal violence erupted in New Delhi and in parts of Punjab killing thousands of people.

The Congress chose Indira's son Rajiv Gandhi as the next leader and Prime Minister. He loosened government restrictions on the industry and encouraged science and technology, effectively spurring the birth of India's IT and BPO industry. However, India's masses did not benefit from these reforms and unemployment was on the rise. In 1989, elections only gave him a plurality and VP Singh became prime minister. He increased reservation quotas for low-caste Hindus, against which the opposition party BJP (Bharatiya Janata Party) protested; he had to resign and Chandra Shekhar took over for a few months, but his government collapsed when the Congress withdrew support.

2.2.6 Age of Reforms[92]

In the midst of an election campaign in May 1991, a female suicide attacker killed Rajiv Gandhi. Waves of shock and sympathy went through the country and carried the Congress party to victory. The party choose Narasimha Rao as its 'stopgap leader' to head a minority government. Nobody expected much of this seventy year old intellectual, quiet, and dull prime minister. Notwithstanding, he was about to unleash the biggest revolution in India since independence in 1947.

The financial crisis had been long looming. Rajiv Gandhi's government had spent profligately. When oil prices went up during the Gulf crisis, India had no foreign exchange reserves left to buy oil. This in turn lead to a flight in capital by an estimated twenty million nonresident Indians, many of whom had invested in

---

[92] Cf. [Das 2000, p. 213-227; Guha 2007, p. 694-695]

high interest accounts in Indian banks. Narasimha Rao understood that India was bankrupt, and as a first decision appointed Dr. Manmohan Singh as finance minister who had earned himself a doctorate from Oxford University in which he had suggested that India should move towards a more open trade regime;[93] he had been professor for economics and international trade at Panjab University in Chandigarh, then the governor of the Reserve Bank, and had also headed the South-South Commission in Geneva; This was the same Manmohan Singh who – in 2007 – was to become prime minister of India. Palaniappan Chidambaram, with an MBA from Harvard University, became commerce minister. The crisis was an opportunity for change; and change was necessary, as foreign exchange reserves were down to two weeks of import. A USD 2.2 billion emergency loan from the IMF was granted against a part of India's gold reserves, which were flown out to London. This had even hit the opposition leaders: gold is the ultimate symbol of trust and honor in India and pawning the national gold reserves to stay afloat was close to national humiliation.[94] The rupee currency was devalued by 20%, export subsidies were removed, the trade side of the 'Licence Raj' was abolished and replaced by Exim scrips, which allowed exporters to earn foreign exchange for part of the value of their exports. They could use them to directly import goods or sell them in the market, and other producers could buy them instead of applying for an import license. A year later, Exim scrips were replaced again by dual exchange rates that helped to further eliminate bureaucracy. Principal secretary A.N. Varma was tasked with de-licensing the industry and allowing foreign investments. Within two years, the fiscal deficit came down from 8.4% of GDP in 1990–91 to 5.7% in 1992–93, inflation decreased from 13% to 6%, and foreign exchange reserves shot up from USD 1 billion to USD 20 billion; foreign investment began to double each year.[95]

However, once the crisis had passed, the pressure diminished and reforms stopped or slowed down to an incremental pace. Privatization was not completed, labor reforms were not introduced, the agriculture or insurance business was not opened to the market. Subsidies once again started eating away the health and heart of the Indian country. India's infrastructure was not improved, and civil servants kept on asking for bribes. But since Narasimha Rao's reforms, India has learnt to appreciate the efficiency of a free market; there is broad consensus about the need for incremental and careful reforms.

The Congress Party was defeated in the elections of 1996. For many years no single party was able to win a majority; India faced unprecedented political instability.[96] The BJP started to play Hindu sentiments and campaigned against Muslims. In December 1992, this culminated in the demolition of Babri Masjid, a mosque in north India, leading to widespread violence in the country. The BJP

---

[93] Cf. [Guha 2007, p. 694]
[94] Cf. [Das 2000, p. 215]
[95] Cf. [Das 2000, p. 220]
[96] Cf. [Das 2000, p. 226]

realized that it had to become moderate in order to stay in power. Under the leadership of Prime Minister Atal Behari Vajpayee it followed a restrained path and concentrated on the IT sector.

2.2.7   Recent Events

Nuclear Tests 1998

In May 1998, the new government under Vajpayee conducted a series of underground nuclear tests, prompting Pakistan to go for nuclear tests immediately thereafter. The US and Japan imposed economic sanctions pursuant to the Nuclear Proliferation Prevention Act.

Kargil War 1999

In February 1999, the Indian prime minister Atal Behari Vajpayee traveled to Lahore in Pakistan by bus; he discussed increasing trade and more liberal visa regulations with his Pakistani counterpart Nawaz Sharif. However, no progress was made on the border issue in Kashmir. Despite the initiated talks, Pakistani paramilitary forces and Kashmiri insurgents began to infiltrate the Line of Control (LoC) that serves as a de-facto border between the two states. They were first detected by Indian shepherds in May 1999 who were scanning the mountains with binoculars in search of wild goats. Two weeks later, an armed conflict between both nations took place in the Kargil district of Kashmir. The Indian Army and Air Force successfully attacked Pakistani positions, and the navy prepared to block the Pakistani port of Karachi. Pakistan found itself in a prickly position with only 6 days of fuel left and covertly planned a nuclear strike on India. These news alerted the USA, and President Bill Clinton issued a strong warning to Pakistan's prime minister Nawaz Sharif, who had traveled to Washington to look for possible solutions. On returning to Pakistan, Nawaz Sharif formally called off the operation and Pakistan withdraw its forces behind the LoC. President Clinton's clear and firm demands not only averted a nuclear conflict on the subcontinent but rekindled relations between the USA and India.[97]

The aftermath of the conflict saw increased defense spending in India and a rise of the Indian stock market. It also provided material for Bollywood filmmakers and many movies cover this conflict, e.g. LoC Kargil, Lakshya, Dhoop, Mission Fateh, and Fifty Day War.

For Pakistan the war brought economical and political instability. On October 12, 1999, a bloodless coup d'etat by the Pakistani military placed army chief General Pervez Musharraf in power, ousting prime minister Nawaz Sharif. "The

---

[97] Cf. [BBC 160502]. Note that other authors, e.g. [Guha 2007] do not explicitly mention the nuclear threat in connection with the Kargil war.

Indians were not best pleased with these developments; for it was Musharraf who was believed to have masterminded the Kargil operations".[98]

Military Standoff with Pakistan 2002

In March 2000, President Bill Clinton visited India and Pakistan; the day after he landed in New Delhi, terrorists attacked a village in Kashmir. Even in July 2001, when President Musharraf visited Agra, terrorists again struck the valley. "This was becoming a pattern – whenever important dignitaries visited New Delhi the violence in Kashmir would escalate".[99] When US Secretary of State Colin Powell visited India in October 2001, terrorists launched a grenade assault on the Jammu and Kashmir assembly. And in December, four suicide bombers attempted to blow up the Indian Parliament. The attacks on both places brought an end to the political dialogue between India and Pakistan.

In the spring of 2002, military exchanges between Indian and Pakistani troops along the LoC became more frequent. The military build-up at the border intensified; India had 500,000 troops and Pakistan 120,000 troops in the region. Concerns about a nuclear exchange returned and the USA recommended all non-essential citizens to leave India.[100] In June, India accepted President Musharraf's pledge to end militant infiltration into India and war was averted.

Change from BJP to Congress

Simultaneously, in February 2002, a train carrying mostly Hindu Fundamentalists was burned down by a Muslim mob near the station of Godhra in Gujarat; the riots started the next day and let to more than 1,000 people dead[101] and 150,000 displaced.[102] The BJP-led state government was accused of not doing enough to stop Hindu mobs attacking Muslims.

But India's fast economic progress and a peace initiative with Pakistan increased the popularity of Vajpayee's government. In 2004, he recommended early general elections. Unexpectedly, the Congress party came back to power. President of the Congress, Italian born Sonia Gandhi, who is widow of Rajiv Gandhi, declined to take the post and opened the path for Dr. Manmohan Singh to become prime minister. With the benefit of hindsight, Vajpayee's feel-good slogan 'India is shining' and his promise to bring prosperity through market-led growth, did not find the approval of the village population who felt left behind in the economic progress. Dr. Manmohan Singh is the first Sikh to hold the position of prime minister in India. He currently continues economic liberalization and infrastructure projects; his tenure will end in 2009.

---

[98] [Guha 2007, p. 678]
[99] [Guha 2007, p. 679]
[100] Cf. [Howard 2002]
[101] Cf. [BBC 110505]
[102] Cf. [Brass 2005, p. 388]

Realignment with the USA and China

The growing Indian economy is a strong reason for a shift in foreign policy and especially a friendship with the USA. During the Cold War, the USA leaned towards Pakistan, and India towards the USSR. The nuclear tests of 1998 more or less marked the end of India's independent foreign policy. Initially, the USA objected but later came to accept India's nuclear status. Indian leaders took to speaking of common democratic values. But there was also economic self-interest from both countries: India's growing wealth meant a large market for American goods and the USA is by far the greatest outlet for India's IT and BPO industry.[103]

The driving force for the growing friendship between India and China is also of an economical nature. Chinese electronics and plastic goods show an increasing presence in Indian shops, whereas India exports drugs and cosmetics to China. In 2003, Prime Minister Vajpayee recognized Tibet as an integral part of China, and China returned the favor by accepting that the Himalaya state of Sikkim was part of India. His visit was returned in 2005 by Chinese Prime Minister Wen Jiabao, who called for an alliance between the Indian software and Chinese hardware industry to ensure that the twenty-first would be an Asian century.[104]

2.3   Government and Political Parties

Today the Indian Union is a parliamentary and democratic republic based on a federal system. Compared to the USA, the central government has greater power in relation to the states. It is patterned after the British parliamentary system, which is not surprising considering India's colonial past. Defense, foreign policy, and atomic energy are dealt with by the central government, whilst law and order remains the responsibility of the state governments. Science, technology, education, and environment are the responsibility of both governments.[105]

Head of state is the president who is elected for a period of five years. He nominates the prime minister and the cabinet. The congress is made up of the Council of States (Rajya Sabha) and the House of People (Lok Sabha). The Council of States was established in 1919, and with independence it developed into a second chamber with 250 representatives – 238 from the federal states and union territories and 12 directly nominated by the president. Every other year, one third of the Council's members leave and are replaced with new members asked to service for six years; it is headed by the vice prime minister. The House of People comprises a maximum of 552 members serving for five years. The prime minister heads the ministers and consults the president; hence the real power lies with the prime minister.

---

[103] Cf. [Guha 2007, p. 714-715]

[104] Cf. [Guha 2007, p. 716]

[105] Cf. [Sahay 2007, ch1.2]

The governors of the 28 federal states are appointed by the president for a period of five years. Every state has its own parliament and constitution. Seven union territories are directly administered by the central government.

Important political forces are:

- The Congress. Established in 1855 as Indian National Congress (INC), it is the oldest national party which gained importance under Gandhi and Nehru. It became the biggest and ruling party in 1980 under the leadership of Indira Gandhi, and moved to the opposition later under Italian born Sonia Gandhi. Since 2004, it is again the leading power with prime minister Dr. Manmohan Singh. While Manmohan Singh is one of the world's finest economists (see chapter 2.2.6), it is said that Sonia Gandhi is the real power behind him.[106]
- Bhartiya Janata Party (BJP). Established in 1952, BJP is a Hindu nationalist party that officially supports secularism but nevertheless sees India as a Hindu state. This rather radical approach got the party to power in 1998, which it surprisingly lost again in 2004. Their 'India is shining' campaign did not manage to convince the rural population who felt left behind in the country's economic advancement (see chapter 2.2.6).
- Communist Party. There are two arms: the Communist Party of India (CPI) had strong ties with the Soviet Union during the cold war. In 1964, the Communist Party of India Marxist (CPM) split from CPI. CPM is more of a Marxist oriented party and today stronger than CPI. The communist parties are open to the free-market economy and acknowledge the country's governing powers and have thus managed to participate in forming the government.

In addition, there are several hundred smaller parties that sometimes are of only local relevance.

India has a fairly standard system: legislature, executive, and judiciary – each being independent of the other to allow for checks and controls. India's judicial system came to live under the British and thus its concepts and procedures resemble those of Anglo-Saxon countries. The apex judicial authority is the supreme court which is vested with powers to enforce fundamental rights and guard the constitution. Then there are high courts in every state and lower courts at town level. In addition, alternative dispute resolution mechanisms are in place to help resolve pending court cases through arbitration or conciliation.[107] In recent years, the judiciary has taken on its role more actively and as the general populace has lost confidence in the bureaucracy of the executive, public interest litigation[108] has become quite common.[109]

---

[106] Cf. e.g. [Vermeer/Neumann 2008, p. 20]

[107] Cf. [Sahay 2007, ch1.2]

[108] Public interest litigation: concerned citizens file suits in court on matters of public and social interest, although they may not be directly affected.

[109] Cf. [Chhokar 2007, p. 977]

2.4   Economic Situation

After independence, India had been more or less a centrally planned economic system for almost four decades. The economy was controlled and regulated by the government. Initial and tentative steps in liberalization and easing of controls were taken in the mid-1980s. However, far-reaching changes have only taken place from 1991 onward.[110] Along with the opening of the markets came the rise of materialism together with a desire to get rich quickly. It has blurred the distinction between right and wrong, resulting in a fairly large-scale and deep-seated corruption (see chapter 4.5.4). This is not only confined to government officials but also some IT engineers inflate their CVs with jobs, skills, and experiences they have never had.

The present day economic situation in India looks promising with a GDP annual growth rate of 8.5%.[111] Domestic demand is increasing and propelling the economy upwards. The service sector industry, of which IT and BPO are a major part, contributes to 55% of economic output (see Figure 2-4) and grows at a rate of close to 10%. The agricultural sector with a contribution of less than 20% to the GDP is an area of concern. Despite favorable monsoon seasons in the past years, the sector only shows a meager growth rate of 2.3% and still occupies roughly 60% of the country's workforce. Mismanagement of irrigation, surface water, and an inability to increase productivity are some of the problems the sector faces.[112] This means many farmers face unbearable income situations. 25% of India's population lives below the poverty line; the unemployment rate is estimated at 7.2%.[113]

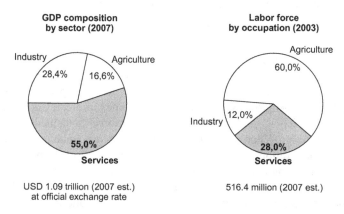

Figure 2-4. Composition of the Indian economy[114]

---

[110] Cf. [Chhokar 2007, p. 976]; see chapter 2.2.6 for a sequence of events
[111] Cf. [CIA Worldbook]
[112] Cf. [CIA Worldbook; Kapoor 2007, ch1.3]
[113] Data for 2007, cf. [CIA Worldbook]
[114] Cf. [CIA Worldbook]

As the fourth-largest economy in the world based on purchasing power adjusted GDP,[115] India is naturally an attractive destination for global investors. However, in the past its rigid policies were a significant hindrance for foreign direct investment (FDI). As a result of rigid and ambitious reforms, India has managed to position itself as a front-runner in the Asia-Pacific region. In 2005, the FDI policy was liberalized and now allows up to 100% FDI stake in certain ventures. [116] Prime Minister Dr. Manmohan Singh "... believe[s] that India needs a lot more foreign direct investment than we've got, and we should have the ambition to move in the same league many other countries in our neighborhood are moving. We may not be able to reach where the Chinese are today, but there is no reason why we should not think big about the role of foreign direct investment ...".[117]

But in India itself, there is "... widespread irritation that the Indian economy is [...] often seen in the West as being principally driven by armies of underpaid 'cybercoolies' working night shifts in call centers."[118] If India wins a cricket match, it's a national issue, and if Indian companies buy a Western company, it marks a symbolic moment. In February 2007, the Tata Group bought Corus, the British Steel company, for EUR 10.1 billion. The deal came exactly a century after Jamsetji Tata, founder of the Tata Group, first proposed making steel girders for the British-run Indian railways in 1907. The colonial administrator Sir Frederick Upcott had scoffed at this idea: "Do you mean to say that Tata's propose to make steel rails to British specifications? Why, I will undertake to eat every pound of steel rail they succeed in making."[119] Indian newspapers discussed the Tata-Corus deal under shrill headlines, such as 'India Poised for Global Supremacy', 'The empire strikes back', and 'Global Indian Takeover'.[120] Sixty years after independence the colonial past still pricks national pride. But with one deal India has turned from a service-driven economy to a manufacturing behemoth. And one year later, in early 2008, the Tata Group made headlines again when buying the brands of Jaguar and Land Rover from Ford.

The wealth of the Indian economy becomes now a subject of debate in the USA. In 2004, it was Democratic candidate John Kerry who built his campaign on fears of more Americans losing jobs to India should President George W. Bush be re-elected. He promised to save American jobs from being 'bangalored'.[121] In May 2008, both US President George W. Bush and US Secretary of State Condoleezza Rice (partly) justified the global rise of the food prices by the increased spending capabilities of India's growing middle class. This immediately

---

[115] Cf. [CIA Worldbook]; India's GDP based on purchasing power parity is estimated at USD 2.965 trillion for 2007.

[116] Cf. [Sahay 2007, ch1.2]

[117] [Gupta 2005]

[118] [Johnson 2007]

[119] British Colonial Administrator Sir Frederick Upcott, as quoted in [Johnson 2007]

[120] Cf. [Johnson 2007]

[121] Cf. [Guha 2007, p. 716]

prompted Indian politicians and newspapers to attack Bush, compare the food calories of an average American with those of an Indian, and demand India's right to eat. Minister of State for Commerce Jairam Ramesh said: "George Bush has never been known for his knowledge of economics. And he has just proved once again how comprehensively wrong he is. To say that the demand for food in India is causing increase in global good prices is completely wrong".[122]

As a matter of fact, the food and energy crisis of 2008 shows once more how economically vulnerable India is even after 61 years of independence. By mid 2008, inflation has pierced the 11-percent mark and reached its highest point in 13 years. India is spending roughly a third of the total tax revenue of 2007 on energy subsidies alone, the direct and indirect food and fertilizer subsidies are higher than budgeted, and as a result India is threatening its fiscal deficit and entire growth story. [123]

---

[122] Minister of State for Commerce Jairam Ramesh, as quoted in [TOI 040508]
[123] Cf. [Mehra/Fitter/Rajendran 2008, p. 28]

3 The Society and Culture in India

Any attempt at describing society and culture in India must begin with three assertions:

- Formally, India only came into being just over 60 years ago. The region in which Indian culture, society, and civilization has developed, has long been a loose and informal confederation. India is more a cultural unit than a political entity.
- In its history, the physical boundaries of this cultural unit were almost always larger than what India is today.
- India is a composite of multiple influences in a civilization that has continued to evolve for more than 5,000 years – and is still in the process of evolving as a living and changing culture.[124]

This chapter briefly describes the mosaic of Indian society and culture.

3.1   Caste System

In all societies, many people want to feel superior to others and find someone to do the hard and dirty work for them at low wages. All societies have some sort of hierarchy.

However, in India, societal hierarchy has been established as the caste system; it is believed to date back to the ancient law giver Manu in the Vedic period around 1,500–1,000 BC.[125] It effectively fragments the social and political life. Today, it is still the central organizing feature of life in the countryside, whereas the upper and middle classes in the cities tend to gloss it over.

The Brahmin (priest, teacher) is at the top of the ladder, followed by the Kshatriya (warrior, ruler, landholder). Third comes the Vaishya (businessman) and the Shudra (laborer, artisan) is last. Below these four castes are the casteless Untouchables and Tribals (Figure 3-1).

	Caste	Connotation	Percentage
1	Brahmin	Priest, teacher	
2	Kshatriya	Warrior, ruler, landholder	15%
3	Vaishya	Businessman	
4	Shudra	Laborer, artisan	50%
	Casteless	Untouchables, tribals	20%
	Other religions	Muslim, Sikh, Christian, Parsee, etc.	15%

Figure 3-1. India's caste system[126]

---

[124] Cf. [Chhokar 2007, p. 971-972]

[125] Cf. [Chhokar 2007, p. 974]

[126] Cf. [Das 2000, p. 140]

This classification system of four castes (varnas) holds around 300 local communities (jatis). The term varna means color and jati stands for birth. There is frequent confusion over these terms; the jatis actually matter in people's day-to-day lives and their members broadly identify with the varnas of ancient literary and religious texts. People of one jati share common religious rituals, food habits, and will not marry anyone from outside their defined group. Jatis can rise in social scale and upgrade from one varna to the next as they become more prosperous. The conversion to Buddhism, Christianity, or Islam does not necessarily liberate one from the caste system; in the villages, people carry on as before.

This system of varnas and jatis has made it possible for a vast variety of people on the Indian subcontinent to live together over many thousand years. In the caste system, a group acknowledges its differences and thereby integrates itself into the society. If someone eats beef, this person has to accept being classified as an Untouchable – and in this classification this behavior is tolerated. Correct behavior and adhering to these norms is called dharma. This is the reason for tolerance and peaceful diversity.[127]

There is a big difference to other cultures, e.g. the Christian culture where the ten commandments of the bible represent expectations for correct behavior. In India, there is no such common rule book for everyone, but the definition of right behavior depends on the community that individuals belong to.[128]

Shortly after India gained its independence, the concept of untouchability was officially abolished in 1950 and its practice made a criminal offense. Action programs were launched by liberal-minded leaders and roughly 20% of seats in colleges, universities, and jobs in the public sector and government were reserved for the former Untouchables, who now call themselves Dalit (the oppressed).

The next development regarding the caste system occurred in 1990. The politician Vishwanath Pratap Singh was looking for an electoral platform to differentiate himself from other politicians. The casteless Dalits already had a political voice and the upper caste had managed to look after themselves nicely for the past three thousand years. He discovered his chance in the backwardness of the Shudra caste, in which half of the country's population was laboring as barbers, carpenters, goatherds, artisans, and farm labor. The Shudras were lacking a political voice. He promised reservations in government jobs and in the education system based on their 'backwardness'. This movement spread with enormous speed and horrified the upper castes. Suddenly, fewer and fewer jobs and seats in universities would be available based on merit. The outcome was a caste war with students building barricades and dozens burning themselves. However, none of the political parties dared to support the students. Their effort was to no avail, the logic of the ballot box was too strong. Today, 50% of the government jobs and seats in colleges are based on criteria other than merit.[129] "[...] backward castes

---

[127] Cf. [Das 2000, p. 141]

[128] Cf. [Vermeer/Neumann 2008, p. 83]

[129] Cf. [Das 2000, p. 146]

are no longer a persecuted minority; they are the majority. Earlier, they suffered caste oppression, but now democracy has converted their advantage in numbers into enormous political clout. As a result, there is a continuous clamor for more quotas."[130]

The question is to what extent the caste system affects the ability of India's IT companies to operate? Does the caste system affect project hierarchy, teamwork, and deliverables?

Obviously the caste system has influenced the practice of leadership in India over the centuries. Warrior-kings belonged to the martial group of Kshatriya, and for them the ability to lead and win wars was essential. However, the kings were often guided by high priests, who were Brahmin and had an exalted position in the king's court. This pattern of leadership continued until very recently.[131]

Administrative and military jobs were always open to all castes. Farming was possible for everyone except for Brahmins, who were not expected to touch the plow. Studies by Western sociologists in the beginning of the 20th century have shown that a lower caste does not prohibit an individual to take up a modern occupation and that untouchables have moved to jobs like carpentry, black-smithing, and white-collar occupations.[132] In India, businesses are mainly family-run and require trust; a kin from one's own community is regarded more trustworthy. Hence, many business leaders have tended to hire employees from their own communities. Even though caste is the last thing on the mind of modern professionals, many employees are hired through recommendations from other employees as a safe recruitment channel. In one company, this can easily lead to an aggregation of employees from a particular community; it may promote divisiveness in the enterprise and can hinder effective teamwork.

While the caste system may be a reason for peaceful diversity, it also segments humans and builds a rather fragmented society. It used to kill enterprises by giving knowledge monopoly to Brahmins and delegating work to the lower castes.

While interviewing employees, one is usually unaware of their caste. The best person for the job is recruited. However, companies need to report the percentage of their employees belonging to certain lower and backward castes proving that they do not favor upper castes. This legal requirement was established recently and directly relates to a political campaign run by Vishwanath Pratap Singh in 1990.

On the other hand, the caste system may have contributed positively towards the success of the Indian IT and knowledge industry. Brahmins have had several thousands of years experience in dealing with abstract philosophical, religious, and spiritual concepts. The information age thus taps into the strengths of Brahmins, whereas product development and production in the industrial age might have suffered from the caste system.

---

[130] Cf. [Das 2000, p. 147]

[131] Cf. [Chhokar 2007, p. 975]

[132] Cf. [Das 2000, p. 142]

3.2   Role of the Family

The family continues to be one of the basic units of Indian society.[133] It is the anchor point of the entire life and for most social interactions.

Extended Family

The Indian concept of family is in stark contrast to the Western world where it usually connotes a nuclear family of two adults and their kids. In India, family always means the extended family. Most people live in joint families under one roof or in one apartment. On marriage, it is quite common for the son to remain at home and for his new wife to join him there. Even when their offspring is born, they mostly remain at home with the parents and sometimes even grandparents. Many young families sleep in one room together with their kids. But just as well as in the Western world there are looming conflicts between mother-in-law and daughter-in-law; they have to find ways of adjusting to each other in an environment of confined space.

As much as there are historical reasons for living in joint families, it is also a matter of convenience. There is always someone at home to look after the kids, supervise the maid, and get things done around the household. In the urban world of the IT cities, staying in a joint family may also be a financial necessity, as living space has become tremendously expensive and almost unaffordable.

However, the concept of family extends beyond the walls of the house, to aunts, uncles, and cousins. Sometimes these words denote real aunts, uncles, and cousins, but many times also very distantly related people. Still, in India, one stays connected to all these relatives – even if they are spread across the world. In the Western world, people usually meet more distant relatives at weddings and funerals only.

Family and happenings in the family come on top of the priority list of every Indian. Employees request their vacation around cousin's weddings, and if an elderly person in the family is sick, the employee might stay away from work or decline a business trip in order to take proper care of the relative. As a manager in the Indian industry, one has to strike a balance and mostly agree to the employee's request; otherwise, one would lose face, trust, and the employee might even escalate matters by putting in his papers and thereby undoubtedly risking his professional career for family-related matters. Family comes first, professional obligations come second.

Hierarchy in the Family

Social hierarchy is also evident in the family. Respect for elders is an important part of India's cultural heritage. Lines of hierarchy and authority are clearly drawn.

---

[133] Cf. [Brodbeck/Chhokar/House 2007, p. 1032]

People who are older and of higher status are still often treated with respect and deference.[134] It is very common to see a successful and highly qualified IT project manager to touch the feed of an elder person in the family. This is regardless of professional achievement and simply driven by age. It is still common for younger siblings to address older siblings by respectful terms rather than by name. In the Hindi language, children are asked to address their parents using the respectful 'aap' form rather than the more informal 'tum' they would use with their friends or which parents would use with them. In general, elders rank above juniors, and among people of similar age, males outrank females. The mother of a household is in charge of her daughters-in-law; a newly arrived daughter-in-law has the least authority. People learn to command others and in turn expect to receive directions from more senior members.

Networking and creating synergy among family members are typical characteristics of the Indian society. Family loyalty and unity is emphasized and a highly regarded ideal.

Traditionally, especially the older generation has not planned financially for retirement. In addition, inflation has made the older generation's saving relatively worthless. It was generally accepted that the retired parents' upkeep is the responsibility of the younger generation. IT companies cater for this requirement; the company health insurance does usually not only cover the employee, spouse, and children, but also includes the dependent non-working parents. This is now changing and today's professionals far less rely on their kids for their old-age upkeep.

The role of Women

A woman's role depends on the social class. In the lower middle class every day is a struggle for survival. The wife needs to take care of the kids, do all the household chores, and additional work for a better off household as a servant, maid, or cook to earn a few extra rupees. The husband will have occasional employment as a factory worker, security guard, or driver. However, there are also many cases where the husband is an unemployed drunkard and frequently beats up his wife. In the middle class, the husband will be regularly employed, the wife will either stay at home and look after the kids and the household, or if they live in with their parents, she may also have a professional job and the grandparents will raise the children. In the upper class, the household is taken care of by servants. It is not uncommon for a well-off household to employ a maid servant, a cook, a gardener, and a driver. If the wife follows the traditional role model, she will be busy socializing and looking after the well-being of the extended family.

Today, employees in the Indian IT industry are sourced from all three social levels. It is not uncommon for a driver's son to work alongside the foreign-born daughter of an established businessman. And apart from these rather stereotyped

---

[134] Cf. [Chhokar 2007, p. 992]

role models, there are of course many successful women in the IT industry and other businesses in India.

Marriages

Marriage is considered an institution and not the decision of two individuals who have fallen in love. It is the job of the parents to identify suitable partners. Most young professionals continue to accept this form of arranged marriages; many Indians have only seen their spouse once or twice before marriage and only in the presence of many relatives. Such a gathering is called a marriage interview, which can best be described as a cross-examination of features and capabilities. It is not uncommon for the girl's parents to ask for the pay slip of the boy. Also, the HR department of IT companies frequently receives calls from parents who inquire about the professional performance of a possible marriage candidate. The western process of dating, living together, and then deciding to go through the legal formalities of marriage are very rare in India. There is even a special term for this in Indian English, 'love marriage' as opposed to arranged marriages. But even if the girl and the boy have found each other 'unaided', the approval of the parents is deemed necessary.

Marriages also bring along implications for IT companies. Some husbands ask their wives to stop working and stay at home. Hence, the likelihood of a woman to put in her papers increases after the wedding. It is to be noted that such cases are on the decline and today, many women come back to work a few weeks after marriage and even after giving birth.

Divorce rates in India are among the lowest in the world. Only 1.1% of marriages are divorced, up from 0.74% in 1990.[135] In rural villages the rates remain very low, but they are shooting up in the urban sphere. Indian culture is going through a change. Today, women in urban India are better educated and many of them hold jobs that secure their economic independence. They are confident enough to walk out of bad marriages unlike the earlier generations who practically tolerated anything. Hence, more divorce cases are now coming to court, though this does not necessarily mean that there was no discord in the marriages of the earlier generations.

3.3   Educational System

History

For thousands of years, India has been a major place of learning. The Gurukul system of learning is one of the oldest in the world, where students reside together with the teacher (guru) in his house and extended family (kula). Students from the Brahmin and Kshatriya castes were taught orally by the teacher and also helped him with his daily household chores. The advent of the first millennium saw

---

[135] Cf. [DivorceRate ---]

higher education flourishing in university centers. Nalanda, the biggest of these centers, handled all branches of knowledge and housed up to 10,000 students and 2,000 teachers at its peak. In the 18th century, education was widespread and available to all levels of society through schools at temples, mosques, and in villages. The British did not recognize or support these traditional indigenous structures of learning, and since then the education system was on the decline. In the 19th century the British established the current Western-style education system and founded many colleges in India. After independence, education was first the responsibility of the states and in 1976 became a joint chore of the central government and the individual states.

Structure

Today, schooling lasts for 12 years in three stages (see Figure 3-2). Reaching out to the comparatively well off, the private sector has started activities for pre-primary education: lower and upper kindergarten. Often kindergarten becomes an integral part of regular schooling.

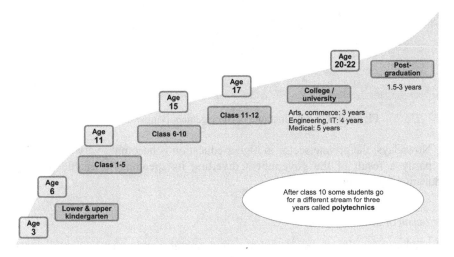

Figure 3-2. Indian education system

Higher education offers the opportunity to specialize in certain fields, including technical or engineering studies. The quality of India's universities varies extremely. The top schools for technical and management education, such as the seven Indian Institutes of Technology (IITs), the seven Indian Institutes of Management (IIMs, see Figure 3-3), and for example the Indian School of Business in Hyderabad (ISB), have world-class status and rank among the top universities in Asia. In the world-wide ranking of the Times Higher Education Supplement, the IITs and IIMs are at position 57 and 68 respectively.[136] These universities take pride in stringent selection processes and accept only about two percent of applicants. Apart from these examples of educational excellence, there is a rather steep decline in quality in the remaining 200 universities and 12,600 colleges.[137]

Typically, Indian students graduate and join the IT industry at the age of 21, which makes them appear immature compared to some Western graduates. For instance in Germany, a typical (male) graduate will be at least 26 years of age.

Figure 3-3. Indian Institute of Management Bangalore (IIM-B)[138]

Nowadays, the private sector in higher education is becoming very strong; this is partly a result of the government diverting its spending to enable primary education for the masses.

Criticism of Indian Education System

The Indian education system, together with the parents and society at large, places emphasis on passing examinations with high percentages. Very few institutes place importance on independent out-of-the-box thinking, developing personality, and creativity. Many schools and universities still follow the system of rote learning, a learning technique focusing on memorization through learning by repetition and as a consequence avoiding a deeper understanding of the subject. The education boards have recently been trying to improve the quality of education

---

[136] Cf. [Times 2006]

[137] Cf. [Müller 2006, p. 72]

[138] Photo by author

by intensifying practical and project work. However, even this tends to be memorized or even plagiarized by 'smart' students.

The hierarchical society in India puts a lot of pressure on students to perform well and score high percentages in their exams. The percentage scored can very well make the difference for whether students are allocated a seat in engineering and can thereafter hope for a job in the IT industry – or have to take up studies in general commerce which will later only allow them to fill less lucrative positions, e.g. as customs officers at the airport. A very high score and excellent performance in additional tests may reserve a place at one of the prestigious institutes, from which a highly-paid first job at Wall Street in the USA is very much in reach. There is an alarming increase in the number of students who cannot bear this competition and commit suicide every year.

The general corruption prevalent in India also has an effect on the education system. Lucrative seats in engineering or medical studies are sometimes sold for high prices. But even for admission to a fairly good kindergarten, the principal may request an additional unaccounted payment for 'the good of the school'.

Most teachers conduct tuition lessons on the school premises after hours in order to increase their meager salary. The tuition industry is driven by high competition in the board examinations where every mark counts, and the loss or gain of one mark determines whether or not students can join the college of their choice. Some teachers use this pressure to force students into their own tuition classes, sometimes by downgrading their marks in school.[139]

Ragging is a widespread phenomenon in India's educational system; it is a verbal, physical, or sexual aggression by more senior to junior students. Ragging incidents have included stripping of all clothes, public sexual acts and sodomy, merciless beating, forced in-taking of drugs, forced imposing of rules such as not removing shoes for months.[140] Complaints make the situation even worse for junior students; singling out a protesting student is a common feature in ragging. In most institutions ragging is rather harmless, not more than cleaning the senior's room or taking off a shirt, it is conducted during a fixed period of time, sometimes only on one day. Once this is over, seniors suddenly become good friends and turn into guardians for the junior students. But "Ragging is an archaic method of interaction with several harmful effects. [...] There are many other healthy ways of interaction which are more effective and without human rights abuse."[141] In 2001, the Supreme Court of India issued a definition of ragging with recommendations to abolish it,[142] and in 2007 has ruled that college authorities and functionaries are now responsible for maintaining a ragging-free environment

---

[139] Cf. [Mukherji 2008]

[140] Cf. [Agarwal et al. 2007, p. 14]

[141] [Agarwal et al. 2007, p. 14]

[142] Supreme Court of India, Writ petition No. 656 of 1998, 4 May 2001, www.noragging.com/laws/supreme-court-judgement.html (accessed 23 Mar 2008)

in colleges.[143] However, it is feared that many colleges now try to cover up ragging incidents to avoid public embarrassment in the media.[144]

Role of the IT industry in Education

NASSCOM – the IT industry association – collaborates with the government to increase the scope and scale of the IITs and IIMs.

Companies also have a vital role in IT education. Prior to assigning young graduates to customer projects, they offer between four and twelve months of corporate education. Besides specialized training on IT topics such as SAP®, ABAP, Java, and office applications, the focus is on personal development, e.g. English communication skills and intercultural awareness.

3.4   Key Indian Beliefs, Values and Avoidances

Figure 3-4 summarizes the general key beliefs, values, and major dislikes/ avoidances in the traditional Indian society.

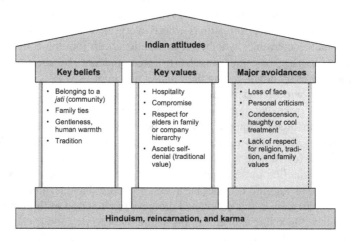

Figure 3-4. Summary of Indian attitudes

Reincarnation and karma are important concepts and values in the Hindu and Sikh religion. Where and if someone is reborn as a human, animal, or plant mostly depends on the credit points (punya) one has collected in the previous life through good deeds. Karma is about managing a deliverance (moksha) from the cycle of reincarnation (sansara) and also an explanation of the suffering in the current life. Therefore, karma is not a good or bad act but the consequence of one's deeds.

---

[143] Supreme Court of India Item No. 33, Court No. 4, Section XIA, 16 May 2007, www.noragging.com/laws/supreme-court-order-may-2007.html (accessed 23 Mar 2008)

[144] Cf. [Agarwal et al. 2007, p. 13]

Indians believe in doing their best and leaving the rest to fate. If something does not go according to plan, one would not get too worked up about it as it would be seen as fate determined by the doings in the previous life.

The Hindu gods can also help to escape the sansara, and this is the reason why people pray to them, asking them to enable an earlier escape from sansara or at least grant a better reincarnation. Hence, death in the Hindu logic only means a material death with the soul continuing to exist in another form. The body is mortal, the soul is immortal.

The concept of karma can make Indians appear somewhat laid back because of their equanimity to accept things the way they are; they show great coping skills. Hyperactive and worried foreigners are sometimes asked to adjust a little. 'Simply adjust madi' is also the name of a radio program of a local radio station in Bangalore.

The continuing commercialization of the Indian society – largely sparked by the IT boom – brings prosperity to India's middle classes. But it also brings along megacities, overcrowding, corruption, atrocious working conditions, and environmental pollution, if not disasters. Life becomes consumerist and banal, alienating the individual from its former family ties and traditional values. Pursuit of material wealth has redefined the purpose of knowledge. Integrity is replaced by corruption, humility by display of achievements, asceticism by showing off wealth. Mobility requirements for onsite assignments weaken family bonds, leave no time for religion, and weaken interest in community life. In short: comercialization threatens the traditional Indian way of life and values. "It is no good hoping that Indian values and the Indian way of life will survive intact. [...] Modernization has its positive and negative consequences, and we have to live with them."[145]

---

[145] [Das 2000, p. 151]

4 India's IT & BPO Industry

4.1 Development of the IT & BPO Industry

4.1.1 Early Steps Towards Becoming a Computer Economy[146]

In the early days of India's independence, agriculture contributed to 55.4 percent of national income, compared to only 16.6 percent in 2007.[147] More than 30 years ago, India decided that if it was ever to become a global player and developed country, it would first have to become an information technology country and build on its historical reputation in mathematics. The central planning in the 1970s actually helped to kick off a long-term plan, focusing initially on education and training. Having first ensured the availability of human resources for the IT market, India's government then wanted to create a business-friendly environment for the IT services industry. But it also wanted to ensure that foreign direct investment would fall in line with India's development priorities. The Foreign Exchange Regulation Act (FERA) became effective on January 1, 1974, and was India's means to achieve this objective. In 1977, business became in fact so uncomfortable for foreign companies that IBM decided to pull out entirely from the country. IBM had commenced operations in India in 1955 with long-term objectives for growth and increase of market share through an improved competitive stance. The Reserve Bank of India (RBI) had analyzed IBM's activities in India and concluded that IBM had to reduce its foreign equity to 40 percent. The Government of India contended that IBM was reaping very high profits from importing the then already obsolete and outdated IBM 1401 computer system which was sold and leased at standard global rates. IBM was repatriating these profits without transferring any sophisticated technology to India. Additionally, IBM India had to pay headquarter expenses to the parent company, and the Government of India understood this as repatriation of hidden profit. IBM was willing to partly adhere to the FERA and submitted a proposal for restructuring its business. However, then Prime Minister Morarji Desai communicated to IBM that no exception was possible. IBM was not willing to accept these terms and reluctantly decided to withdraw from India; IBM ceased operations in India on May 21, 1978.[148] Following IBM's departure from India, changes in the international business climate forced the government to set new policies for the development of the computer industry in India. By 1988, IBM was again actively seeking and securing new business in India and formally returned in 1991 by forming an alliance with Tata,[149] which they later bought out.

---

[146] This chapter builds on [Messner 2008a, p. 17-18], a previous publication by the author.

[147] Cf. [Chandra/Rau/Ryans 2002, ch12; CIA Worldbook]; see chapter 2.4

[148] Cf. [Negandhi/Palia 1988]

[149] [NYT 1991]

4.1.2   Years of Bodyshopping

In 1991, the long running fiscal deficit precipitated an economic crisis in India (see chapter 2.2.6) and as a result the government relaxed controls over the international movement of capital enabling foreign companies to operate subsidiaries with a major foreign stake of ownership in India. This was when multi-national IT players started coming to India (see chapter 4.3.3); but the intensive ramp-up of their resources started only after the year 2000.

Indian IT firms led by Infosys, Tata Consultancy Services (TCS), and Wipro began to outgrow the limited domestic market and serve the needs of the foreign IT services market. Indian IT professionals were deployed as temporary onsite workers to clients in the Western world who in turn were able to produce software code significantly cheaper than with computer professionals from developed countries. This business model quickly became known as *bodyshopping*.[150]

The new institutional environment in India allowed Indian companies to move from debt financing to raising capital on equity markets; this gave them the ability to head for more aggressive growth strategies and further leverage the advantage of wage arbitrage. However, it still took the export market till the year 2001, i.e. till the Y2K boom, to outgrow the domestic market in terms of revenue (see Figure 4-2).

The Indian IT industry started as a labor-arbitrage body shop, but is now moving into knowledge-intensive services. Indian IT engineers have not only learnt how to solve problems, but have gained experience in re-engineering processes and making process flows more effective.

While the advantages of wage arbitrage and a lack of IT engineers were major drivers on the demand side, in India itself the growth of the IT and BPO industry was further leveraged by two factors:

- Introduction of the Software Technology Park (STP) scheme in 1999 with major tax savings for the export market (see chapter 4.1.3).
- Software process improvement (SPI) through adaptation of quality models like ISO and CMM to provide process support and control to handle growth (see chapter 4.1.4).

4.1.3   Software Technology Park Scheme

In 1999 the Government of India established a scheme called *Software Technology Park (STP)* which exempts the export-oriented IT market from paying tax on their export revenue as per Section 10(A) and (B) of the Income Tax Act; details of the requirements and benefits are given in Figure 4-1.

Considering that India's domestic market is extremely price sensitive, the benefits to be realized under the STP scheme are even more of a reason for an

---

[150] Cf. [Sako 2006, p. 3]

Requirements for recognition as STP	Benefits
• 100% export oriented undertaking (EOU) for software development; export through data communication link or physical record transfer • Includes export of professional services, i.e. onsite assignments of consultants • Not more than 25% of software to be sold in India domestic market (in value terms) • Minimum export performance of 250,000 USD for 5 years (or five times the value of imported goods) • Can be set-up by a state government, public or private sector undertaking; either in an STP complex or as a stand-alone unit • Custom bonding procedures to be followed	• Profit and gains derived from export of software are fully exempt from tax in India till 31st Mar 2010; the tax can be as high as 48% • Duty free imports of infrastructure (computers etc.) from outside India • Excise exemption on goods (e.g. furniture) bought from India domestic market • Foreign equity up to 100% permissible • Computer systems can be used for training purposes inside the STP

Figure 4-1. Software Technology Park (STP) scheme

Indian IT company to look for offshore revenues. And when India started to move into offshore business process outsourcing (BPO), the Indian industry coined the term ITES, which stands for IT Enabled Services.[151] In simple language, it was argued that a workplace in a call center is equipped with a computer and therefore BPO – now named ITES – should enjoy the same tax benefits as IT development.

The STP scheme was originally planned for 10 years and supposed to end in 2009. Heavy profit concerns of the industry have led A Raja, minister for communications and IT, to ask finance minister P Chidambaram for a 10-year extension on the ground that the IT and BPO industry need some more years to mature. In April 2008, it was announced that the scheme would – for now – be prolonged for another year until March 2010.[152]

4.1.4 Software Process Improvement

The Indian software industry has been maturing in many dimensions. In the value chain it started as a subcontractor for manpower and shifted to doing complete coding or testing phases of projects. In the early 90s, the quality norm ISO9000 was introduced and the Indian software industry quickly recognized its potential to improve its quality processes while at the same time establishing a unique selling proposition on the international market. When CMM was introduced in the late 90s, almost the entire Indian IT industry went for a re-certification and within a few years, many software companies matured to level 4 or level 5. More than half of the total high-maturity organizations in the database of the Carnegie Mellon Software Engineering Institute (SEI) are from India.[153] While Software Process Improvement (SPI) usually is a slow process, the fast adaptation in India has many reasons.[154]

---

[151] Cf. [Davies 2004, ch3]

[152] Cf. [Business Line 300408]

[153] Cf. [Jalote 2001, p. 1]

[154] For a detailled list of reasons see [Jalote 2001, p. 2-5]

On a worldwide basis, the services sector has responded strongly to SPI as it is directly driven by customers. With mainly international customers, the Indian IT & BPO industry felt the need to follow global standards and frameworks. Selling the offshore model as opposed to onsite staff augmentation meant customers had to be convinced that a company thousands of miles away can service them in good quality; a globally accepted quality model was a key factor in this argumentation. Managing subcontracted work required monitoring structures and some formality at the offshore interface in order to reduce risks.

The high growth rate had to be managed by solid and controlled processes. Software was at the core of the business and thus SPI got the attention of management who wanted to improve quality in order to fight effects of commoditization; the value proposition had to be changed from cost arbitrage to quality. Due to the early adoption of ISO, people in many companies have taken quality to their hearts and contributed actively to further improve on quality management systems, which then lead to the adoption of the various CMM levels.

The average age of IT engineers, BPO employees, and managers in the Indian industry is very young. This is largely due to the young age of the industry itself and because of the rapid growth of the industry in the last 10 years; this has created opportunities and also an organizational necessity for employees to move up the career ladder faster. Younger people are generally more receptive to change and improvements, but they also need more guidance, supervision, and control; SPI provided a framework to cater to both requirements. On top of this, Indian managers would have come into contact with quality frameworks earlier in their career as developers and provide backing for SPI initiatives.

India's IT industry does not only attract computer scientists but also graduates from related disciplines in engineering and commerce, who are given a three-month induction program to software development. As opposed to studies in computing science, where students first learn programming and technology, such induction programs focus on software engineering right from the beginning. In other words, the process-based approach to software development is embedded into employees at a very early stage.

Last but not least, the Indian collectivistic culture (see chapter 1.2.2) supports conforming to established frameworks. Indians also do not mind getting measured as much as some Western nations, and there are fewer concerns about misuse of collected data.

Today, showcasing a quality certification is no longer a distinguishing factor or selling proposition for an Indian IT company, but it has become a selling necessity driven by peer pressure as customers have started to expect Indian companies to be certified at the highest maturity levels.

4.1.5 The Boom Time

Gradually, Indian software firms such as Infosys were moving from bodyshopping to offshore development contracts. Indian IT engineers would no longer travel onsite to work as a means of staff augmentation but would perform the development work from Offshore Development Centers (ODCs) in India. This offered an even greater cost arbitrage to the advantage of both, the Indian companies as well as their clients. Against the cost advantages, the clients perceived greater risks because they could no longer directly control staff and their deliverables. As highlighted in chapter 4.1.4, the Indian IT industry invested heavily in improving management and quality assurance processes.

Indian companies are now trying to secure a local presence in foreign markets in order to become true multinational players and get access to higher-end decision makers, thus acquiring more knowledge-based projects and not only product development assignments. They are beginning to compete with companies like Accenture, Capgemini, EDS, and IBM who in turn have also spread their geographical reach and have set up ODCs in India; traditionally, they do not only concentrate on the implementation but devise strategies for technology solutions. Such high-end work not only requires domain experience but also domain expertise which is still mainly available in the Western world.

Today's worldwide IT service market size amounts to USD 819 billion.[155] Within this market, offshore delivery is growing at 14.5% in Europe and 18% in North America, thereby soaking up more and more market share.[156] Revenue from the Indian IT and BPO industry is marked by sustained double-digit revenue growth and in 2008[157] it reached USD 64 billion (see Figure 4-2 and Figure 4-3) with a compound annual growth rate (CAGR) of 33.3% for the total market, 28.3% for the

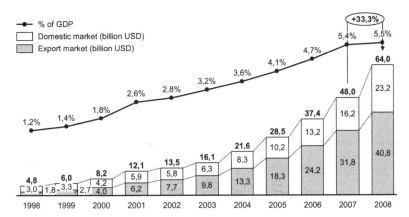

Figure 4-2. India IT industry performance over the last ten years[158]

---

[155] As estimated by Gartner, the research company, for 2008, cf. [Hale et al. 2008]; this is up from USD 748 billion in 2007 and USD 677 billion in 2006.

[156] Cf. [Thun 2008a, p. 3]

[157] Relates to the Indian financial year 2007-08 ending March 31, 2008.

[158] Data from [Nasscom 2007; Nasscom 2008]. Figures include IT services, engineering services, research and development (R&D), software products, ITES-BPO, and hardware. Attention: 2007 relates to the Indian financial year from April 2006 to March 2007; 2006 relates to April 2005 to March 2006; etc.

export market, and 43.2% for the domestic market alone. There is also strong optimism in the industry to achieve a target of USD 60 billion for the export market by 2010.[159]

Multi-national companies have announced an investment of more than USD 10 billion in the next few years. In Bangalore alone, every month, an estimated 10 foreign companies open shop. Along with the revenue growth, the number of employees in the Indian IT industry is also rapidly increasing; the year 2008 has seen 24% more employees in this sector than 2007 (see Figure 4-4). There is high pressure on the HR functions in the IT industry to meet these staffing requirements. They have already entered a vicious circle of quality vs. quantity (see chapter 4.4).

	Export		Domestic	
	2007	2008	2007	2008
Software	22.9	29.5	7.1	10.1
BPO	8.4	10.9	1.1	1.6
Hardware	0.5	0.5	8.0	11.5
Total	**31.8**	**40.8**	**16.2**	**23.2**

in USD billion / Indian financial year
figures may not add up due to rounding off

Figure 4-3. Revenue break-up of the Indian IT industry[160]

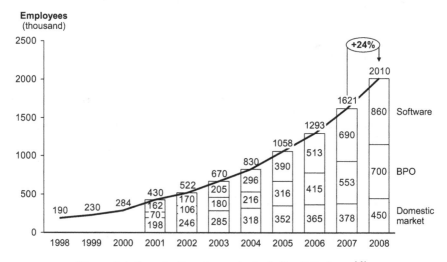

Figure 4-4. Growth of employees in the Indian IT industry[161]

---

[159] Cf. [Nasscom 2007, p. 1-2; Nasscom 2008, p. 1]

[160] Data from [Nasscom 2008]

[161] Data from [Nasscom 2007, p. 1; Nasscom 2008, p. 4]. Figures do not include hardware. Attention: 2007 relates to the Indian financial year from April 2006 to March 2007; 2006 relates to April 2005 to March 2006; etc.

Figure 4-5. Office of SAP® LABS in Bangalore (Whitefield)[162]

Figure 4-6. Office of Capgemini in Bangalore (Outer Ring Road)[163]

---

[162] Photo by author
[163] Photo by author

Regarding infrastructure, leading MNCs and Indian companies alike have invested into (near) world-class buildings and office infrastructure; Figure 4-5 to Figure 4-6 show typical software development centers. Generally, call center operators and IT engineers both work in large offices on their computers placed in compartments divided by shoulder-high partitions (Figure 4-7). Besides competitive salaries, chances for competency and managerial development, a healthy and positive work environment is equally important to the company's employees in India.

Figure 4-7. Office of Capgemini in Mumbai (Vikhroli West)[164]

4.1.6 Critical Years Ahead?

The Indian IT industry is a number game; everything revolves around headcount and charge-out rates (COR). The fantastic revenue growth of the last ten years was

---

[164] Photos by Capgemini

mainly due to an explosive increase of manpower (Figure 4-4). The daily charge-out rates of the Indian software developers to the Western customers, however, were only adjusted to the rise and fall of the rupee currency.

Figure 4-8 shows a revenue productivity[165] of 3.43% for the export-oriented IT industry in 2008.[166] The CAGR of revenue productivity was negative in 2007 and has picked up again in 2008 with 3.36%. Revenue productivity for the export-oriented BPO industry was only 1.56% in 2008. It demonstrated a meager CAGR of 0.06% in 2007 and 2.51% in 2008. Most of the revenue growth of the last years was contributed by adding more people, which is a less scalable and difficult-to-sustain business model.[167]

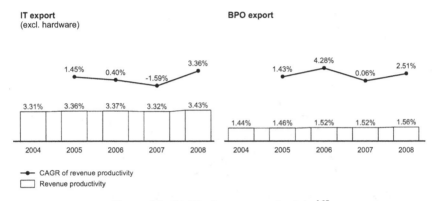

Figure 4-8. CAGR of revenue productivity[168]

Increasing commoditization of IT delivery, competition from other offshore countries and from new me-too market-entrants in India, together with falling charge-out rates of Western consultants due to a worldwide economic recession leaves the Indian IT industry with little choice but to streamline its processes, take an industrialized approach to software engineering, and optimize utilization of its offices and other infrastructure in order to compensate for the steep incline of salaries (see chapter 4.4).

In addition to the above measures, Indian pure-players will need to move up in the value pyramid towards consulting, software products, and R&D services, where the value capture is higher than in systems integration, application development and maintenance, programming and maintenance services, and IT-enabled services. As one moves higher up the value curve, the complexity of required skills and competencies also increases.[169] It remains to be seen how Indian pure-players will manage to compete in this traditional stronghold of MNCs.

---

[165] Revenue productivity is defined as revenues (billion)/employees (thousand) and can be accepted as a good measure for competitiveness, cf. [Umamaheswari/Momaya 2008, p. 129].

[166] Relates to the Indian financial year 2007-08 ending March 31, 2008.

[167] Cf. [Umamaheswari/Momaya 2008, p. 116]

[168] Computed from data in Figure 4-2, Figure 4-4, and [Nasscom 2007; Nasscom 2008].

[169] Cf. [Umamaheswari/Momaya 2008, p. 118-119]

4.2 The 'Silicon Valleys' of India

Tier-I Cities

IT and BPO offshoring companies are mostly clustered around the major cities because of their need for skilled employees who congregate in the major cities. Hence, the industry has grown in various locations in India (see Figure 4-9). The six key cities form a *Northern* and a *Smaller Southern Triangle* and are commonly referred to as tier-I locations for offshoring.

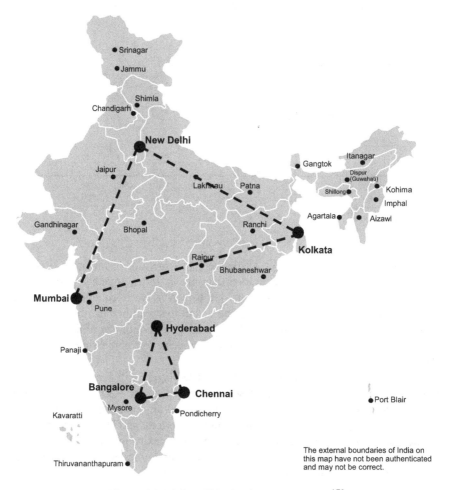

Figure 4-9. Major offshoring locations in India[170]

---

[170] Cf. [Messner 2008a, p. 18-19]

In India's north the focus is on three regions: Mumbai, Delhi, and Kolkata. The Delhi metropolitan region is usually termed as the National Capital Region (NCR) and comprises the cities of New Delhi, Noida, and Gurgaon. The city of Kolkata is an upcoming location with increasing importance for outsourcing organizations. Despite its poor international reputation stemming from its historical association with poverty, it today boosts of a good infrastructure at lower operating costs than in other established locations.

In the south, IT development and BPO is concentrated on the technology triangle of Bangalore, Hyderabad, and Chennai. Bangalore is often referred to as the Silicon Valley of India; it has grown from a garden city, where pensioners would move to spend their retirement years, to a supercharged city of rapid growth. Chennai and Hyderabad are beginning to earn a strong reputation in BPO services. In both cities, the creation of new office space in 2008 sees a high increase compared to 2007. In Bangalore, the growth rate is stagnating or keeping pace with the previous year (see Figure 4-10). Due to high rentals in central business districts (CBD), most companies are shifting from prime to secondary or even tertiary locations in the outskirts of the cities. As a result, very little additional office space is created in the CBDs.[171]

Location	Addition of office space in 2007	Addition of office space in 2008 (est.)	Rental in CBDs per sqm (INR and USD)	
Bangalore	1.2m sqm	0.9m sqm	860 INR	20 USD
Chennai	0.9m sqm	1.4m sqm	840 INR	20 USD
Delhi (incl. Gurgaon, Noida)	1.3m sqm	1.4m sqm	3,660 INR [172]	87 USD
Hyderabad	0.4m sqm	0.7m sqm	700 INR	17 USD
Mumbai (incl. Thane, Powai, Navi Mumbai)	n.n.	1.6m sqm	4,840 INR [173]	115 USD

Figure 4-10. Growth of office space in IT centers[174]

Tier-II and tier-III Cities

The congestion in realty structures together with high human capital costs has forced the IT and BPO companies to look out for smaller cities. The respective

---

[171] Cf. [Sivan 2008]

[172] CBD Delhi: Connaught Place.

[173] CBD Mumbai: Nariman Point, Fort, Cuff Parade.

[174] Data extracted and converted from an analysis by realty consultant CB Richard Ellis, as quoted in [Sivan 2008]

governments haven taken initiatives in providing the smaller cities with infrastructural facilities and in creation of Special Economic Zones (SEZs). The promising future of these cities drives investors to invest into property predicting long-term gain in the years to come.

Some of the tier-II cities are in close proximity to the established silicon valleys. In the Mumbai region, the city of Pune (Maharashtra) has scooped up some work previously performed in Mumbai itself. Pune is an independent city itself, but sufficiently close to Mumbai to allow business with clients based in Mumbai. Mysore (Karnataka) is an upcoming location some 150 km from Bangalore; its infrastructure is still cheap compared to Bangalore, and it is also an attractive location for employees.

Other tier-II and tier-III cities with an importance for the IT and BPO industry are Ahmedabad (Gujarat), Bhubaneswar (Orissa), Chandigarh (Punjab), Cochin (Kerala), Coimbatore (Tamil Nadu), Panaji (Goa), Indore (Madhya Pradesh), Jaipur (Rajasthan), Kozhikode (Kerala), Mangalore (Karnataka), Nagpur (Maharashtra), and Trivandrum (Kerala). These cities provide cost advantages of 15% to 30% through lower wages, less attrition, and lower real estate costs.

Skeptics contend that the industry will not find many skilled human resources in these cities as most of them have already shifted to bigger cities in search for better opportunities. However, once things start moving towards the tier-II and tier-III places it can be safely assumed that a reverse migration will take place. If there are job opportunities, people will only be too happy to leave the congested mega-cities behind and opt for a more peaceful life in the tier-II and tier-III cities, which may happen to be closer to their home towns as well.

For firms entering India for the first time, tier-I cities are likely to prevail for some time as they provide higher comfort levels.

4.3   Operating Models

The market landscape of IT and BPO companies operating in India is highly fragmented; they can best be grouped by three different clusters:

- Captive offshore centers are direct subsidiaries of Western companies delivering services only for their parent company.
- Firms of Indian origin (FIOs) are IT & BPO companies native to the subcontinent.
- Multi-national IT & BPO companies that have either bought FIOs or founded their own subsidiaries in India.

The captive offshore centers are by far outstripped by the growth of external offshore delivery companies. There is a very high number of small and medium suppliers operating in the IT service market; the top 10 suppliers (in terms of revenue) share a mere 25% of the market.[175]

---

[175] Cf. [Gartner 2007, p. 7]

4.3.1   Captive Offshore Centers

The trend of establishing a company's own facilities in a low-cost location is known as captive offshoring; it was triggered by early success from companies such as Texas Instruments and Motorola. Between 2000 and 2005, more than 200 companies from across the globe and across verticals have established such captive centers in India; another 100 companies plan to follow suit.[176]

They are mainly concentrated in Bangalore, New Delhi NCR, Mumbai, Chennai, and Hyderabad (see Figure 4-11), i.e. in cities offering the best infrastructure, business environment, and possibilities of recruiting from the job market. Nine out of ten existing captives plan to grow headcount at 50% per annum or more.[177] Their reasons are manifold:[178]

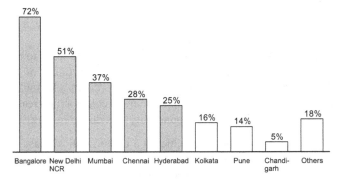

Figure 4-11. City-wise distribution of captives in India[179]

- It is 'in' to go to India, the market is asking for it, and the competition is doing it as well.
- Captive offshore centers provide better control and protection of intellectual property together with power to keep the Indian management 'on a shorter leash'.
- Stunned by the high profitability of Indian companies, firms compare the cost-to-company of Indian employees with the charge-out-rate (COR) of IT service providers and believe they can further reduce costs by doing it themselves.
- Many companies think it is easier for them to ensure consistent processes, quality, and culture within their own captive center. They also suggest that they can have better access to experienced staff compared to an established IT service provider with its shallow hierarchical pyramid and big number of junior employees.

---

[176] Cf. [Apte et al. 2007, p. 2]

[177] Cf. [Subramanian/Atri 2006, p. 8]

[178] Cf. [Apte et al. 2007, p. 2]

[179] Some companies have captives in more than one location; data from research by [Rajeevan et al. 2007, p. 9]

Forrester, the market research company, estimates that 60% of the captive centers in India are struggling.[180] Captives typically suffer from the following three inhibitors:[181]

- Initial management support dwindles and the business model collapses. If there is no continuous pressure from top management, control freak operational managers will refrain from moving work offshore. As a result, the captive unit will not reach its critical mass and the business case will fail. In addition, the company would have hired and trained employees who then start sitting idle.
- Sky-rocketing attrition drives HR costs. From an Indian perspective, work coming to offshore captive centers is mainly maintenance of old systems and very rarely on new technologies and new product development. Given the current market situation in India, this leads to immediate and increased attrition. Because of their limited size, it is difficult for captives to match the clear career paths that established offshore IT serviced providers offer; this in turn leads to increased attrition at senior levels.
- Process integration failure between front and back-office leads to quality issues. Processes designed to work within one closed department of the company suddenly crumble when deployed at a global level. In addition, there are no fine-tuned and established tools to support remote collaboration readily available. This results in quality issues and productivity loss due to rework.

The captive model can work if it achieves a certain critical mass within one to two years of its launch. This so-called captive critical mass (CCM) is around 350 to 500 employees for application development and maintenance activities and 250 to 300 people for a BPO operation.[182] The CCM figures will rise in the years to come, as along with a continuing offshoring boom resources in India will become scarcer.

4.3.2   Firms of Indian Origin

In 2005, 84% of offshore IT delivery was performed by Indian owned companies.[183] Such companies are sometimes also referred to as firms of Indian origin (FIOs)[184] or more commonly as Indian *pure players* (see Figure 4-12). Consequently, stock evaluations for pure players have sky-rocketed over the last years.

---

[180] Cf. [Apte et al. 2007]

[181] Also see [Apte et al. 2007, p. 6-8; Iyengar 2006, p. 5-6; Subramanian/Atri 2006, p. 8] for problems undermining captive centers.

[182] Cf. [Apte et al. 2007, p. 6; Iyengar 2006, p. 2-3]; these figures do not apply if the captive center performs highly specialized or niche work.

[183] Cf. [HSBC 2007, p. 8]

[184] Cf. [Umamaheswari/Momaya 2008, p. 113]

Company	Employees in India	Total number of employees	Percentage of employees in India	Percentage of Indian IT workforce
Infosys	71,000	89,000	80%	4.36%
TCS	70,000	108,000	65%	4.29%
Wipro	*	80,000	*	*
HCL	*	46,000	*	*
Satyam	*	42,000	*	*
Cognizant	41,000	56,000	73%	2.52%
Hexaware	6,000	6,900	87%	0.37%
iGate	4,200	7,300	58%	0.25%
Sapient	3,700	5,800	64%	0.23%

Figure 4-12. Employee figures for FIOs (2007)[185]

One of the key things that separate FIOs from multi-national companies is the lack of innovation focus. While the top Indian pure players are consistently praised for their technical skills and on-time delivery, they cannot be rated very highly as business solution leaders; their spend on R&D is very small in comparison to MNCs.[186]

4.3.3 Multi-national Companies

Established multi-national companies (MNCs) in the IT & BPO service domain have replicated the offshore model and counter the emergence of Indian pure players. MNCs have already built up a massive presence in India, but despite high growth, they continue to trail behind the pure players in terms of growth and profitability; the five largest international players[187] together account for less than 9% of the Indian IT workforce (see Figure 4-13) and together they are just a little bigger than the two largest Indian pure players[188] combined. While they have a better strategic positioning in the global market, they are challenged with adapting the heart of their operating model to offshore delivery.

---

[185] With the exception of Infosys, the media communication of the other Indian pure players did not reply to a request for employee figures; the data provided is based on careful research in publicly available studies and reports. Any errors are not intentional and only due to lack of information; a star (*) signifies that information is not available. The percentage of total Indian IT workforce is calculated as employees in India divided by the total Indian IT workforce of 1,630,000 in 2007, cf. [Nasscom 2007, p. 1]

[186] Cf. [Umamaheswari/Momaya 2008, p. 123]

[187] IBM, Accenture, EDS, Capgemini, and CSC

[188] Infosys and TCS

Company	Employees in India	Total number of employees	Percentage of employees in India	Percentage of Indian IT workforce
IBM	53,000	200,000	27%	3.25%
Accenture	35,000	170,000	21%	2.15%
EDS	25,000	140,000	13%	1.53%
Capgemini	17,500	80,000	22%	1.07%
CSC	15,000	91,000	16%	0.92%
LogicaCMG	3,000	39,000	8%	0.18%
Atos Origin	2,500	50,000	5%	0.15%
TietoEnator	600	16,000	4%	0.04%

Figure 4-13. Employee figures for MNCs in India (2007)[189]

4.4   The Phenomenon of Overheating

Even though India has been developing its export-oriented software development sector for more than a decade, India produced far fewer graduates from computing science and related engineering disciplines than required to accommodate to the exponential growth of the country's IT industry.

Figure 4-14 shows the number of engineering graduates that India's universities and colleges produce with 4-year degree and 3-year diploma courses. While the absolute number of IT graduates is slowly rising, the percentage of IT-related degrees to all engineering degrees is on the decline. A reason for this can be the stricter entry requirements for new students in IT related disciplines.

	2003	2004	2005	2006
Engineering graduates	215,000	284,000	348,000	382,000
- thereof with degree	112,00	155,000	210,000	235,000
- thereof with diploma	103,000	129,000	138,000	147,000
- thereof with IT related degree	95,000	100,000	111,000	117,000
- thereof with IT related diploma	46,000	65,000	70,000	76,000
Percentage IT-related (all)	65%	58%	52%	51%
Percentage IT-related (only degrees)	85%	65%	53%	50%

Figure 4-14. Engineering graduates[190]

---

[189] As per information received by Thun and the author from media communications of the individual companies in October 2007, cf. [Thun 2008a]; figures for EDS, CSC and Atos Origin are updated based on new research in various publicly available studies and reports. Figures of Capgemini contain acquired companies Kanbay and Indigo, figures of EDS contain Mphasis, and figures of CSC contain Covansys. The percentage of total Indian IT workforce is calculated as employees in India divided by the total Indian IT workforce of 1,630,000 in 2007, cf. [Nasscom 2007, p. 1]

[190] Nasscom Strategic Review 2005, as quoted in [Gereffi et al. 2005, Appendix]. An IT-related degree is considered to be a course of studies in the area of electronics, instrumentation, computer science, telecommunication, information technology, instrumentation engineering, and computer application.

Figure 4-15 shows the number of fresh IT labor supply entering the workforce for the years 2003 to 2006. It shows that the IT workforce is steadily increasing but it also shows that many students from non-IT or even non-engineering related disciplines are trying to get a foothold in this lucrative industry. Quite a number of graduates leave India and continue their studies abroad or start a career there. An estimated 40,000 IT graduates have left the country and now work in the USA. This effect has been coined the 'brain drain'. But in recent years, the recession in Europe and economic slow-down in the USA have helped to somewhat improve the quality of India's workforce. The USA is no longer viewed as the perfect destination to live in and pursue a career, and many Indians are now moving back to their home country.

	2003	2004	2005	2006
IT professionals entering the IT workforce	80,000	94,000	103,000	109,000
- thereof with degree	55,000	58,000	64,000	68,000
- thereof with diploma	25,000	36,000	39,000	41,000
Non-IT engineers entering the IT workforce	40,000	40,000	40,000	40,000
Graduates from other disciplines entering the IT workforce	30,000	30,000	30,000	30,000
Total fresh IT labor supply	**150,000**	**164,000**	**173,000**	**180,000**

Figure 4-15. Fresh IT labor supply[191]

When one compares the new market entrants to the industry's requirement for new employees, it shows a widening and frightening gap of skilled IT labor. From 2006 to 2007, the demand for new employees has grown by 40 percent. However, this steep growth is only satisfied by a meager expansion of 4 percent on the supply side.

In emerging markets such as India, the pool of suitable talent for multinational companies (MNCs) shrinks further because of a lack of fluent English skills, an educational emphasis on theory at the expense of practical knowledge, and a lack of interpersonal skills which do not go well together with Western expectations. This shrinking factor is estimated at 75% for Indian engineering graduates and at 90 percent for students with generalist knowledge. In China, the situation is even worse with only 10% of the engineering graduates deemed suitable for employment in MNCs. However, Poland and Hungary show a comparatively smaller shrinking factor of 50 percent.[192]

---

[191] Nasscom Strategic Review 2005, as quoted in [Gereffi et al. 2005, Appendix].

[192] Cf. [Farrell et al. 2005, p. 96]

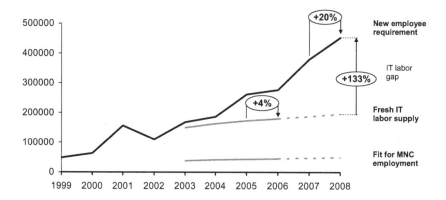

Figure 4-16. IT labor gap[193]

The actual available pool is even further reduced because around half of India's students graduate from universities away from major cities with IT industry and international airline connections. Luckily, Indians are not unwilling to relocate and most young software engineers move to the big IT cities and initially stay in paying guest accommodation. Companies tend to follow one another to locations that already have a track record of providing offshore talent rather than exploring new locations. There are positive effects with a concentration of companies, like improvement in the business environment and infrastructure. But eventually this leads to an imbalance of demand and supply, which in turn produces a local wage inflation and high attrition rates. Wages paid to IT engineers for the same job and qualifications in Bangalore are considerably higher than in Mumbai or Kolkata.

EXAMPLE: By end of 2007, Capgemini has a workforce of 17,500 employees in India, which is 22% of its entire workforce of 80,000.[194] It plans to grow to more than 40,000 employees in India by end of 2010[195] resulting in every third of its employees being based out of India. The employee profile of Capgemini India shows that 30% of employees have less than 3 years of work experience and have been mostly hired directly from university or college. Adding the required 22,500 employees over a period of three years while maintaining the experience profile, means introducing 5,250 lateral hires and 2,250 new graduates every year in addition to compensating normal attrition. Capgemini would thus have to attract 5% of the entire MNC compatible new entrants to the IT workforce every year. Given that Capgemini's current percentage of the overall Indian IT workforce is a little above 1%, this is a real challenge which can only be met through combination of a competitor acquisition, a strong market positioning, and high attractiveness for employees.

---

[193] Dotted lines are estimates based on previous year growth. New employment requirement calculated from direct IT employment figures in [Nasscom 2007, p. 1; Nasscom 2008], plus an estimated 4% annually in order to reflect retirement, job changes to outside the IT industry, and emmigration to other countries, like the USA, for better job opportunities. Fresh IT labor supply is based on NASSCOM Strategic Review 2005 as quoted in [Gereffi et al. 2005, Appendix]. The estimate of 25% for fit for MNC employment is based on [Farrell et al. 2005].

[194] Cf. [Thun 2008a, p. 7]

[195] See e.g. statement by Capgemini CEO Paul Hermelin, cf. [BusinessWeek 150208]

Companies are entering a vicious circle when combating the IT labor gap; three options remain:

- Offer better salary and benefits compared to the competition in order to attract more and better talent and be able to compete with other employers.
- 'Scrap the barrel deeper' and employ less qualified people.
- Set up own corporate universities in order to re-educate new graduates from non-IT related disciplines and/or to train previously non-MNC compatible applicants in the required personal skills.

All these three options lead to higher costs – either through higher salaries, training costs, or rework respectively project overruns caused by a lack of quality.

In addition to the general IT labor gap, there remains a clear scarcity of experienced middle managers. New market entrants often aim to hire their middle management from established operations instead of investing into the mentoring and training of their own staff. Other countries increasingly recruit middle managers from India. This trend is clearly reflected in the increase of wages. On average, entry-level software developers currently earn an annual wage of 270,000 INR (4,000 EUR) and project managers 1,500,000 INR (25,000 EUR). There is hardly any limit to the top; annual compensations for directors and vice presidents comfortably compare with western salaries (see Figure 4-17). In the past, wages

Position	Description	Years of experience	Annual compensation (thousand INR)	Annual compensation (USD)
(Senior) Vice President Outsourcing	Strategic outsourcing of software or IT infrastructure services	20+	7.000 – 10.000	165.000 – 240.000
Vice President Delivery	Delivery management of application software	20+	5.000 – 7.000	120.000 – 165.000
Vice President Quality	Quality assurance, CMMi certification, risk management	15+	4.500 – 6.000	105.000 – 140.000
Director Testing	Delivery management for testing assignments (application, system software, storage, networking)	15+	3.500 – 4.500	80.000 – 105.000
Software Quality & Testing Manager	Management of testing projects	8 – 15	1.200 – 3.500	30.000 – 85.000
Senior System Administrator	Unix, Solaris, HP, Storage, Windows	8+	1.500 – 1.800	35.000 – 45.000
Senior Software Architect	J2EE, .NET, Unix, C++	8 – 15	1.800 – 4.000	45.000 – 95.000
Project Manager	SAP application software development	8 – 12	1.300 – 1.600	30.000 – 40.000
R&D Professionals (with Ph.D. / M.Sc.)	Algorithm design, data modelling, data analytics, speech recognition	1 – 15	800 – 4.000	20.000 – 95.000
Software Engineer	Application development or maintenance	0 – 1	200 – 300	4.700 – 7.000

Figure 4-17. Salary bandwidth in the Indian IT industry[196]

---

[196] Information on compensation bandwidth derived from www.pnvassociates.com/IT Openings. htm (accessed 19 Mar 08), [Messner 2008a, p. 28], and other contacts with recruiting agencies in India.

increased up to 20% every year at the entry level and at 5% for project managers;[197] for 2008 the average salary increase is forecast at 14.4%.[198]

4.5   Potential Downsides

There is a tremendous opportunity for captive offshore companies, FIOs, and MNCs in India; however, they are facing some unique local challenges while acting in a global arena.

4.5.1   Infrastructure

India's infrastructure – or rather the lack of the same – is the main concern for senior managers of multinational companies.

Among the various infrastructure constraints, power supply is probably the most fundamental, as electricity is clearly indispensable for the IT industry. Major cities suffer regular brownouts, especially during summer when demand for electricity surges. Better off homes and businesses hum with the sound of diesel generators, while workshops and others face darkness and silence. Peak demand exceeds supply by about 10,500 megawatts, or 11.6%.[199] The establishment of business parks with power supplies backed up by diesel generators has helped to soften the issue (see Figure 4-18).

Other infrastructure constraints, such as water, roads, and ports are significant bottlenecks for the manufacturing industry. In fact, one of the reasons the software and services industry was able to take off in India was that they do not heavily depend on these types of infrastructure.[200] However, new airports and better airport management become increasingly important: due to the rise of the software industry and the need to transfer knowledge by sending analysts and developers to Europe or the US, every year some 250,000 additional seats have to be added to flight capacity to and from India.[201] Both Bangalore and Hyderabad have opened new international airports in the first half of 2008. Unfortunately, the new Bangalore airport is located far outside the city with no railway or adequate road connections ready for its opening, which is why jokingly people already refer to the project as the only airport worldwide that can only be reached by air.

The modernization of roads is most visible in the golden quadrilateral project, aiming to link Delhi, Mumbai, Kolkata and Chennai with a 3,635-mile four-and-six lane highway. Estimated costs are USD 6.25 billion and this is only the core element of a nationwide plan to pave and widen 40,000 miles of highway at an estimated total cost of USD 60 billion.[202]

---

[197] Cf. [Messner 2008a, p. 28]

[198] Cf. survey by Haygroup as quoted in [PTI 2008]

[199] Referring to financial year 2005-06, cf. [BCG Wharton 2007, p. 1]

[200] Cf. [Basu 2004, ch10.3.2]

[201] Cf. [Müller 2006, p. 65]

[202] Cf. [BCG Wharton 2007, p. 2]

Figure 4-18. Diesel backup generators at RMZ Ecospace, Bangalore[203]

Commuting within the city is a sheer disaster that employees have to face on a daily basis, as do foreign visitors when they travel between the airport, hotel, and office. In Mumbai, the twenty kilometer ride from the airport to downtown never takes less than ninety minutes passing many shanties along the road and Asia's biggest slum. In Bangalore, employees spend up to one hour for a commute of two kilometers along busy roads like Airport Road. Missing sidewalks make it impossible to cover the stretch as a pedestrian. It is not only about losing time and impact on the economy, but perceptions are also affected. While cities like Mumbai, Delhi, and Kolkata provide at least a public metro system, in Bangalore work on the first line commenced only in 2007. IT companies need to run their own bus and taxi lines through the city to shuffle employees to work and back. It is needless to say that frequent stops and cost optimizations to pick up as many employees as possible with one bus only add to the commuting time. Frequently, such buses are stuck in traffic jam and delayed, making strict adherence to core working hours nearly impossible.

Telecoms remained a government enterprise until very recently, and it was only the rise of India's software industry that has drawn attention on the dramatic changes in the telecommunication sector. Sector reforms started in 1991, until then telephones were considered a luxury in India with the waitlists stretching for years. After four years of reforms, in 1995, only one in hundred Indians had a telephone. But between 2000 and 2005, India added about 18 million landlines and 73 million mobile connections. Teledensity is now 11.5% in rural and 34.7% in urban areas.[204] Mobile telephone connections are among the cheapest in the

---

[203] Photo by author
[204] Cf. [BCG Wharton 2007, p. 4]

world, with every worker, maid, and driver able to afford one. The Telecom Regulatory Authority of India estimates that on average 338,000 landlines and 2.3 million mobile phones are added each month.[205] Still India's telecom infrastructure is in a poor state; international links and bandwidth need to improve for the Indian IT industry to realize its growth projections.

In most Indian metropolitan areas, the infrastructure development now keeps pace with the growth in the city. But it is just about keeping pace, it is not catching up the backlog, and it is definitely not running ahead.[206]

For India to stay ahead of other offshoring countries, a lot more and faster investment in the infrastructure is required. Only the government can mobilize funds to upgrade airports, roads, utilities, and the communication network. According to an interview with the Prime Minister Dr. Manmohan Singh in 2005, "[...] we need an investment of about USD 150 billion in the next seven or eight years to realize our ambition to provide our country with an infrastructure which is equal to the economic and social challenges that we face. I'm not saying that everything is in place, but I think that [...] we have set in motion the processes through innovative public-private partnerships to explore new pathways to make the infrastructure ambitions a realizable goal."[207]

4.5.2 Currency Risk

A major issue in India offshoring deals is the currency risk, i.e. the risk of exposure due to volatile exchange rates of the Indian rupee (INR); a rise in the value of the Indian rupee eats into the profits of the Indian service companies who charge their customers in USD or EUR but have their own internal cost structure in INR.

At the beginning of 2007, the USD was at 44.25 against the INR, then the INR gained strength, and the USD hit 38.10 in September 2007. Some Indian pure players were obviously not well-hedged against this currency shift and looked for alternative ways of securing profit margins, e.g. asking people to work overtime and bill longer hours – or come in on a Saturday to clock extra days.[208] Naturally, this had evicted much criticism among the IT employees and many were wondering if they would also have to sacrifice their Sundays if the trend was to continue. As one blogger put it: "This is ridiculous. [...] This is like going back to the colonial days, where the worker was paid peanuts for his whole day slogging. [...] so what if people have money but no time to enjoy it!"[209]

However, in July 2008 the USD is again at 43.16 against the INR (see Figure 4-19).

---

[205] Data refers to 2005, cf. [BCG Wharton 2007, p. 5]

[206] Cf. [Gupta 2005; Sankhe 2007, p. 51]

[207] [Gupta 2005]

[208] Cf. [Hamm 2007]

[209] http://www.siliconindia.com/shownews/36472 (accessed 14 Jul 2008)

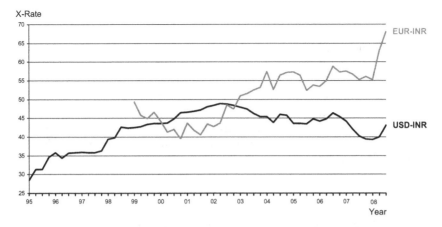

Figure 4-19. Exchange rates EUR and USD against INR[210]

4.5.3   War, Terror, and Violence[211]

War[212]

India and Pakistan have fought over the territory of Kashmir in two wars in 1947–48 and 1965. Since then, many smaller conflicts have taken place in the region, including suicide attacks of religious militant fighters. The last full-scale war between India and Pakistan took place in 1971, and the threat of a nuclear conflict is the key restraint on both countries. In the last years, Indian relations with Pakistan have continued to improve, with full diplomatic relations restored in May 2003.

Other borders are also under dispute, occasionally flaring into the public consciousness. The border of the Indian states of Assam and Meghalaya with Bangladesh saw violent skirmishes in April 2001. The long running border dispute with China on the frontier with the Indian state of Sikkim was peacefully resolved in July 2003.

Today, much more than Pakistan, Indian defense experts view China as the real long-term military threat. Both countries are competing for the same strategic space in the Indian Ocean Region (IOR); China is hugely dependent on the oil shipping sea lanes passing through this area. China actively continues to help Pakistan with its missile and nuclear programs, possibly intending to checkmate India. It also encircles India by assiduously forging maritime linkages with

---

[210] Source for historic exchange rates: www.gocurrency.com

[211] This chapter builds on [Messner 2008a, p. 20-21], a previous publication by the author; updated and extended.

[212] See chapters 2.2.5 to 2.2.7 for more details.

Eastern Africa, Seychelles, Sri Lanka, Bangladesh, Myanmar, and other countries in the region. The Indian defense establishment believes that it will not be long before the Chinese navy begins to make active forays in the IOR.[213]

Terror

Even though Al-Qaeda accuses India of killing Muslims in Kashmir with US support and has put New Delhi on its list of targets,[214] the chances of Al-Qaeda mounting a full-scale attack on India appear rather slim. However, the Subcontinent is increasingly becoming the breeding ground for Islamic terrorists.

On December 28, 2005, Prof. emeritus Dr. Munish Chandra Puri of IIT Delhi was shot while attending a conference at IIT Bangalore. Three other scientists and a lab assistant were seriously injured in the attack. The shooting was declared a terrorist attack, making it the first in Bangalore. Two years later the police declared a confirmed link to the terrorist organization Lashkar-e-Tayyaba (LeT),[215] which is one of the largest and most active Islamic militant organizations in South Asia. Founded in Afghanistan and currently believed to operate from Pakistan, their primary objective is to end Indian rule in Kashmir.

The seven bomb blasts in the Mumbai suburban trains on July 11, 2006, were also carried out by Lashkar-e-Tayyaba (LeT) together with the Students Islamic Movement of India (SIMI).[216] 209 commuters died and 714 were injured. SIMI was founded in India in 1977 and aims to 'liberate' India from western materialistic cultural influences and convert the country to an Islamic society. The organization is now feared to be infiltrated by Al-Qaeda. Earlier bomb blasts in Mumbai occurred in December 1992, when hundreds of people were killed and the city was paralyzed by religious violence triggered by the destruction of the Babri Mosque. In 1993, serial bomb blasts killed more than 250 people and damaged the Bombay Stock Exchange; these were believed to be orchestrated by mafia don Dawood Ibrahim in retaliation for the demolition of the mosque. Similar bombings occurred in 1998.

One of the suicide car bombers, Kafeel Ahmed, who drove a car into Glasgow airport on June 30, 2007, was an engineer from Bangalore working towards a doctorate in computational fluid dynamics. In 2005 and 2006, he had been working as a senior designer with Infotech, an outsourcing company in Bangalore.[217]

On July 25, 2008, the city of Bangalore itself became a target of eight serial low intensity bomb blasts, leaving one dead, eight injured, and dislocating economic activity.[218] One day later, the city of Ahmedabad in Gujarat was hit by

---

[213] Cf. [Pandit 2008]

[214] As declared in an Al-Qaeda video by Azzam Al Amriki in August 2007, cf. [Bagchi/Mohan 2007]

[215] Cf. [TOI 110208]

[216] Cf. [CNN 011006]

[217] Cf. [TOI 060707]

[218] Cf. [TOI 250708]

serial bomb blasts killing 55 people; SIMI is believed to have masterminded the operation and the police have arrested suspects three weeks after the attack.[219] On September 13, 2008, the heart of India's capital New Delhi became the scene of another bomb attack resulting in 20 people dead and many injured; once more a subgroup of SIMI has claimed responsibility.

The recent increase in deadly attacks has made India one of the worst sufferers of terror attacks worldwide. The menace of terrorism does not only disrupt social harmony, but challenges India's integrity and attractiveness as an offshoring destination.

Violence

There are frequent clashes between Hindus and Muslims in the country leading to widespread violence. In December 1992 and January 1993, tensions rose between Hindus and Muslims in Mumbai. 900 people died in the riots and some 200,000 fled the city. The riots did not only affect slums but also apartments and other gated complexes.

In addition, riots between different castes occur sporadically. In June 2007, a full-blown caste conflict took place between Rajasthan's dominant tribes, the Meenas and the Gujjars. The Meenas considered themselves to suffer from quota benefits in both, government and educational institutions, if the Gujjars were to be granted a similar status. "Large Meena mobs were seen traveling on tractors, armed with country-made guns, pickaxes and other weapons, heading towards the areas where the Gujjars had created road and transport blocks. Their aim was to attack the Gujjars and remove the obstruction and render their protest futile. The violence has spread despite the heavy army and paramilitary deployment and the shoot-at-sight orders in Sawai Madhopur and Bharatpur districts."[220] As a result, the Jaipur-Agra highway very much resembled a war zone.

In February 2008, activists attacked migrant workers as the local Samajwadi party held a rally in Mumbai. A vitriol-laced campaign against North Indians followed and as a result, around 10,000 people from Mumbai and 25,000 from Pune fled for their homes, mostly in Uttar Pradesh and Bihar.[221] "Fear continues to grip hundreds of North Indian laborers here, who are availing of every possible mode of transport to reach their hometowns [...] affecting many projects of the construction industry which employs skilled and unskilled labor from Uttar Pradesh and Bihar."[222]

---

[219] Cf. [Hindu 160808]

[220] [TOI 020607]

[221] Cf. [TOI 140208; TOI 240208]

[222] [TOI 240208]; adapted to US English

4.5.4   Criminalization of Politics, Businesses, and Public Life

Transparency International ranks India with a score of 3.3 in the corruption perception index. This score measures how business people and country analysts perceive the degree of corruption among public officials and politicians; it ranges from 10 (highly clean) to 0 (highly corrupt).[223] The Bribe Payers Index by the same institute ranks export countries according to the propensity of firms to bribe when they operate abroad. India falls into cluster four along with Taiwan, Turkey, Russia, and China, i.e. its companies are highly likely to bribe when they operate outside India.[224]

Criminalization of Politics

"With corruption and criminalization, Indian politics has also increasingly fallen victim to nepotism. Once, most parties had a coherent ideology and organizational base. Now, they have degenerated into family firms."[225]

Many criminals enter politics in order to gain influence and ensure that charges against them will be dropped. Because of their financial clout, they are able to make it big in the political arena. Political parties tap criminals for funds and in return promise them patronage and protection. Also, members of the mafia have shown that they are able to convert their power into votes. Voters in some areas of India are forced to vote for the local strongman and political parties are not averse to supporting members who promise election wins. According to unofficial studies, in 1996 as many as 39 members of parliament, including four ministers, faced criminal charges. An investigation revealed that 72 of the 500 candidates for the Lok Sabha (lower house of parliament) elections in 1998 had criminal pending proceedings against them.[226]

The Election Commission operating under order of the Supreme Court has now made it mandatory for political candidates to disclose details of any criminal background, their assets, liabilities, and educational background. While this is certainly a step forward, it is more about disclosing than disqualifying. The background of political candidates has become a non-issue to voters; politicians are seen to be corrupt and criminal.[227]

Politicians are also competing in giving away free goods and services to win voters. In February 1997, the Chief Minister of Punjab Prakash Singh Badal gave away free electricity and water to farmers. He had lived up to his electoral promise, but twelve months later Punjab's fragile state finances were destroyed and there was no money to pay salaries to civil servants.[228]

---

[223] Cf. [Lambsdorff 2007, p. 324-330]

[224] Cf. [Mak 2007, p. 331-334]

[225] [Guha 2007, p. 685]

[226] Cf. [Ramachandran 2004]

[227] Cf. [Ramachandran 2004]

[228] Cf. [Das 2000, p. 313]

"Sixty years after Independence, India remains a democracy. But the events of the last two decades call for a new qualifying adjective. India is no longer a constitutional democracy but a populist one."[229]

Criminalization of Businesses

The costs of corruption are manifest in many parts of the Indian economy; it delays execution, raises costs, and destroys morality. Examples for corruption in businesses include: [230]

- The chartered accountant pays some money to the financial authorities on behalf of the owners of a small business in order to get the income tax declaration filed and the reimbursement processed.
- A restaurant owner wants to open a bar and sell beer and wine. The government officials request three times the nominal fee for a liquor license as bribe.
- Indian truckers pay something like USD 5 billion annually as bribes to keep their freight flowing.[231]

Some Indian companies and many multinational companies[232] claim to have taken the high road against corruption, but many firms find it extremely difficult to get anything done without paying just that little bit extra. Most firms only try to stay clean of bribes on the surface and practice 'bribe-laundering', i.e. somewhere down the line of subcontractors and vendors someone would have paid a bribe, covered it under a different sort of expense, and issued an invoice for it.

Corruption and Criminalization of Private Life

Government officials and sometimes also employees of private companies use their power to grant or deny services to enrich themselves by accepting bribes. According to Transparency International, India is one of the most corrupt countries in the world.[233]

Here are a few examples of corruption in daily life:[234]

- When going for a two-wheeler driving license, a college student refuses to pay bribes to the examiner and fails the exam twice. With appropriate bribes, a driving test is limited to starting the car and moving it from one side of the road to the other.

---

[229] [Guha 2007, p. 691]

[230] Please note that these examples are not invented; the author has either witnessed them during his tenure in India or heard about them from very reliable sources.

[231] According to estimates by Transparency International, cited in [Wharton 2007]

[232] Cf. e.g. [Vermeer/Neumann 2008, p. 216; Wharton 2007]

[233] Cf. [Lambsdorff 2007, p. 324-330]

[234] Please note that these examples are not invented; the author has either witnessed them during his tenure in India or heard about them from very reliable sources.

- An Indian returns from the USA and wants to get an Indian driving license issued based on his American license. He employs an agent to help with the process at the concerned department who charges INR 2,000; he walks in and out of the offices freely, preparing the necessary paperwork for the government officials; the required license is issued within a few days. It is rumored that government employees pay a high bribe for a lucrative job at the motoring department and have to make the business case work by accepting bribes in return.
- The principal of a kindergarten requests unaccounted admission payment for the 'good of the school'. When questioned by the parent, the principal says: 'What do you want? I have 600 applications; I can take the next one who is willing to pay.'.
- The telephone line in a new house has noise disturbance. Complaints to the concerned telecom department result in refusal to accept any responsibility. However, the engineer visiting the house knows a little workaround. He takes INR 600, does a little bit of rewiring, and within 10 minutes there is a clear telephone line: 'Do not tell anyone; my company does not allow me to do this rewiring'; however, following the official process did not bring any results.
- After a car accident, the agent of the insurance company asks for a bribe. 'If you do not pay, I will report that you have parked the car illegally.' After some negotiation, the car owner and the insurance agent agree on the car being repaired in one garage where the agent gets a commission.

Interestingly, in none of the above cases a rule was actually bent in favor of the person paying the bribe; the money has only made things happen faster or happen at all (speed money).

Some IT and BPO employees behave in a criminal fashion to cheat their way into reputable organizations. 11,000 INR (260 USD) gets one a favorable two-year job certificate on company letter head with a real signature allowing entry into the next company at a more senior level and with a better pay. Detective agencies hired by firms to detect such employee fraud are not always effective and sometimes accept bribes themselves in order not to report the applicant.

Theft of public goods plays a major role as well. Electricity consumers simply hook their homes and businesses illegally to the transmission grid, or bribe corrupt employees of the State Electricity Board (SEB) to look the other way. In a ten year period up to 2002, 40% of the power generated in India was stolen. In the financial year 2003–04, the SEB had losses of USD 4.7 billion, or nearly 1% of India's gross-domestic product (GDP).[235] The rate at which this happens varies greatly by region. In the more advanced states like Tamil Nadu and Kerala, 80% of subsidized government food reaches the poor. However, in India's second poorest state Bihar with a population of 75 million, more than 80% of the food is stolen.[236]

---

[235] Cf. [BCG Wharton 2007, p. 3]
[236] Cf. [Luce 2007; Wharton 2007]

The public media is uncovering many cases of corruption and slowly the perception of India as a corrupt society is changing. "But to the extent that change in cultural norms will be needed to root out corruption, it will take a persistent, long, drawn-out effort. While economic change is easier to achieve, cultural change is much slower and more difficult. This is compounded by the rearguard actions of those who are beneficiaries of the status quo."[237] Today, India is still one of the most corrupt societies in the world.

4.5.5   (In-)security of Data[238]

Allegations that Indian call center employees are stealing credit card and other personal data frequently make the headlines, culminating in news about companies withdrawing their operations from India. In the dynamics of taking business processes offshore, such objections are quickly raised – sometimes only to hinder offshoring and stop jobs being lost. In the heat of the discussion, a riposte is often equally poorly researched and it is hence necessary to look at the measures companies in India take to avoid malicious behavior, and the facts of data protection legislation.

IT companies in India conduct comprehensive background checks before offering employment to candidates. To support the tracking of employment history, in early 2007, NASSCOM – the National Association of Software and Service Companies in India – launched a national skills registry for IT professional. Security compliance programs, comprehensive security audits, authentication, and sometimes even physical access control on project level have become commonplace in the software industry and are supported by workshops aiming to enhance employees' knowledge and awareness of data misuse.

In addition to preventive measures, there are several laws which apply to data theft and misuse in India. Complaints can be filed for theft, cheating, criminal breach of trust, dishonest misappropriation of data, or criminal conspiracy under the provisions of the Indian Penal Code (IPC) of 1846, and for hacking under the Information Technology Act (ITA) of 2000. Offences under IPC and ITA allow for an arrest without warrant, are non-bailable, and as penalties carry fines as well as imprisonment from one year to life sentences. Civil proceedings for copyright infringement under the provisions of the Copyright Act (CA) of 1957 and the Specific Relief Act (SRA) of 1963 are also initiated in case of data misuse. Penalties under these acts can range from hefty fines to temporary and permanent injunctions.[239] The Indian government is currently in the process of amending the ITA to address data privacy and security issues. These provisions will allow for control processes to ensure adequate integrity, security, and confidentiality of electronic data.

---

[237] Saul P. Steinberg Professor of Management Dr. Jitendra V. Singh, The Wharton School, University of Pennsylvania; as quoted in [Wharton 2007]

[238] This chapter builds on [Messner 2008a, p. 25-26], a previous publication by the author

[239] Cf. [Manghan/Wugmeister/Titus 2007]

While laws are in place to address data security issues, the Indian legal system as such remains a concern. Delays are common, and it can take more than ten years for a case to be resolved. More than three million cases are pending in India's 21 high courts, and in subordinate courts across the country an astounding 26.3 million cases remain open.[240] The next question is how many of these so-called white-collar crimes actually get reported to police; enterprises generally tend to avoid getting police into their premises and creating any trace with the public media.

4.6   Business Continuity Management

Offshoring exposes companies to different levels of risk compared to their home countries. One criterion for decisions on offshore locations is the ability of a firm to continue its core operations even under adverse conditions, which can be caused by the following events:

- War, terror attacks, and communal riots. The exterior and interior threats to peace on the subcontinent are detailed in chapter 4.5.3.
- Strikes. Political parties or unions frequently organize strikes (*bandhs*) affecting retail businesses, transportation (bus, taxi), and the supply of essential goods.
- Natural disasters. Some major IT cities are located in zones with seismic activities and are therefore prone to earthquakes.[241] Heavy monsoon can uproot trees, cause walls to collapse, and temporarily flood streets knee-deep with water.
- Industrial disasters. Many hazardous industries are located in close proximity to residential and business areas.
- Epidemics and pandemics. During the monsoon rain diseases spread quickly; examples are diarrhea, Madras eye, malaria, chikungunya, dengue fever, and leptospirosis.
- Power supply. The demand for electricity by far outstrips supply which leads to scheduled power cuts.

Due to a stretched infrastructure, an occurrence of any of these problems has a much greater impact on India than it would have on a country in the developed Western world.

The biggest threat for business continuity lies in employees unable or scared to come to work. During communal riots or even during local strikes, curfews may be in place that make it impossible and unsafe to leave the house. Transport strikes occur frequently, affecting the company vehicles shuffling employees between home and work. The absence of a reasonable public transport system renders commuting nearly impossible for employees during such days.

---

[240] Cf. [HeadlinesIndia 2007]

[241] Cf. [Arya 2000, p. 1270]: Cities in high damage risk zone (MSK VIII): Chandigarh and New Delhi; moderate damage risk zone (MSK VII): Bhubaneshwar, Kolkata, Lucknow, Mumbai, and Trivandrum.

Companies are sometimes forced to shut down during extreme weather periods like the annual monsoon rain. In 2005, without any previous weather warnings, heavy rains hit Mumbai and resulted in the international airport being closed for thirty hours. Many offices had to remain closed for several days. Some employees were taken by surprise, did not leave office on time, and had to be housed on site.

In July 2008, the monsoon rain arrived later than usual in the federal state of Karnataka leading to critically low water levels in many rivers and reservoirs. As a result, the hydroelectric power plants could not produce enough electricity and the city of Bangalore faced scheduled power outages of seven hours and more each day. Residential complexes, businesses, and all IT parks had to switch on their diesel backup generators for extended periods of time. On July 24, 2008, the petrol stations in Bangalore and surrounding towns had run out of diesel. Some IT companies had to issue a business continuity warning because they were either running low on diesel for their own backup generators or they could not shuffle employees to work because some taxis and buses had already stopped operating. Luckily, the monsoon rains commenced over the weekend and helped to ease the power situation.

An outbreak of the Avian flu would cause a pandemic with disastrous effects in India because of the dense population and stretched health facilities. Employees would be scared to leave home and go to work.

Most of these scenarios can be classified as location outage. Nonetheless, it would be useless to maintain a backup site in another part of the country (i.e. *active-passive scenario*) and plan to transport employees there. First, employees would not even consider leaving their families in the lurch and would refuse to relocate to the backup site. Second, transportation facilities would be extremely stretched, if not unavailable. Third, roads or railway tracks may be blocked.

This seems to call for a *mobile-backup solution* where employees are to work from home in case of disaster. But even this has its own limitations in India.

- Already during normal times, Internet and the power supply to private homes is hardly stable.
- So-called high-speed Internet for home-use comes at a speed of no more than 256 kbit/sec which is merely twice the speed of ISDN.[242]
- The IT & BPO industry in India does not provide laptops to all its employees as desktops are still cheaper. Also, laptops are considered critical in terms of data storage and hence, in order to adhere to STP regulations (see chapter 4.1.3), their serial numbers together with the employee's ID and name need to be entered into registers by security personnel every day.

Looking at all these shortcomings, a successful business continuity plan in India can only rely on an *active-active scenario* in which the team and tasks are distributed across two locations right from the beginning. This is a cumbersome

---

[242] This is slowly changing; beginning of 2008 the first affordable offers for faster Internet connections are seen in India.

setup during normal operations; distributed delivery within distributed delivery models has to be managed and business travels within India are neither popular with the employees nor time-efficient. However, for critical offshore endeavors this is the only way to ensure a speedy recovery in case of location outages.

A (partial) country outage, e.g. caused by a nuclear war with Pakistan, cannot be covered by any of these scenarios and has to be dealt with an international backup scenario.

5 Human Resources

5.1 Aspects of Human Resource Management

The foundations of the human resource (HR) function in India dates back to 1926 when the Trade Union Act formally recognized the workers' union in an attempt to show concern for labor welfare. In 1932, the Royal Commission recommended the appointment of labor officers, and the Factories Act of 1948 laid down the duties and qualifications of labor welfare officers.[243] In today's HR function, the influence of social contacts and the belonging to communities remains prominent and creates an interesting clash with the pressure to comply with the requirements of modern and international professionalism.

This chapter looks at the following aspects of HR management from an Indian IT and BPO industry perspective:

- Recruitment
- Training
- Performance appraisals
- Compensation management
- Employee turnover and retention management.

5.1.1 Recruitment

Recruitment and selection of the employee base is important to support the planned growth of the Indian IT and BPO industry. However, in India these things work somewhat differently from the Western world. There are two major important recruitment channels:

- Campus recruitment. Young employees are mostly hired through campus recruiting. The hiring company presents itself at colleges and universities to students around six months before graduation. Interviews are conducted and job offers are made directly on campus. In the Indian IT industry, such employees are commonly referred to as 'freshers'.
- Recommendations. Word-of-mouth is equally important and pumps in many good CVs at all levels. There are serious financial benefits of between 10,000 and 30,000 INR (240 to 710 USD) for successful recommendations; this sounds a lot compared to the local salaries, but for many IT companies it is the most cost-effective way of hiring new staff. Companies get up to 50% of its new hires[244] through this channel.

---

[243] Cf. [Budhwar/Luthar/Bhatnagar 2006, p. 344]
[244] Cf. [Vermeer/Neumann 2008, p. 142]

Other channels are also used:

- Advertisements. Job advertisements on billboards (see Figure 5-1) and in the intra-regional newspapers Times of India, Deccan Herald, and The Hindu mainly focus on creating awareness in the IT community, but also generate between 10,000 to 20,000 replies[245] per advert; external agencies are therefore employed to identify the most promising application.
- Walk-in interviews. This is another specialty of the Indian IT industry. Through newspaper or sometimes even radio advertisements, people are encouraged to simply show up at the company's premises or in a well-known hotel on a specific day. A multi-step screening process is established and successful candidates can walk out with a job offer.

Figure 5-1. Company awareness advertisements on billboards[246]

A job is considered a business deal in India; if someone receives a better offer from another company, the first contract is often considered to be of no interest and void. This leads to the astonishing fact that people sign a contract but never show up for work. Also, there is a high number of employees quitting or simply disappearing within the first two weeks in a new job; they may have got a better offer somewhere else. The battle against attrition thus already begins before employees actually start their new jobs.

---

[245] Cf. [Vermeer/Neumann 2008, p. 142]
[246] Photo by Capgemini; Bangalore, Outer Ring Road

The salary offered to the new employee has to be carefully considered. It is very important to keep the structure intact, if not for fairness then for cost containment; salaries are very openly discussed in Indian companies, and a higher salary for a new employee soon becomes a benchmark for the existing employees.

The probation period usually lasts 6 months. In the IT industry it is very uncommon to lay off staff within the probation period; if employees do not show the promised skills, they are mostly asked to put in their papers which supports the face-saving culture of India and creates less administrative or even legal problems for the company. However, in the call center industry, the average retention rate after the probation period is only around 85%.[247]

5.1.2   Training

The rapid expansion of the IT sector sees a need for a growing investment by IT companies in the development of their existing and new employees, both in terms of technical as well as managerial skills. In India, IT companies now keep aside between 3% and 5% of revenues for training programs.[248] Combined, the Indian IT industry spends USD 216 million annually on training, which is about 21% of the world IT training budget.[249] In the BPO industry, the rapid growth and the offering of high-end BPO services require companies to provide new employees with in-depth training; domain competencies are no longer available 'off-the-shelf'. All topics related to training, e.g. training needs analysis, organization of training courses, and their evaluation, are usually the responsibility of the learning & development department, a sub-section of HR.

Well designed training programs together with clear career paths have become a major instrument for retaining employees. Sometimes it is possible to convince employees to continue working on an important but technically or personally unchallenging project by offering them training on a new technology in return.

Official certifications like PMP® by the Project Management Institute, or application technology related certifications by Microsoft®, Oracle®, SAP®, etc. are sometimes more important to show on the CV of IT developers than formal university degrees. If the company sponsors such trainings, very often they request the employee to sign a bond, i.e. to agree to stay with the company for a certain period of time or to pay back the prorated costs of the training. On the other hand, as companies are looking for good return on training investment, they often require trainees to pass a written test after the training.

5.1.3   Performance Appraisals

A formal and structured approach to conducting performance appraisals is common in most IT and BPO companies in India. The immediate superior is

---

[247] Cf. [Budhwar/Varma/Singh/Dhar 2006, p. 889]

[248] Cf. [Naukrihub 2007]

[249] Cf. IDC report as quoted in [Naukrihub 2007]

referred to as *N+1* and appraises the employee. In round-table meetings between all unit managers, these appraisals are calibrated to enable comparability, increase fairness, and also to pursue company growth targets, stay in line with the monetary promotion budget, and counter competitive market pressure.

Especially in the BPOs but also in some IT companies, employees hardly contribute towards setting their own goals;[250] goals are mostly pre-defined and formalized for each and every career level.

However, the main drawback of a Western appraisal system in India is that it is contrary to the face-saving culture where nobody likes to give bad feedback (see chapter 6.5.4); in fact, it is perceived by some managers as a necessary evil. In addition, most subordinates are not used to receiving negative feedback or being told about areas of improvement. Appraisal results play an important role in calculating the annual bonus package and next year's compensation. Call centers sometimes rank their junior employees and make this list available to everyone. While the top employees are considered role models, the bottom part receives additional training, mentoring, or a formal performance warning. As a result, appraisal discussions often end up in an argument and both parties part with hard feelings. "However, considering the nature of the [...] industry, most HR managers are convinced that performance appraisal is essential and believe that over a short period of time employees either accept it as a fact of life or quickly adapt."[251]

5.1.4   Compensation Management

Companies usually have a standard wage structure with a pay and benefit scheme that is attached to grade, education, total work experience, and employee performance and skills.

During the annual or bi-annual compensation rounds, many factors have to be taken into consideration for deciding upon the average pay hike. Most companies try to align their compensation package to market trends by receiving information from regular surveys, looking at the inflation rate and consumer price index (CPI), and benchmarking themselves against the paymasters in the industry. In addition, the effect of the pay hike on the charge-out rates (COR) of consultants to clients needs to be taken into account in order to stay competitive in the international market. If a company has high employee growth targets, it will need to pay slightly more than the market average to retain and attract more employees.

5.1.5   Employee Turnover and Retention Management

Most Indian IT companies show surprisingly low attrition rates in their company presentations which are at the same level as in Europe or North America. On the other side, the press often cites horrifying cases where entire companies had to

---

[250] Cf. [Budhwar/Luthar/Bhatnagar 2006, p. 353]
[251] [Budhwar/Luthar/Bhatnagar 2006, p. 352-353]

close down because of high staff turnover. The truth is somewhere in between; reliable studies show average attrition rates of 20–30% across industries and peaks of 35% in BPO and 44% in the financial services sector.[252]

On the one hand, the business model of the Indian IT industry with its employees expecting fast promotion, good salary hikes, and early management responsibilities largely depends on attrition. However, companies need to retain good people to build a stable project environment. To achieve this goal, retention initiatives are institutionalized and focus on three main areas: compensation, motivation, and career development.

Reasons for Attrition

Studies on attrition in India[253] highlight a number of reasons for employees leaving and changing companies in the IT and BPO industry:

- Career growth perspective. Employees who feel bereft of career opportunities or simply do not see their career path clearly laid out for them are likely to look for better options.
- Boring work. Especially in call centers and in the application maintenance field, work is quickly considered boring, monotonous, and without sufficient opportunities for additional learning. Indian employees typically work in isolation from management decisions; unfortunately, the 'de-skilling' of work on offshored business processes and the trend towards industrialization of IT delivery only aggravate this feeling.
- Relationship with superiors. A trustful and caring relationship with the superior can motivate employees to stay longer in a company and overcome periods of less motivation. However, most management systems in India act as closed systems, i.e. they are not ready to take feedback and interact with the employees.
- Burnout stress syndrome (BOSS). Erratic working hours and night shifts cause problems with employees who are married and have families, leading to difficulties in normal socialization and identity crisis. Female employees are not expected to work on night shifts by their families, causing friction with male team members who have to come to office during the less attractive working hours. Young call center agents find it difficult to handle tough customers, do not understand the customer's accent, or cannot align themselves with the different culture, leading to unsuccessful calls and demoralized agents. Indian software engineers are not used to collaborating with colleagues from more task-oriented cultures (see chapter 1.2.2), resulting in frequent misunderstandings about the true intention of communication.
- Marriage. Directly after marriage, the attrition rate among female employees is comparatively high. Many women quit their professional careers to look after the household chores, the well-being of the husband, and raising of the children.

---

[252] Cf. [GlobalTalentMetrics 2008]
[253] E.g. [Budhwar/Varma/Singh/Dhar 2006; GlobalTalentMetrics 2008]

Pay is not a major primary driving factor for attrition. Employees do usually not look for a new job opportunity because they feel underpaid; instead, it is some of the above reasons which drive them to the competition. And if they manage to get a better offer, a substantial pay hike then becomes the deciding factor to put in the papers and move on. From this viewpoint, a long-term retention bonus,[254] which is a yearly cash bonus on continued employment with the company to stern attrition on middle and senior management levels, will not be very effective.

Combating Attrition

Combating the phenomenon of attrition starts with hiring the right employees. Companies are diverse in terms of what they offer, and should select the employees that best fit them. Eight organizational factors (Figure 5-2) influence prospective candidates to make their joining decision – and also later to stay with the company. Organizations should therefore select candidates whose preferences and aspirations are in line with what the company has to offer.

Good job content and planned career growth are key drivers for both retention and attrition, and hence an employee development plan and institutionalized job rotation programs can act as great retention levers. If employees are provided adequate learning opportunities and see realistic promotion opportunities on the horizon, they are less likely to look for alternate options in other companies.

Frequent feedback, coaching, and mentoring should be an integral part of managerial support along an individual's career development; this encourages employees as they progress and learn new skills.

Public recognition is important to ambitious young employees; rewards should be transparent and given for exceptional individual or team performance in line

Organizational factors	Description
Job content	Clarity of expectations; attractiveness of technologies/products; learning opportunities; challenging and interesting work; image of end-customer
Career growth	Promotions; growth in people management; offered trainings; onsite postings to attractive locations
Pay and company policies	Salary scales; employment bonds; performance ratings and rewards; employee benefits; personal Internet/email at work; quality of food etc.
Placement and transfer	Bench time; mismatch between skills/training and assignments; posting in secondary cities; night shifts; task allocation; transfer to other teams
Work culture	Work-life balance; freedom; monitoring; helpful managers; style of communication; feedback; support by peer colleagues
Top management	Visibility of top management; recognition and appreciation from top management
Managerial support	Concern for people; cooperation; mentoring; appreciation; career guidance
Brand image of company	Reputation of the company; social prestige associated with working for the company

Figure 5-2. Organizational retention factors[255]

---

[254] Cf. [PTI 2008]
[255] Adapted from [GlobalTalentMetrics 2008]

with the organizational values, beliefs, and targets. Such rewards may also be non-monetary, e.g. a 'project star award' for an individual top performer or a trophy for the team that has received the best customer feedback (Figure 5-3).

Creating a fun atmosphere at work enables the – mostly young – employees to relate to their college days; companies are conducting singing or drawing competitions (Figure 5-4) and reserve the last Friday afternoon of every month for a party.

Figure 5-3. 'Super team' trophy being awarded during annual party[256]

Figure 5-4. Drawing competition[257]

[256] Photo by Capgemini

When an organization is able to create an appealing employee brand, Indian employees will receive more social recognition from their peers, friends, and families. In turn, the company benefits from higher work quality and finally lower employee turnover. Figure 5-5 shows how an international branding campaign with customer focus has been turned into an employee branding campaign in India; the Indian advertisement was displayed on billboards along major roads and in newspapers to create awareness about employment attractiveness.

Figure 5-5. Local adaptation of Capgemini branding campaign[258]

For the same reason some IT and BPO companies have begun to organize annual company events not only for their employees but for their extended families as well. The thought process behind this substantial expenditure is that if parents believe their children work for a reputed and good company, they will keep them from quitting too quickly.

5.2   Hierarchy

India being a high-power distance country (see chapter 1.2.1), its IT & BPO industry has introduced a sophisticated hierarchical system with many levels. It is important to note that subordinates do not perceive their superiors as facilitators but as someone giving directions, expert advice, and as an ultimate decision maker – or at least as someone who is able to get a decision from his respective superiors.

Most IT companies know at least the following job titles:

- Associate consultant. New workforce is recruited from college as associate consultants and typically given about 3 months of technical and soft-skill training, followed by a period of around 2 months of work-shadowing, where they are first exposed to real-life assignments without delivery responsibility. During this time they are referred to as 'freshers', and afterwards they have to prove themselves as team members in projects.

---

[257] Photo by Capgemini
[258] Source: Capgemini

- Consultant. After one or two years on the job, associate consultants expect to be promoted to the level of consultant. Consultants focus on developing technical skills and specialize in a certain area; they may already coach associate consultants on their first assignments and such early management skills are the main driver for a promotion to senior consultant. As most of them are still unmarried, they are also very keen on onsite assignments in the Western world to gain international experience for their CV, see the world, and to make some extra money.
- Senior Consultant. Senior consultants will be technical experts in their chosen area but slowly move towards managing teams. In IT delivery factories, senior consultants can already lead teams of up to 20 people and this is the main driver for promotion to the next level. However, the interaction of senior consultants with clients is limited to technical issues; for any issues around resource or project planning they will be backed up by a manager. Good senior consultants are often sent on onsite assignments as offshore coordinators working liaising with the client, understanding business requirements, and coordinating the technical work directly with a manager in India.
- Manager. After 6 to 10 years of job experience, the promotion to manager brings along the much-awaited move from dealing with technical issues to pure management. Managers will no longer concern themselves with development work or specifications; instead email and phone become their main work tools. They now lead larger teams of up to 80 staff, are involved in day-to-day client activities, and have delivery responsibility. Managers also coordinate training requirements, provide appraisals for their subordinates, and suggest promotions.
- Senior Manager. As soon as managers run projects with a few managers reporting to them, the promotion to senior manager is due. They now get involved in proposals, competency development, and may take up responsible for a service line. From now on promotion to the next three levels is quite automatic and not too difficult in a growing industry, where most targets are around increasing headcount.
- Associate Director/Director. The responsibilities of an associate director and a director do not differ much; they will both have a handful of senior managers reporting to them and they can take most decisions without financial implications.
- Vice President. This level brings about responsibility for several clients, countries, or technologies – together with accountability for profit and loss.

The organizational structure of the BPO industry is similar and has the following common job titles:[259]

- Process Associate
- Junior Officer

---

[259] Cf. [Budhwar/Varma/Singh/Dhar 2006, p. 888]

- Business Executive
- Team Developer/Senior Executive
- Assistant Manager
- Manager
- Assistant Vice President
- Vice President.

It is not uncommon for companies to introduce in-between levels, e.g. a consultant 1 and 2, a senior consultant 1 and 2, etc. This offers the possibility to promote and motivate employees at least every one and half or two years.

Promotions do not come with pay hikes alone, but also with visible status symbols, e.g. company-paid cell-phones, extended medical care insurance for dependents, laptops instead of work stations, and separate cabins instead of open-office space. Sometimes company cars with dedicated drivers or company flats are also offered to senior staff.

5.3   Leadership and Management

Indians see leadership and management as different. Leadership is felt to be broader and at a higher level than management. Leaders are expected to inspire people and get them to excel. The main focus of managers is to get the job done through people.

Leaders in the Indian Society

Leaders are a very common topic of discussion across all sections of Indian society. While a discussion about political leadership is probably the most common, leaders in other areas like sports, religion, and owners of businesses are also discussed. "The importance of leadership is also attested to by the fact that statues of a variety of leaders – political, social, and religious – are erected all over, from big cities to small towns. A large number of public-service institutions such as hospitals, schools, colleges, and airports are named after leaders. Portraits of historical and religious leaders are often voluntarily displayed in public places such as shops, cafes, and offices."[260]

Gandhi was a prime example of a political leader who converted materialistic weaknesses into spiritual and political strengths. His style of leadership was charismatic, inspirational, visionary, and value based.[261] In recent years, political leadership in India has become discredited through corruption, expedience, and misuse of caste or religion for vote-gathering or self-serving purposes.

Traditionally, Indian private companies were owned and managed by a family belonging to one of the traditional business communities, notably the Gujaratis, Parsis, Sindhis and Marwaris. There are big business houses whose founders and

---

[260] [Chhokar 2007, p. 978-979]
[261] Cf. [Chhokar 2007, p. 979-980]

successors are widely admired. Examples are the house of Tatas, the house of Ambanis (Reliance), or the house of Vijay Mallya (UB Group, Kingfisher). These communities developed a high level of internal trust with a close network for business opportunities, loans, information, and other resources. As some of these family businesses grew and endeavored onto the international business scene, their leadership now reflects a juxtaposition of two divergent cultures. In many of these companies the top leadership positions – especially that of the CEO – are still in the hands of family members. However, they have mostly been internationally trained with university education at U.S. or U.K. premier institutes.[262]

Organizational Leadership – A Worldwide Comparison

The GLOBE[263] study examined organizational leadership; it identified first and second order factors and attributes (see Figure 5-6).

According to the findings of the survey, the following leadership attributes rank highest in India: visionary, integrity, administratively competent, performance

Leadership factors	Leader attribute items
(1) Charismatic / value-based	
- Visionary	Foresight, prepared, anticipatory, plans ahead
- Inspirational	Enthusiastic, positive, morale booster, motive arouser
- Self-sacrifice	Risk taker, self-sacrificial, convincing
- Integrity	Honest, sincere, just, trustworthy
- Decisive	Willful, decisive, logical, intuitive
- Performance oriented	Improvement-oriented, excellence-oriented, performance-oriented
(2) Team oriented	
- Collaborative team orientation	Group-oriented, collaborative, loyal, consultative
- Team integrator	Communicative, team builder, informed, integrator
- Diplomatic	Diplomatic, worldly, win-win problem solver, effective bargainer
- Malevolent *(reverse scored)*	Hostile, dishonest, vindictive, irritable
- Administratively competent	Orderly, administratively skilled, organized, good administrator
(3) Self-protective	
- Self-centered	Self-centered, nonparticipative, loner, asocial
- Status consciousness	Status-conscious, class-conscious
- Conflict inducer	Normative, secretive, intragroup competitor
- Face saver	Indirect, avoids negatives, evasive
- Procedural	Ritualistic, formal, habitual, procedural
(4) Participative	
- Autocratic *(reverse scored)*	Autocratic, dictatorial, bossy, elitist
- Nonparticipative *(reverse scored)*	Nondelegator, micromanager, nonegalitarian, individually oriented
(5) Humane oriented	
- Modest	Modest, self-effacing, patient
- Humane orientation	Generous, compassionate
(6) Autonomous	
- Autonomous	Individualistic, independent, autonomous, unique

Figure 5-6. Leadership factors and attributes[264]

---

[262] Cf. [Kakar et al. 2002]

[263] See chapter 1.2

[264] Cf. [Hanges/Dickson 2004, p. 131,137]

orientation, and inspirational. The lowest ranking attributes are malevolent, self-centered, non-participative, autocratic, and face saver. It is important to note that this is the ranking within India.

If compared with other countries, India's highest ranking attributes are self-sacrificial, face saver, self-centered, and malevolent (see Figure 5-7).[265] Interestingly, the lowest ranking attributes of Indian leaders are still rather high compared to other nations.

Indian leaders manage to balance, accommodate, and integrate contradictions between thoughts and actions; they do not necessarily lead to dissonance and confrontation.

Face saving has great importance in Indian autocratic leadership. For instance, Indians can keep secrets much longer than their Western counterparts. Even lying can be acceptable if it serves a just purpose. If the team or the business can be protected by bending the truth, this is very much acceptable.

The high inter-country ranking of the attribute self-centered has its roots in the historical value and belief systems in India that focused on the importance of understanding oneself.[266]

Relationship orientation is more important for effective leadership than performance or task orientation.[267] When building a team, one would usually prefer team members whom one can trust and is comfortable to interact with over team members with a perfect skill-fit but not on the same wave length.

There is a comparatively high commitment by employees and also senior managers to the leadership of their companies. In fact, they almost adore and idealize their CEOs. Because of the socialization pattern in the family, Indians are more likely to be inclined to perceive the leader of a company as a wise, caring, dependable yet demanding figure – just like the elders in the family or social community. However, today this idealization of leaders is no longer completely blind to their deficiencies or the organizational needs they might not fulfill.[268]

In short, the most effective leadership style in India combines charisma, action orientation, autocracy, bureaucracy, collective relationship orientation, being a problem solver, self-starter, entrepreneur, and visionary. This appears a difficult task for one person to fulfill. But in Indian organizations, individualism coexists with vertical collectivism.[269] This is seemingly contradictory, but it is the co-existence of values that in other cases would be mutually exclusive, which makes Indians effective leaders in their world.

---

[265] Cf. [Chhokar 2007, p. 994]

[266] Cf. [Chhokar 2007, p. 996]

[267] Cf. [Chhokar 2007, p. 1004]

[268] Cf. [Kakar et al. 2002]

[269] Cf. [Chhokar 2007, p. 1004-1005]

Leadership factors	India	Australia	Austria	Finland	France	Germany	Great Britain	Nether-lands	Sweden	Switzer-land	USA
(1) Charismatic / value-based	**5.85**	**6.09**	**6.02**	**5.91**	**4.93**	**5.84**	**6.04**	**5.97**	**5.84**	**5.93**	**6.12**
- Visionary	6.02	6.24	6.13	6.29	5.06	5.99	6.23	6.30	6.05	6.12	6.28
- Inspirational	5.93	6.40	6.34	6.42	5.22	6.15	6.44	6.38	6.31	6.25	6.35
- Self-sacrifice	5.45	5.14	5.03	4.22	3.98	4.87	5.02	4.79	4.81	4.88	5.16
- Integrity	5.99	6.36	6.46	6.52	5.14	6.12	6.20	6.52	6.29	6.36	6.51
- Decisive	5.83	6.02	5.96	5.97	5.06	5.78	5.96	5.87	5.59	5.86	5.96
- Performance oriented	5.96	6.35	6.23	6.04	5.10	6.11	6.41	5.95	5.96	6.08	6.46
(2) Team oriented	**5.72**	**5.50**	**5.74**	**5.83**	**5.11**	**5.49**	**5.67**	**5.73**	**5.73**	**5.60**	**5.80**
- Collaborative team orientation	5.51	5.52	5.67	6.35	5.11	5.48	5.33	5.42	5.98	5.25	5.38
- Team integrator	5.83	-	5.34	5.54	4.73	5.05	6.16	6.01	5.50	5.59	6.03
- Diplomatic	5.70	5.56	5.43	5.40	5.01	5.08	5.40	5.43	5.27	5.27	5.46
- Malevolent *(reverse scored)*	2.35	-	1.54	1.47	1.95	1.68	1.71	1.62	1.52	1.60	1.55
- Administratively competent	5.98	5.41	5.80	5.32	4.52	5.51	5.15	5.43	5.44	5.51	5.63
(3) Self-protective	**3.77**	**2.99**	**3.07**	**2.54**	**2.81**	**2.96**	**2.96**	**2.88**	**2.80**	**2.93**	**3.15**
- Self-centered	2.63	1.91	1.99	1.55	1.86	2.10	1.88	1.75	1.79	2.00	1.97
- Status consciousness	4.18	3.82	3.86	3.15	3.25	3.72	3.61	3.93	3.30	3.81	3.60
- Conflict inducer	4.24	-	3.57	3.10	5.11	3.59	3.47	3.26	3.33	3.36	3.53
- Face saver	3.57	2.67	2.56	2.05	2.19	2.36	2.48	2.23	2.39	2.46	2.66
- Procedural	4.10	3.56	3.36	2.87	3.17	3.00	3.38	3.22	3.19	3.00	3.90
(4) Participative	**4.99**	**5.72**	**6.00**	**5.91**	**5.90**	**5.88**	**5.66**	**5.76**	**5.54**	**5.95**	**5.93**
- Autocratic *(reverse scored)*	3.10	2.28	2.11	2.10	2.36	1.95	2.42	2.08	2.41	1.91	2.03
- Nonparticipative *(reverse scored)*	2.93	-	1.90	2.08	1.86	2.28	2.27	2.41	2.51	2.20	2.10
(5) Humane oriented	**5.26**	**5.11**	**4.93**	**4.29**	**3.82**	**4.44**	**4.88**	**4.85**	**4.78**	**4.77**	**5.21**
- Modest	5.33	5.09	5.05	4.52	4.27	4.27	4.80	4.71	4.59	4.88	5.24
- Humane orientation	5.17	5.12	4.80	4.06	3.29	4.61	4.95	4.98	4.96	4.65	5.19
(6) Autonomous	**3.85**	**3.95**	**4.47**	**4.08**	**3.32**	**4.30**	**3.85**	**3.53**	**3.97**	**4.13**	**3.75**
- Autonomous	3.85	3.95	4.47	4.08	3.32	4.30	3.85	3.53	3.97	4.13	3.75

Scale of 1 to 7

Data based on [Chhokar 2007, p995-996] for India; [Ashkanasy 2007, p314] for Australia (2nd order calculated by author); [Reber/Szabo 2007, p129] for Austria; [Lindell/Sigfrids 2007, p94] for Finland (2nd order calculated by author); [Castel/Deneire et al. 2007, p573] for France; [Brodbeck/Frese 2007, p174] for Germany; [Booth 2007, p348] for Great Britain (financial industry only; 2nd order calculated by author); [Thierry/Hartog et al. 2007, p239] for Netherlands (2nd order calculated by author); [Holmberg/Akerblom 2007, p51] for Sweden (2nd order calculated by author); [Weibler/Wunderer 2007, p273] for Switzerland (2nd order calculated by author); and [Hoppe/Bhagat 2007, p512/514] for USA

Figure 5-7. Ranking of leadership factors

Having said this, Indian managers in leadership positions in the Western world frequently face substantial problems, as their leadership style and their competency is not compatible with the requirements of the Western industries.

In spite of many changes in India, Indian executives have not yet been fully 'westernized', i.e. made compatible with the way 'Westerners' are thinking and acting. When Western management styles are adopted, it often appears to remain superficial, leaving the core personalities unchanged. In cases of stress, Indian managers might fall back on more traditional ways of getting things done.

Dependability on Personal Relationships

The concept of dependability is also different. In the Western world, superiors depend on tasks to be successfully completed by their subordinates – and for them the completion of the task is more important than a stable relationship with the subordinate. In India, however, managers fully rely on their people and on the relationship with them. This leads to a completely different definition of dependability: in India, what counts is how well connected superiors are to their subordinates and how much they can rely on them personally.

To build and cement such relationships, superiors often attend weddings or religious ceremonies in the extended family of their subordinates.

Practical Implications for Foreign Managers

Managers and leaders from other cultures need to be prepared to interact with a wide range of organizational and leadership practices in India. One reason is the sheer size of the country, the complexity of its society, and all the variations within it. Another reason lies within the coexistence of collectivist and individualist values. This often creates unpredictable situations.[270]

Foreign IT project managers interacting with India will probably go through three phases of surprise:[271]

- Initially there is the surprise and often shock on how things work – or do not work – and how different they appear from the home culture.
- The second surprise is due when foreigners become a little more familiar with the operations in India and acquainted with individuals; differences do not seem to be that big anymore and a number of similarities to the home culture are found. This is because the Indian culture is so broad that in it almost everyone finds something seemingly familiar.
- In the third phase, one discovers that despite a lot of similarities, the root cause and driving forces for the behavior are entirely different. This leads to a deeper understanding and appreciation of India as a country, people, and culture.

---

[270] Cf. [Sinha 1997; Chhokar 2007, p. 1005]

[271] Cf. [Chhokar 2007, p. 1005]

"The resultant prescription for dealing with India [...] is to expect differences, to accept differences, and also to respect differences, without overlooking similarities."[272]

Management of Teams in India

In many Western cultures, employees expect a management framework to guide them in their work. In India, however, employees require and demand a detailed job description. The importance of the job is underlined by explaining and assigning the task more than once; without repetition the task will be treated as unimportant and probably not taken up at all.

Once a task is assigned, the manager cannot assume that the task is actually taken up, worked upon, and brought to a successful completion. Instead, constant monitoring and frequent feedback is required. This does not necessarily have to be a formal review meeting but could happen in the shape of a short chat, an email, or a telephone call.[273]

EXAMPLE: After a workshop, the American project manager Kevin casually tells one of the Indian team leaders Santosh that he would like to see the key findings documented in a short presentation. He then rushes off to the airport. A week later, Kevin calls Santosh and expresses his disappointment about not having received the presentation yet. Santosh is surprised.

ANALYIS: Santosh did not understand what Kevin exactly meant with his request and because seemed in a hurry at this moment, he kept quiet. He thought that if this presentation would be important for Kevin, he would come back to him nonetheless. But as Kevin did not mention the presentation again, Santosh thought that it had lost importance for Kevin.

SUGGESTIONS FOR IMPROVEMENT: In this intercultural context, Kevin should have tried to get a strong confirmation from Santosh that he is going to take up the work on the presentation. In addition, he could have sent him an email referring to the short discussion they have had and thus re-emphasized the importance of his request.

It may also happen that a deadline passes by and that there is still no feedback from the Indian team. Somewhere in the past weeks there was a problem, the Indian colleague has probably requested for input but did not receive an immediate reply. And he keeps waiting for this reply... without sending a reminder, without escalation; he just waits for his counterpart to come back with a solution.

EXAMPLE: An Indian IT engineer works on a portal implementation for a project in Europe. He is based out of a software development center in Bangalore and his task was assigned by the project leader in Europe. At some point of time he encountered connectivity issues and because of technical reasons could not continue with his work. By chance his line manager in India asked him about progress of his work and he told that he has a connectivity issue and is waiting for a response. The conversation went like this: 'When did you send out the alert to your project leader?' – 'Some one or two weeks ago.' – 'When exactly?' – 'On September 17....' – 'So this is more like two to three weeks, right? What did you do in the meantime?' – 'I have a problem, I am waiting for a

---

[272] [Chhokar 2007, p. 1006]
[273] Cf. [Vermeer/Neumann 2008, p. 145]

reply.' – 'Did you call your onsite project leader? Did you send out another reminder?' – 'No, I am waiting for the reply. The project leader is probably busy.' – 'Can you please call immediately?' – 'Shouldn't we wait for another two days and see if the project leader replies?'[274]

ANALYIS: This example shows two relationships which do not work effectively. First, the Indian IT engineer does not have a good rapport with his onsite project leader; they do not communicate on a regular basis and if at all only via email. He is apprehensive to reach out to the Western onsite project leader; there is no established trustful relationship. The Western onsite project leader is probably uncomfortable or too busy to immediately call the IT engineer in Bangalore to get more information about his work on the assignment, issues, and their potential impact. Second, the relationship between the Indian line manager and the IT engineer also suffers from a lack of interaction; they do not seem to communicate on a regular basis as well.

SUGGESTIONS FOR IMPROVEMENT: (1) The Indian IT engineer and the Western project leader need to establish a better relationship. Ideally this can happen through an onsite assignment of the IT engineer where he gets to know the business context, customer, and key contact people. (2) The relationship to his line manager seems to be suffering as well. In this case the Indian IT engineer was a 'lone soldier' working 1:1 for the Western project leader and did not receive any coaching by a more senior IT engineer in India; probably there was no project budget available for management overhead when setting up the project. The hierarchical distance to the line manager was simply too big for him to escalate small little problems like connectivity issues. Hence the viability of such small offshore assignments should be scrutinized very carefully; they neither meet the aspirations of Indian IT-engineers, neither do they fit into the hierarchical structures of Indian IT companies, nor do they allow for a compelling business case.

Team motivation in India is a very different and difficult story. Through their upbringing, school, and university education, Indians have learnt to excel and be successful as individuals; trusting others, cooperating, or simply delivering a project as a group is not part of the curriculum. When forming teams in the IT industry, each team member has to first understand that anyone aiming to do the job alone would not be successful. Team spirit can best be instilled through regular informal team outings, e.g. a dinner at a relaxed place, a bowling or go-cart evening, or some outdoor adventure activity.

But team managers also need to pay tribute to the fact that India is a very competitive society; because of the sheer number of people, individuals need to excel and prove their worthiness to the current and potential future employer. Excellent contributions of individuals or small teams should be highlighted by nominating someone as 'employee of the month' or giving away 'star awards', a certificate coupled with a small monetary gratification.

Managing by Asking Questions

A good Indian manager controls by asking questions. This is not only a good way of getting a grip of the project status but also for exchanging ideas. Powerful questions make Indians think proactively, follow a line of thought, and one also gets a much better buy-in.

---

[274] Extract from a conversation witnessed by the author.

Good questions to ask are:[275]

- What information (input) do you need to complete the project on time?
- From which areas and colleagues do you need input?
- Which alternatives do you have?
- How can I support you?
- What has been achieved in the project so far?
- What issues did you face? How can these be avoided in the future?
- What are your priorities in the project?
- How does this approach ensure quality?

Managing Private Life of Employees

In India there is no clear separation between business and private life. Likewise, managers are expected to take an interest in the private lives of their employees – and help to solve problems. When Indian IT engineers are scheduled to travel to an onsite assignment, they will, for example, have to take care of their spouses. Even today, most wives are in a role of dependency, they are not expected and not able to cope for three weeks or months alone at home. Instead, the husband is obliged to take care of her and maybe ask the in-laws to take her back for some time and look after her. Of course, this is a no-go shortly after marriage because the community may think that the husband is not in a position to properly take care of his wife.

All these activities are about managing expectations, logistics, and time. Indians discuss such issues very openly with their bosses, they do not only expect suggestions but also that the project plan is adjusted to their personal requirements.

But if managers succeed in accommodating the individual's private needs, there will be a strong bond between subordinates and boss and employees will go the extra mile for the boss, if required.

5.4   Typology of Employees

At an aggregate level, Indian call center agents and IT engineers may appear to have similar needs around working on latest technologies, career progression, earning good money to afford luxury goods, enable their parents a comfortable life-style, and securing their own old-age retirement. Work and career is mostly a vehicle for achieving these material goals; there is hardly any intrinsic motivation found through the content of work alone.

Notwithstanding, the workforce can be further segmented along a (1) combination of factors they value when selecting, staying, or leaving a job; (2) their experience with the West; and (3) their level of formal education.

---

[275] Adapted from [Vermeer/Neumann 2008, p. 156]

Value Factors

Factors people value when selecting, staying, or leaving a job can be used for segmenting the workforce; a recent study by Global Talent Metrics in cooperation with the Indian Institute of Management Bangalore and AlignMark has identified six clusters that account for 66% of the Indian white collar workforce (see Figure 5-8).[276]

Employee segment	Percentage*	Description
Demanders	16%	Demanding with very high expectation from their employers. Want best pay, a top brand company, a high-growth career path, and constant recognition
Just a job	13%	Opposite of demanders. Looking for a job that pays moderately with relatively low expectation across other factors
Start ups	12%	Looking for exciting work, learning opportunities, fast growth, and building value relationships. Do not value pay and brand
Work not pay	11%	Expect high career growth, challenging work at a prestigious company with good management. Do not necessarily expect best pay in the market
Mercenaries	9%	Purely motivated by pay as the only factor: want the highest pay irrespective of what work they do and where they work
Cash and brand	5%	Like mercenaries, but also extremely conscious about the brand name and image of the company for social recognition

* Percentage of Indian white-collar workforce

Figure 5-8. Value factors for employee segmentation[277]

It is a good idea to map prospective employees or team members to these clusters and then compare with what the company or project has to offer; this will help to combat attrition (see chapter 5.1.5).

Experience with the West

When interacting with Indians, an important distinction has to be made between those who have spent a considerable time working in the West, those who have been on short-term project assignments abroad, and those who have not yet had this opportunity.[278] Within these three broad sets the familiarity with Western ways of communicating, working, and dealing with problems obviously decreases.

When traveling abroad Indians, begin to notice that a lot of ways in which they have previously behaved are not reflected in Western countries. When they behave in their traditional Indian way, people look at them strangely – and they are more likely to adjust their behavior. In short, they become westernized and because of this adaptation Westerners find it easier to collaborate with them. Of course, one

---

[276] Cf. [GlobalTalentMetrics 2008]

[277] Adapted from [GlobalTalentMetrics 2008]

[278] The author proposes three levels of experience with the West; cf. [Storti 2007, p. 6] who only distinguishes two types of Indians.

can never expect a full Westernization and even though Indians adopt Western behaviors at the surface, they will revert to their Indian self in some cases when they are under a lot of pressure. Western business colleagues should hence not mistake a few changes at the surface for a complete personality change.

Level of Formal Education

The next distinction is by formal education, which broadly divides the workforce of the Indian IT and BPO industry into three different layers:

- Some degree from an institute of higher education. These colleagues have gone to some rather unknown university outside the big cities, studied for some degree with mediocre success, and attended basic computer training. Lecturers at such universities usually do not have a doctorate degree and have rarely been abroad themselves. The main selling proposition of these employees to the IT industry is that they can speak and write English.
- Degree from a renowned university. India's better universities are mostly located in the big cities, they boost a stringent selection process, and also attract better faculty. These colleagues would have learnt to formulate their own ideas and at work will be able to contribute without too much management guidance.
- Postgraduate degree from a leading management or technology institute. These institutes boast world-class faculty and teach students know-how plus independent thinking in their MBA or MSc programs.

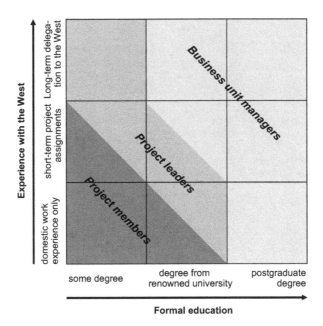

Figure 5-9. Generalized IT & BPO career matrix

While ten years back, the Indian IT industry would have only recruited from the second and third tier on all levels, today, the war for talent and increasing cost pressure forces HR departments to look at applicants from the first layer for most entry jobs. In Indian newspapers this is celebrated as success for the industry.

People from the first layer will find it hard to grow to levels above project leader; on the other hand, a MBA degree from one of the leading Institutes of Management is a fast entry ticket into business unit management positions (see Figure 5-9).

6 Interactions with India

Even if we understand the cultural dimensions, the practical challenges of an international team involving India remain the same: How do you inspire each other? How do you communicate? How do you ensure quality and deadlines? How do you avoid cost overruns? How do you resolve disagreements and disputes? In chapter 1.2, we looked at the big picture of intercultural dimensions; this chapter studies what happens at the workplace when people from different (Western) cultures interact with Indian colleagues.

6.1   Indian Languages and Indian English

India has 15 officially recognized languages[279] and more than 1,600 mother tongues and dialects. Most Indians are brought up by their parents in more than one of these languages. Hindi is the national language and primary tongue of about 30% of the people,[280] but is only widely spoken in the North. In the Southern states Tamil is widely spoken, and there have even been attempts to restrict the usage of Hindi.

The problem of not having one common language has been resolved by the use of English in business; it thus enjoys associate status. It is important in this context to note that recently some regional governments in India have begun to resist using English as a medium of education.[281]

Because Indians do not have one common native language, becoming fluent in one of the Indian languages will be of little help for Western business people. On the other side, an Indian who maintains a good command of a Western language other than English will more easily integrate in the culture of the business partner. French and German are the most sought after foreign languages in the Indian education system. The attractiveness of Russian is on a deep decline, but Japanese, Spanish, and Korean are coming into fashion.[282]

In intercultural encounters with India, all parties are likely to use English as a trade language. However, the use of a pidgin form of English restricts communication to those issues for which this simplified version has words.[283]

Even native English can be misinterpreted; there are so many versions of English in this world, from UK-English to US-English, and Australian English.

---

[279] The 15 official languages are (in alphabetical order): Bengali, Telugu, Marathi, Tamil, Urdu, Gujarati, Hindi, Malayalam, Kannada, Oriya, Punjabi, Assamese, Kashmiri, Sindhi, and Sanskrit; Hindustani is a popular variant of Hindi/Urdu spoken widely throughout northern India but is not an official language; cf. [CIA 2007]

[280] Cf. [CIA 2007]

[281] In September 2006, over 800 schools in Karnataka have been asked to shut down because they use English as their medium of instruction instead of Kannada as the mother tongue of the children. In addition, nearly 600 schools in and around Bangalore have lost their license for violating this policy; cf. e.g. [TOI 150906]

[282] Cf. [Sharma 2004]

[283] Cf. [Hofstede/Hofstede 2005, p. 327-328]

Indian English adds a level of difficulty to this. Most Indians do not speak English at home, but rather their local language. Their English, though fluent and sometimes with a surprisingly vast vocabulary, may thus have some gaps. They also tend to speak very fast and at an even pace without much of intonation, making it more difficult to understand. Some words in Indian English have very different meanings; Figure 6-1 is a comprehensive but by far not exhaustive listing of this phenomenon.

What Indians say ...	... and what it really means
Crore	Ten million
Lakh	Hundred thousand
Cousin-brother	Male cousin
Eve-teasing	Sexual harassment of a woman
To pre-pone a meeting	To move to an earlier time, i.e. the opposite of postpone
Rank holder	Someone who is at the top of his class at university
To crib about something	To complain about something
I have a doubt about the project plan	I have a tiny question – but I definitely will not question the entire project plan
Done!	I will start doing it tomorrow
Yes	Yes, I have heard you
Can I make a move?	I think we are done. Can I leave?
Where are you put up?	Which hotel are you in?
Where do you stay?	Where do you live? In which part of town is your house?
I don't take fish	I don't eat fish
What is your good name?	What is your name? This is a Hindi legacy where the word 'shubh naam' means auspicious name.
To send a document across	To send a document over
Out of station	Out of town, on a business trip or on vacation
Tell me!	How can I help you?
Shall we order for food?	Shall we order food?
To pass out of university	To graduate from university
Restaurant cum bar	Restaurant with attached bar; cum is a Latin word which was earlier used in British English

Figure 6-1. Discovering the real meaning of Indian English[284]

EXAMPLE: Figure 6-2 shows a prime example of a culturally driven misunderstanding in written English. Frank sends a short email to Frank acknowledging the receipt of a presentation and expressing his disappointment about a lack of consolidated KPI figures. In his email he uses

---

[284] Expanded from [Messner 2008c]

the colloquial phrase 'it's a shame', which in international English means nothing but 'it's a pity'. His Indian colleague feels somewhat guilty about this shortcoming, spots the word 'shame' and gets a painful humiliation sensation. He then reacts very strongly by sending an email to Frank's boss Robin complaining about Frank putting shame on the India organization and not knowing English properly.

From: **Frank Bauer**
To: **Manoj Agarwal**
CC: **Robin Casocavallo**

Hi Manoj,

thank you for your presentation; but it's a shame that we cannot get a consolidated overview of the KPIs.

Any chance to escalate this in your organization?

Thanks,
Frank

From: **Manoj Agarwal**
To: **Robin Casocavallo**

Robin,

please find below the requested information.

Being two different legal entities, we have some challenge in compiling India level KPI data. The portal is updated at the end of every quarter. Definitely we are also not satisfied with this situation. But it is certainly not shameful. Hence Frank's remark is unnecessary and demoralizing. We hope Frank knows its meaning (English).

Regards,
Manoj

Figure 6-2. Example of language driven miscommunication[285]

ANALYSIS: Obviously there are previous undercurrent hard feelings between Manoj and Frank so that a simple colloquial phrase could cause Manoj to completely misinterpret Frank's intention and overreact. Interestingly, Manoj does not reply directly to Frank but escalates the matter to Frank's boss without putting Frank on cc. This shows how Indians rely on hierarchy to resolve any issues. Manoj also wrongly assumes that as an Indian his English his by far superior than that of his German colleague Frank.

SOLUTION: Depending on Robin's level of intercultural India awareness, his time to fully read Frank's first email, and his command of English, Frank's reputation with his boss Robin is affected. Frank would be well advised to personally discuss difficulties in intercultural communication with Robin and thus do damage control within his reporting line. He could choose to ignore this incident in his previous communication with Manoj or formally apologize and state that he had never intended to demoralize anyone. An explanation of how the phrase 'it's a shame' is used in international English will probably not be very effective as Manoj will feel lectured, further humiliated, and his resentment for Frank will only increase.

In terms of pronunciation, the most noticeable feature of English spoken in India is its syllabic rhythm,[286] which can be a source of comprehension difficulty among other English speaking people, especially when the conversation is going fast.

The grammar of Indian English also shows some anomalies.[287]

---

[285] Original communicaton received by the author; names changed and content slightly altered
[286] Cf. [Crystal 2003; Lawler ---]
[287] Cf. [Lawler ---]

- The progressive tense is used in instead of static verbs: 'I am understanding it' – instead of 'I understand it'; 'She is knowing the answer' – instead of 'She knows the answer'.
- Sometimes prepositions are directly translated from Hindi: 'pay attention on' – instead 'pay attention to'; 'discuss about the situation' – instead of 'discuss the situation'.
- 'Isn't it?' and 'no?' are used as general tag questions: 'You're going, isn't it?' – instead of 'You're going, aren't you?'; 'He's here, no?' – instead of 'He's here, isn't he?'
- The word order can be different: 'Who you have come for?' – instead of 'Who have you come for?'; 'They're late always' – instead of 'They're always late'; 'My all friends are waiting' – instead of 'All my friends are waiting'.
- The past perfect tense is sometimes used where the past tense is more appropriate: 'I had gone for a meeting' – instead of 'I went for a meeting'.
- The conjunctive 'I would' is used instead of the more affirmative 'I will' or 'I am': 'I cannot reply to your email as I would be attending a meeting on Monday and Tuesday'.

6.2   Culture Shock India

There are many things which strike people from other cultures when they interact with Indians for the first time.

- Lack of order and structure. Life functions differently in India, everything seems to run in its own rhythm. Following schedules, adherence or existence of rules cannot be taken for granted. Everybody follows their very own destination, logic, and rhythm.
- Decibel level. Indians tend to speak all at the same time and at much louder volumes than necessary. People are used to living and working in overcrowded spaces and it is thought to be important to raise ones voice in order to catch attention.
- Display of emotions. Indians control their emotions far less than foreigners do. Uncontrolled outbursts of irritation, overwhelming appreciation, open anxiety, and declaration of loyalty can be a challenge to deal with.
- Respect for hierarchy. Elders in the family enjoy a special superior status because of their seniority. Most organizations have a very steep hierarchy and authority is often not questioned.
- Lack of private sphere. Colleagues at work and also total strangers surprise you with questions about your age, work experience, marital status, number of children – and even your income. All this is not viewed as a violation of personal space in India. Colleagues at work are very much aware on where their peers stand in terms of monetary compensation.
- Juggling of appointments and multitasking. Appointments are not necessarily written in stone, as they are more considered like a tentative reservation that

can be cancelled without notice if anything more important comes up. It is very rare that a teleconference starts at the scheduled time; most Indian participants will dial in five to fifteen minutes later. When in a meeting, Indians will not switch off their cell phones but take each and every call – it might be an important one. This goes as far as telephone calls being answered while visiting the restroom.

- Peace over truth. In cases of conflicts or disputes, the value of peace comes before truth. This means that you will not be told the complete truth or be told an adjusted version of the story in order to allow the Indian to keep face and continue with a harmonic relationship. Facts can be twitched and turned, if it serves a good purpose; there is not only one version of truth.

When foreigners arrive in India for first time, more observations get added to this list:

- Chaotic traffic. Simply put, traffic is complete madness. First, there is an absence of basic rules like right-before-left, there are no speed limits, and red lights are more of a suggestion. Second, everybody seems to be (and actually is) taking care of their own advantage only. Two-wheelers and auto-rickshaws squeeze through vehicles. If there are pedestrian walkways, they appear to serve as a bypass for motorbikes rather than a safe place for pedestrians.
- Air pollution. Emission control exists in the books but is only half-heartedly enforced as people find innovative ways around it. Trucks and buses spit out black clouds of smoke. The chimneys of factories do not have filters installed, thereby reducing the costs of production at the expense of the environment and human health.
- Low priority to hygiene. Indians can live with hygienic conditions that Westerns find unimaginable and repellent. Dusty roadside food stalls and butcher shops, open drainages clogged with garbage, children of the poor playing on garbage heaps, no organized waste removal system, filthy hygiene in some hospitals, slums, absence of sufficient and clean public toilets, and people urinating on the roadside are just some of the things that strike every first-time visitor to India.
- Poverty and class disparity. Children and mothers with babies persistently keep knocking at car windows queuing up in front of traffic lights to get a rupee or two, thus seeking to ensure their survival for today. Badly handicapped persons or ones with open leprosies hang on to trousers of passers-by and beg for money. Slums are mostly illegal constructions, sometimes right in the centre of the city. There is no clean water supply and despite some huts boosting a television set, electricity is mostly illegally tapped. On the other side of the wealth spectrum, there are many rich people in India who openly showcase their wealth. Where else would one spot a Porsche Carrera at walking speed maneuvering around potholes? The better-off younger generation has become very brand-conscious, sporting the latest brands from around the world.

- Body language. Male Indians offer very long handshakes, walk holding hands, or enjoy a post-lunch nap on the lawns with their feet entangled. Even software engineers sit very closely while solving a coding problem in front of their computers. However, they all do not mean to send out any signals about homosexuality. On the other side, even married couples do not commonly demonstrate their affection publicly.
- Quality and ethic of labor. Artisans and other so-called skilled workers are not trained formerly. Instead, they often follow the footsteps of their fathers or uncles. Work is a time-passing opportunity for them to earn money, but not a profession in which they want to excel and thrive.
- Superstitious believes. There are many good and bad omens, auspicious and inauspicious timings to control daily and also project activities. Tuesdays are generally avoided and even the barber shop will be empty on this day; but Fridays are considered fortunate days. The new moon signifies the start of a growth phase and is therefore a good day to commence a new endeavor.

But then there are also many wonderful things about the Indian culture that foreigners find positively overwhelming. Indians are extremely hospitable and adjust themselves to the convenience of others. According to an old adage, a guest is to be treated like god. Indians appear to be a happy people; regardless whether they live in artificial gated complexes surrounded by security guards or in slums, they accept life as an illusion, thereby giving less weight to material inadequacies than their Western counterparts. Last but not least, the availability of cheap household help, good and fresh food, and the colorful clothing of women make India – at first glance – irresistible in the eyes of many foreigners.

6.3   First Business Contacts

Reaching Out to New Business Partners

It is common in the Western World to reach out to new business partners via email, telephone, or the new networking tools such as linked-in or xing.[288] One will usually get personal appointments with previously unknown colleagues or business partners.

But in India, people are hesitant doing business with someone they do not know. Simply asking someone in an Indian organization for an appointment will not be very successful. If the request is at all answered, one will be redirected to a subordinate – and the way to the top is blocked for a long time. This behavior sounds strange and arrogant to Westerners, but it is part of the India business culture where a strict protocol is followed.

The best way to overcome this hurdle is to ask for an introduction or recommendation, while considering hierarchies at the same time. Both the desired

---

[288] www.linked-in.com or www.xing.com

contact partner and the recommender have to be at the same hierarchical level as the Westerner asking for the appointment.

This process can be very time consuming and the Westerner may be under pressure from his own organization. It is extremely difficult for Westerners to report back home that getting an appointment and some basic information from the Indian company is taking a long time.

EXAMPLE: A Swiss IT service provider is working on a proposal for a client and requires input on certain aspects of offshore delivery from its Indian subsidiary. The Swiss bid manager Hugo sends out an email to the competency lead Santosh in India, but there is no reply. It takes two reminders for Santosh to finally reply to Hugo and ask one of his subordinates, Prashanth, to support Hugo. In the meantime, the client deadline has come closer and Hugo has gone ahead with the proposal without input from India.

SOLUTION: There would have been two ways to better handle this situation and avoid the deadlock. First, Hugo could have explained his request to a colleague already known to him in India. This could have been either a local employee or an expatriate colleague from Switzerland. This known contact partner would have phoned up Santosh and explained to him about Hugo's quest. Ideally, he would have organized a telephone conference between the three of them and established the connection. Second, if Hugo was working on a real tough deadline and did not have enough time for the relationship building, he should have approached his business head Peter who then would have contacted his counterpart Srinivas in India. Srinivas would have instructed Santosh to support Hugo. As Santosh would have received this request 'top-down' from his superior, he would have given it highest priority and immediately worked on it.

Meeting Your Indian Colleague for the First Time

The first impression is important in India. It all starts with the airline, the class of travel, and the hotel you have chosen. Indians are very status conscious, and how much your company spends on your airfare and the hotel accommodation directly reflects your status in the organization – at least in the eyes of your Indian counterpart.

After a long trip and lots of new impressions on the way from the airport to your hotel, you finally reach the office of the Indian company. Cost savings are also taking place in India; today you will mostly be greeted by a security guard whose command of English is questionable. His main concern will be that you enter your name and the laptop serial number into a register. These are not only security requirements to protect the company from theft of data and assets, but mainly legal requirements due to classification of an export oriented business and tax benefits under the software technology park (STP) scheme (see chapter 4.1.3).

When you finally meet your Indian colleagues, they will greet you with a long handshake. Handshakes in India last much longer and can extend to a few minutes of conversation. Just leave your hand in theirs, it is very common in India. But if you are to meet a woman, do not extend your hand to her unless she clearly offers it to you. Traditionally, men and women do not shake hands for a greeting; instead, you can slightly bow your head and show that you acknowledge her. The traditional greeting of 'namaste', i.e. the folding of your palms, looks silly on most foreigners and is also not common practice in the Indian IT industry. If she is experienced in international business relationships, she might offer a handshake to you. Only then accept it, and it will be much shorter and softer than with a man. As a Western business woman you best wait for your Indian counterpart to make the first step and follow accordingly.

You will be tempted to talk about your first experience in India. All those impressions of poverty, slums, traffic, and masses of people on the road – your contact partner is the first person whom you meet in this foreign country who is a little bit familiar to you, and naturally you feel like opening your heart and asking about everything you have seen. Please remember that it is your colleague's country, they might not have seen the world outside of India – and above all, it is the country their heart belong to. Commenting on inefficiency, poverty, the caste system, and e.g. your taxi driver's stupidity is completely inappropriate. However, you can safely talk about how long you spend in the maddening traffic in the car. This is something your Indian colleagues face every day and they are equally annoyed about it.

In the Western world you would right away go to a meeting room, have a cup of coffee, and start with your presentation or business discussion. In India, please be prepared for an extended warm-up phase. Show respect for the Indian culture, talk about the niceties you have so far experienced during your stay in India, family, sports and especially cricket, and maybe about your plans to see some sights during your visit to India. If you are visiting for the first time, you will probably be shown around in the office and introduced to some senior management. Come prepared and take a lot of business cards with you, you will need them.

It is not a good idea to shorten this warm-up phase, it builds up empathy and creates goodwill with your Indian colleague. Only then you are ready to discuss business.

6.4   Meetings and Negotiations

Preparing and Analyzing the Starting Position

It is needless to say that every meeting should be prepared for. When conducting meetings in India it is especially important to analyze and understand one's own position. The Indian counterparts adapt their willingness to negotiate according to whether they see an advantage in the relationship with you in the short or long term. Especially with one-off businesses, Indians will be very rationale and put their own advantage over fairness or reliability. It is a good idea to work out and prepare for alternatives if the ideal solution is not accepted.

Indians on the other side usually do not prepare for meetings as thoroughly as Westerners do. While Westerners often arrive with a detailed agenda, a presentation with data, and a recommended action plan for the meeting, Indians mostly come with a blank sheet of paper and a pen. They want to get to know you first, understand your goals, and establish a good relationship. A meeting has a different purpose in India. It is about brainstorming for ideas, whereas in the West, it is about presenting facts, conclusions, and agreeing on pre-prepared actions.

Choosing the right strategy for the meeting is also important. While most Western countries follow the prioritization strategy and discuss the important topics first, in India it is the other way round. Topics with less priority are discussed first during the warm-up phase, and a decision will only be made once all topics have been talked about. Consequently in the West, people are more concentrated at the beginning of the meeting. In India, initially people do not listen very carefully as they expect casual small talk or issues of lesser importance on the agenda. They only warm up towards the middle of the meeting.

Negotiations in India can take much longer than in the Western world. The initial offering will be taken down, no matter how lucrative it is. One has to prepare for this and always leave room for negotiation.

Scheduling a Meeting

Meetings in India are always tentative. When sending a meeting request, it is very rare to receive a yes or no as a reply. Most people in India confirm with a tentative reply. It is near to impossible to get a firm commitment more than three hours before the start date of the meeting. On the other side, it is possible to just walk into an office and arrange management meetings at very short notice. Some foreigners in India have adapted to this fact and actually plan their business trips without previously arranging meetings.

Meetings rarely start before ten o'clock in the morning and a day packed with meetings is a bad idea, because already the first meeting will start later than expected and extend beyond the starting point of the next one.

Different responses to meeting requests have different meanings: 'Today' means that the meeting is probably going to take place today or at least within the next 24 hours. 'Tomorrow' signifies that the other party is willing to conduct the meeting. But the appointment will not happen tomorrow; sometime in the following week is more likely. 'Next week' is rather vague and connotes an interest to talk sometime in the future. If the reply is 'in two weeks time', one can be sure that the request will be ignored and that the meeting will not take place in two weeks. This statement of time is best to be translated into 'maybe sometime'.

Starting a Meeting

A Western business meeting usually starts with a few minutes of light conversation. It can be about the weather, sports or traffic. After this, business will start more or less immediately. As mentioned before, the warm-up phase is longer in India. First, nobody will arrive on time for the meeting. Second, the meeting room booking will be messed up. And if a projector for the laptop was booked, one can be sure that it is missing in the room. A typical meeting commences anywhere between fifteen to thirty minutes late. It is very uncommon for the Indian to say

'Sorry, I'm late'. The absence of an apology, however, is not impoliteness on the part of the Indian; instead, the value of punctuality is simply not present in India. One can never be too late for an appointment. During this time, the few people actually present will talk about cricket, tea or coffee, and their families. This is followed by an uncomfortable seating ritual, nobody knows where to sit and usually there are not enough chairs available anyhow. If a brave soul has taken the initiative of sitting down, private discussions will continue over a cup of coffee or tea. Even if holding back the urge to discuss business is difficult for the Westerner, one is advised to leave the official start to the Indians.

Conducting the Meeting

Any meeting with Indians is around the idea of a deal to be agreed. Hence, a shared understanding and establishment of a partnership is more important than action items and meeting minutes. There is a polite and patient atmosphere in meetings. It is uncommon to crack many jokes and put too much pressure on the other side.

The decision process will take longer as well. While in the Western world, the attendees of a meeting are usually entitled to take certain decisions, in India this is a team process where many internal discussion have to be made before a decision or a concession is made. And afterwards it is the upper or top management who has to approve.

During the meeting it is not uncommon for the Indian participants to frequently change languages and switch to either Hindi or one of their other common mother tongues. This is not meant to be impolite but rather shows that something really important has to be discussed.

Indians love to talk, all at the same time, and at great lengths. As a foreigner one is often tempted to shorten things, move on, and to interrupt. But this is the worst thing one can do – let the Indian counterparts finish their lengthy speeches, listen patiently, and resist the urge to interrupt. When it comes to your turn, ask if everything has been said, and only then commence presenting your viewpoint.

It is a good sign if suddenly the Indian counterparts start asking many questions and the speed of the meeting increases; this means that the Indians are interested in the proposal. It is now up to the other side to slow down the discussion and thereby hold up the tension. A good way is to ask questions about competitors and other customers which are mostly being answered honestly at this point in time.

Facial expressions and body language are both very prevalent in discussions in India. Particularly South-Indians have a perplexing habit, when listening to you, of shaking the head in a manner that appears to be saying 'no'. This is named the Indian wiggle. Given the context of the conversation, this can have a variety of meanings: 'yes', 'I'm listening', 'it makes sense what you are saying', 'I agree', 'sounds good', or simply 'go on'.

EXAMPLE: A German delivered a software training to a group of Indian IT engineers in Bangalore and asked them if his presentation made sense and if he could move on to the next topic. The Indians 'shook' their heads, meaning 'go on – we have understood'. The German however took it for a 'no' and started to repeat explaining the same thing. Later, he said he had the feeling that he did not come across very well and had difficulties communicating. The Indians, however, gave the feedback that the German obviously did not know much about the subject and kept repeating the same thing.

Facial expressions can be a play as well. Sometimes the faces reflect sheer horror when a commercial proposal is made; or sometimes anger is displayed very openly. The only possible advice is to not move to the defensive, stay quiet, and not show any reaction at all.

Ending a Meeting

Westerners expect meetings to come to an end after about an hour or at the end of the previously allotted time. In the last 10 minutes, there would be a wrap-up, action items would be allocated, and the date for the next meeting would be settled. But in India, "… we will in contrast be heading very gently for some sort of agreement about what we are to disagree about."[289] Of course, there will also be identified and agreed actions. But even if they are written down, they will later be a subject of reinterpretation, as Indians think that agreed decisions have to be later seen in a new context. There is a simple lesson for foreigners: do not pay attention to meeting minutes or action items as they hold no value. The purpose of the meeting is more to establish a good personal relationship which will then form the framework for a future cooperation.

The meeting does not end with the action items and a handshake. More talking and discussing will take place, all this is part of the meeting and the relationship building process. This goes on until one is finally out of sight. This phase is generally the most important part of the meeting, as the action agreed upon when the lift door closes is the most likely one to be implemented.

Attention Levels During the Meeting

The above observations can be summarized in an attention level diagram (Figure 6-3). People from Western business cultures go into a meeting with a rather high attention level, maintain this level until all high-priority items are discussed and decided upon. As the importance of the agenda points goes down, the attention level drops. Towards the end of the meeting, Westerners expect casual small talk and their attention levels are down. Indians, however, expect extended casual small talk at the beginning of the meeting and hence their attention levels are rather low. After an initial overview of the topics to be discussed, their attention levels steeply increase and remain high till the business partners are waved good-bye at the lift.

---

[289] [Davies 2004, p. 136]

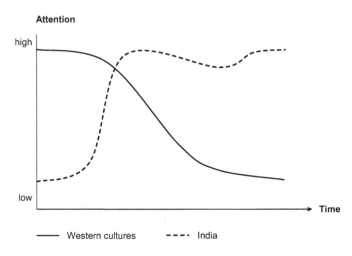

Figure 6-3. Attention level diagram

Assuming the agenda and time schedule of the business meeting is driven by Westerners, the overlap of high attention periods between representatives of both cultures is rather short . When Westerners bring up their high-priority topics, Indians still expect small talk; and when Indians want to finalize decisions at the point of saying good-bye, the attention levels of Westerners have already dropped to the small-talk level.

6.5   Communication Skills

6.5.1   Communication from India

Communication problems between Indian and Western colleagues mostly start with the Indians saying something but their colleagues understanding something entirely different. Both parties believe that they have understood each other because they are conversing in English as a common language. However, the communication still leads to unfortunate misunderstandings as both colleagues walk off on different tracks. Further down the road, this leads to frustration and mutual distrust.

Neither party is at fault; the meaning of words and the way people communicate are culturally determined.

The Indian Word 'yes'

In a collectivist culture like India, preserving harmony and maintaining face are important values in communication. The word 'yes' has become an indispensable word to achieve this purpose. "Simply stated, how can you ever disappoint, upset, embarrass, or offend other people, especially those above you in the hierarchy, if you always respond with 'yes', regardless […] of what you really think or of what the truth might be?"[290] Hence the word 'yes' connotes many different things – but none of them come close to what Westerners mean by 'yes'. In the Western world, 'yes' is an affirmative reply to a question meaning 'I agree' or 'I understand'. And when Westerners hear the word 'yes', they assume that the respondent answers a question in an approving way.

But in India, the words 'yes', 'ok', 'sure', 'no problem', and 'fine' are merely polite acknowledgements that one is listening: 'I hear what you say'; they do not stand for a positive answer. In fact, a negative answer can follow the word 'yes'.

Westerners can easily overcome this communication hurdle by not paying any attention to the word 'yes', by virtually disregarding it, and only listening to what comes next in the response. Maybe it helps to remember that when an Indian says 'no problem', one can very much expect the problems to start.

Figuring Out an Indian 'no'

In India, one is not supposed to give offense or to disappoint the management and hence saying 'no' to something is almost impossible. Telling others what they do not want to hear causes distortion in a relationship and is thus to be avoided.

Therefore, Indians almost never say 'no' or use another blatantly open negative formulation when talking to their subordinates, customers, or Westerners. However, the hierarchical nature of Indian society and organizations allows superiors to be very open and rude to their subordinates; receiving a 'no' from a boss is almost expected and does not disturb the harmony of this relationship.

Indians manage to communicate the 'no'-message in a much more discreet way by not saying 'yes'. Then they do not say anything negative and possibly destroy harmony, but it is obvious to everyone familiar with the Indian culture that nothing positive has been expressed:[291]

- No reply. Not replying to an inquiry, an email, or a letter is a very common form of giving a 'no'. If one sends an email to Indian IT developers asking if they have the knowledge in a certain specialized technical area required for a project assignment, and if one does not receive a reply, this may well mean that they do not have that knowledge. However, as they are unable to say anything positive, they have chosen to ignore the question and hence do not reply. Nothing has been said, only a positive answer has not been given. In India, the message would have been perfectly understood.
- Changing the subject. Another popular way of getting around saying 'no' or delivering a dissatisfying reply is to steer away from the subject and avoid the question altogether. From an Indian perspective, there is something wrong with the question, meaning that it cannot be honestly answered in a positive way.

---

[290] [Storti 2007, p. 35]
[291] Cf. [Storti 2007, p. 43-49]

- Postponing the answer. If Indians try to postpone an answer to a question, this mostly means that they are not willing to answer because they are not in a position to give a positive reply. Keywords to look for are: 'I have to check with my boss', 'I need to look into the details', 'Let me get back to you on this', or 'I'll follow up on this'.
- Returning the question. Repeating the question and thereby returning it back to the speaker is another popular way of avoiding a direct answer. If Indians think that something is possible, they would say so when asked. But trying to avoid the question can signify that they cannot positively commit to the question. Also, turning the question around and asking for the opinion of the questioner is a variant of an implicit negative reply; common phrases are: 'Do you think it's possible?', 'Is it good for you?', 'Will your team be ready?', or simply 'What do you think?'
- Weighing the answer. A slight hesitation is also not a good sign when one hopes for a positive reply. This can take the form of a short silence when the Indian is weighing the answer, a phrase like 'I see', a nervous laugh, or a quick intake of breath.
- Using qualifiers. For Indians, qualifiers do not mean anything specific, though usually the answer is much closer to 'no'. Phrases to look out for are: 'That should be possible', 'Should be ok', 'We'll do your level best', 'We have a good chance to do it', 'We will try', 'Possibly', 'Probably yes' or 'We'll put in all our efforts'.

Deciphering Bad News

Delivering bad news is fraught with implications for maintaining face. Hence, Indians treat this topic with great care which poses a big communication challenge for Westerners who are unable to follow what the Indian tries to say.

In the IT industry, bad news are most commonly about project delays and overruns. But by the time Westerners discover that the Indian offshore team is not able to deliver on time, the deadline is usually very close. Westerners usually overlook seemingly innocent comments from Indians revealing that a project may be delayed. If an Indian raises one of the following topics or concerns, then this will be a good indicator for such a situation:

- The project team has recently become very busy, started to put in a lot of overtime, and even comes in over the weekend.
- Some (!) parts of the project are really successful and ahead of or on time.
- Returning the question of deadline adherence as in asking the Westerner if the project schedule remains convenient for him: 'Is the deadline still good for you?'
- Some small part of the project is facing a problem or was more complicated than originally estimated and therefore may take a little longer.

Conversations around these topics can also be a cry for help. Asking for help is an especially embarrassing situation in cultures where face saving is high on the agenda, as one has to admit of not being capable of or not having the time to deliver something which was promised earlier.

Spotting Indian Initiative

In the eyes of many Westerners, Indians prefer to follow instructions without using their brains. Some Indians may feel uncomfortable telling their Western counterparts that they know a better way of solving a problem. They do not like to be seen as trying to be smart and acting more competent than their superiors who may lose their face by considering (or even accepting) a suggestion from a subordinate.

Indians use coded phrases and right away downplay their idea to let their bosses know about a better option: 'I don't know if this would work ...', 'I am just doing some out-of-the box thinking ...', and 'I know it may sound crazy but can we consider ...'.

Sometimes Indians try to reconfirm if the approach proposed by their bosses will really work: 'Do you think that this will work?'. In fact, this question does not ask for reconfirmation, but it tells the superior that the subordinate may have a different approach in mind. And as mentioned before, the absence of positive feedback on a proposition can also mean that the subordinate has something completely different in mind.[292]

The definition of initiative is also entirely different in India. In the Western business world, initiative means to come up with an idea, act on your own, and to implement it. In India, taking initiative entails identifying the area of improvement and informing your manager about it; but it does not go as far as taking actions on your own (see example in Figure 6-4). At this point in time, Indians like to be requested to take up the implementation as well. This is often overlooked by Westerners and it results in the prejudice that Indians do not take initiative and ownership. However, it just requires this little confirmation from someone up the hierarchy ladder and Indians will put their thoughts into practice.

From: **Arun Bhatterchaja**
To: **Karl Andersson**

Dear Karl,

I want to share with you my thoughts on utilizing functional consultants for our service offering "test factory".

Can we assign a functional consultant to the test factory at offshore? He could review the test scripts from a business process perspective.

This in my opinion will also be a right step towards getting more functional know-how into the team.

Best Regards,
Arun

Figure 6-4. Example of Indian initiative[293]

---

[292] Cf. [Storti 2007, p. 102-105]
[293] Adapted from original communication received by the author; names changed.

6.5.2   Communicating to India

The communication problem goes both ways. Most Westerners are from task-oriented societies with direct communication styles (see chapter 1.2.2). They would not have to worry so much about landing their message if Indians were not from a face-saving culture where especially the more junior people tend to consider Westerners as superior, and as a result act apprehensively, i.e. they do not want to cause disturbance, nuisance, or frustration and prefer to guess what the Westerner means. Sometimes they sit together after a phone-call or meeting with a Westerner and try to figure out what has most likely been said or meant.

This tendency for Indians not to ask for clarifications makes communication extremely complicated. It puts the responsibility on the Westerners to implicitly collect feedback on their communication, monitor themselves, and decide upon the necessity to rephrase. In face-to-face meetings, the best clue is to look at the faces of the Indian counterparts, and a confused or puzzled look will be a good indication that the message did not land and one has to rephrase or explain.

It is all the more difficult in telephone conversations; here the burden falls entirely on the Westerners to monitor their speech. A good way is to ask powerful questions that require the Indian to formulate an answer other than yes or no; from the quality of the answer one can make out if the content of the communication has been understood. Examples of such powerful questions are:

- 'What will be your priorities in implementing this?'
- 'What are the next steps you will take?'
- 'What input do you need from me?'
- 'What obstacles do you foresee?'

Another advice is to ask Indians frequently for clarifications and re-phrasing when you have not understood them and thus implicitly encourage them to do the same with you.

6.5.3   Positive Feedback

The best feedback is always a personal discussion. When starting a project, a face-2-face meeting, videoconference, or at least a telephone call should happen on a weekly basis. The interval can be extended to two or three weeks depending on the progress of the project. In addition, more formal reviews and feedback should also be implemented. The project status with key metrics, successful achievements, and open issues should be reported every two to four weeks. After a few months, it is a good idea to initiate a 360-degree feedback process, in which the Indian employees can anonymously voice their opinion of how they feel about the cooperation with their Western colleagues or with the customer.

India is a land of emotions; positive feedback is almost automatic and embodied in the culture of telling other people what they want to hear. The worst case for any Indian team is a highly qualified German engineer who simply shrugs his shoulders on completion of a tough deadline and starts talking about the next project phase. Delight can be and is expected to be shown openly.

The email in Figure 6-5 (a) shows project feedback by the Indian team leader Sivakumar to one of his subordinates Kiran. In (b) Aravind both thanks the Western engagement manager Christof for sponsoring an incentive gift as well as motivates the team by re-emphasizing how dear the incentive is. In example (c), Susan already provided feedback to Arvin in an email and Arvin now asks for more formal feedback by sending her a form; in (d) he thanks her again for good feedback and stresses on how this will further motivate the team.

Indians wait for overwhelmingly positive feedback and no feedback is essentially bad news. If an Indian does not say something positive when asked for

(a)
| From: | Sivakumar G |
| To: | Kiran Hospet |

Dear Kiran,

Greetings!!! Today is your last day in our project.

It was a wonderful moment we worked together in this project. You had done a wonderful job for our project. I appreciate your sincerity and dedication to the project.

I am thankful to you for making every minute so special in this assignment. I'm looking forward to work together in future. All the best for your next assignment!!!

Thanks a lot & Warm Regards,
Sivakumar

(b)
From:	Aravind Rajkumar
To:	[project-team]
CC:	Christof Appel

Hi Team,

I hope everyone has got their T-Shirt by now. I can see a happy mood in the team after getting their most awaited gift.

Please join me to thank Christof for rewarding us with this beautiful gift for all our good work that we have done on this project. I am sure this encourages us do more good work and make this project a successful one.

Big thanks from the entire BORCON team to Christof.

With Best Regards,
Aravind

(c)
| From: | Arvin Gupta |
| To: | Susan Collins |

Hello Susan,

Thank you for your comments and glad to learn that the output could be used for your discussion with the customer.

Please be kind to fill this feedback to motivate the team members as well as indicate the areas of improvement.

Thanks and Regards,
Arvin

(d)
| From: | Arvin Gupta |
| To: | Susan Collins |

Hello Susan,

Thank you once again, appreciate it!! This should motivate us ☺

Best regards and look forward to working with you on future projects,

Arvin

Figure 6-5. Positive email feedback[294]

---

[294] Original communication received by the author; names changed.

feedback, then this omission most likely means negative feedback.[295] But Western business people and especially non-native speakers of English are often hesitant to send out such flowery feedback, as they are not accustomed to this style of writing. But shorter and less effusive emails are also well received in India and they are frequently forwarded within the team, to peers, and to the management.

No positive feedback can easily lead to frustration among team members; they assume that their performance ratings and their career will get affected (see Figure 6-6). All these aspects are taken into account in a mature rating and promotion process, but the employee's feeling of being left behind and missing a chance is certainly a real one; and at the end of the day this matters to a successful project execution.

    From: Jyothi Rao
                To: Vijay Bangalore

Hi Vijay,

I think I need to talk to you regarding the problems faced by me due to being on the TALK2CAR project.

If I get no good feedback, lower ratings, and if I am not able to prove my potential, I need to leave this project.

This is what I need to talk to you about urgently.

Regards,
Jyothi

Figure 6-6. Concern about lack of positive feedback[296]

6.5.4   Negative Feedback

"Negative feedback, needless to say, has nothing in common with telling people what they want to hear and for Indians, therefore, is practically akin to torture."[297]

Receiving Negative Feedback From India

In most circumstances Indians never say anything negative but simply refrain from saying anything positive. In other words, negative feedback in India is essentially the absence of positive feedback.

Giving negative feedback is even more difficult for an Indian than saying 'no', because this does not only mean to disappoint but also to criticize someone and causing a possible loss of face. Hence, Indians either resort to very lengthy

---

[295] Cf. [Storti 2007, p. 54]

[296] Adapted from original communication received by the author; names changed.

[297] [Storti 2007, p. 53]

circumlocutions that can be difficult to decipher for foreigners or they fall silent. The most commonly techniques used to avoid commenting a topic are:[298]

- Not responding. If an Indian does not reply to a proposal, it can mean negative feedback without the Indian having said anything. An Indian is under strong cultural pressure to say something positive in order to strengthen relationships. Not replying is a courageous step which the Indian thinks will help the Westerners to preserve face. The intercultural problem is that for Westerners negative feedback implies saying something and they do not consider the absence of feedback as negative feedback. For them, no-response is an omission or negligence and they feel the urge to follow-up, which in turn will put the Indian under an even bigger cultural pressure to avoid explicit negative feedback.
- Trying not to answer. By repeating parts of the question, Indians try to defer their reply and deflect from the question. Sample phrases used are: 'Last week?', 'Really? Did you send a suggestion?', 'When exactly did you send it?'. To the Westerner, it sounds like the Indian is in a different world and cannot relate to the topic under discussion.
- Conspicuous pauses. Westerners need messages in the form of words. But sometimes an Indian says nothing or tries to start a new discussion thread; this can mean another attempt to convey an uncomfortable feeling about a proposition by allowing the contact person to save face.
- Suggesting alternatives. When Indians do not provide feedback but suggest an alternative, the real message is that the first idea is not worthy of discussion.
- Expressing some doubt. Asking if something should be tried is as good as saying that the idea will not work. However, it allows the contact partner to save face by taking back their own idea and suggesting not to go ahead.
- Praising the part and dismissing the whole. Praising only a part of the idea allows the Indian to say something positive and at the same time to implicitly suggest dismissing the whole thing. Phrases to look out for are: 'We liked the one part where you mentioned ...' and 'Your slides really look fantastic...'.

At the end of such conversations both parties think that they move forward on parallel tracks. The Westerners believe that the proposal is going to work since nothing negative has been said about it. But Indians assume that they have made it point clear that it will not be feasible and that the Westerners want them to experiment and try it nevertheless. In essence, they are not on parallel tracks but on a collision course.

On the other hand, if an Indian perceives to be in a higher hierarchical position, negative feedback can be very direct and almost rude – regardless if it is aimed at a foreigner or at a colleague in India (see Figure 6-7).

---

[298] Cf. [Storti 2007, p. 55-58]

From:	Amish Satalkar
To:	Claudio Brendani

Claudio,

Once more we are moving in the incorrect way. We cannot work in this manner; if you have a problem talking to Jay G, please let me know.

I do not care about your meeting minutes. We have a different situation now; we need one month to prepare. So please make up your mind and decide fast.

Best Regards,
Amish

From:	Puneet Raja
To:	Sharad SV

Sharad,

I have seen the customer feedback received for your project. This is very bad and far below average.

I expect much more from my project managers and I definitely also expect the same quality of delivery from you.

Regards,
Arvin

Figure 6-7. Uncouth top-down email communication[299]

Giving Negative Feedback to India

When Indians use the above-mentioned techniques for giving negative feedback, they come across as clear and direct to other Indians. However, Westerners perceive them as very indirect. The definition of directness and indirectness becomes relative and driven by culture.

Vice-versa, Western-style indirectness comes across in India as direct; and a direct email from a Westerner is perceived as blunt and insulting. This part of the conversation continuum feels very uncomfortable to Indians.

It is extremely difficult for a Westerner to adapt to the Indian way of giving feedback, but some communication can be worded differently and embedded into an overall appreciation of the cooperation. Another option is to coach Indians on how direct feedback is to be read.

EXAMPLE: Sven Rosenthal is an account manager with an outsourcing company and has just sold an application maintenance project to a European client. The 2nd level support team in India is made up of 15 consultants, headed by Anish Oberoi and growing further. After definition of support processes and initial knowledge transfer, the India team cannot keep up to the response times as agreed with the customer in the SLA. Sven is very worried as his next promotion is linked to the success of this project. Sven feels that the root cause for the problem is in the relative inexperience of the team in India. He sends an email to his team in India clearly expressing his dissatisfaction, putting the blame on the inexperience of the consultants, and requesting a telephone conference (see Figure 6-8-a).

ANALYSIS: This email is harsh by Western standards and very hurtful by Indian norms. The email goes to the entire team and most consultants will feel highly de-motivated as they had put in overtime in the setup phase and believe they are working to the best of their capabilities. Of course, nobody likes to be referred to as a 'green bean'. Anish has lost face with respect to his team members and he is has to tackle a motivational problem in the team.

---

[299] Adapted from original communication received by the author; names changed.

(a)

From:	Sven Rosenthal
To:	Anish Oberoi
CC:	[project-team]

Dear all,

The current 2nd level response times do not evoke standing ovations on my side. This was expected as you have staffed too many green beans without enough experience on this stream.

Please set up a telephone conference for Thursday. We will continue this on a weekly basis until we have reached a satisfying level of quality and response time. I will not accept any more consultants with relevant experience of less than 2 years.

Best Regards,
Sven

(b)

From:	Sven Rosenthal
To:	Anish Oberoi

Dear Anish,

Thank you for setting up the support processes in your team. They look good to me; we have also received first good feedback from our customers.

But did you notice that the response times have recently dropped beyond agreed levels? ☹ I am wondering about the reason and what to do about it? Any idea?

I am back in office tomorrow morning and will call you then – that's 11:30 a.m. in India. Let's try to identify a solution...

Warm Regards & Hello to the team,
Sven

Figure 6-8. Turning harsh feedback into an India-compatible form[300]

SOLUTION: Sven's email could have been written in a more friendly way. The example in Figure 6-8-b sets the stage by thanking Anish for his efforts in setting up the support processes. The negative message is encapsulated into a question and uses a smiley as a softener. Sven also asks Anish for his opinion about the underlying reason and what could possibly be done. Then he tells him that he will call him the next day and refers to the India time zone which is a nice gesture and shows a certain level of interest in the other culture. Sven also refrains from copying anyone else on the email allowing the situation to be handled between the two of them.

6.6   Contracts and Agreements

Contracts not only summarize decisions but they also serve as a basis for litigation in courts.[301] However, in India there are different levels of contracts and agreements. A proper contract needs to be printed on a watermarked stamp paper and signed by both the involved parties as well as a notary. Lawyers help in drafting contracts; and sometimes companies pay them to build ambiguity into contracts so that litigation can be opened more easily.

Contracts not printed on stamp paper are only considered as a memorandum of understanding – and this understanding can change later depending on how things develop. India is a relationship oriented society and a contract is taken as a starting point for a business relationship.

A verbal commitment does not carry much weight in India and can only be considered a non-obligatory declaration of intent; it should always be re-confirmed at least via email.

When drafting a contract, make sure that it is detailed enough and that there is not too much room for interpretation. Special terms, service levels, and key performance

---

[300] (a) is compiled from original communication received by the author; names changed.

[301] See chapters 2.3 and 4.5.5 for the state of the Indian judicial system.

indicators (KPIs) should be well-defined and detailed. In case service levels are not met, corrective action and reimbursement should be clearly agreed upfront.

6.7   Handling Administration

India is probably the most bureaucratic country in the world. People are fond of asking for information, multiple copies of documents, filling forms, filing, and collecting information.

In an interview, Delhi's chief minister Sheila Dikshit gave an example concerning exporting. "There were 17 different forms that had to be filled out to export something. So we had a talk with the relevant authorities and said, 'Please, let's reduce this.' Other countries have 2 or 3 forms, and it's done with. So they set up this committee, and when they came back with a solution, instead of 17 forms, 25 forms had to be filled out. So you see it's the mind-set ...'"[302]

In the IT industry, there are many opportunities for introducing forms. Take some examples: when you are requesting a hotel and taxi transfer from the guest relationship department, in return to your email request, you will receive a detailed excel sheet asking for the purpose of your visit. The same if you are trying to reserve a conference room; you can be certain that your request has to be approved by at least one manager. Forms are not only used for collecting information, full processes are built around forms, they are forwarded within the organization and signatures are collected before the concerned person can actually swing into action. Needless to say that all this takes time, and it is virtually impossible to book a conference room or a taxi transfer one day in advance.

What is the best recipe to react to this kind of bureaucracy? What is the foreigner supposed to do? Frankly speaking: surrender and comply with the processes, you stand no chance to change anything at all. If you complain that you have already provided all required information in your first email, your request will simply not be dealt with. It is best to have an assistant in India who will carefully fit in such kind of information into the required forms.

If you are setting up a team in India, it is best to be proactive and design some selected forms yourself. Propose them to the India team and thus you stand a chance of reducing the number of forms and simplifying processes. However, if your Indian IT partner has stringent quality processes and a quality management system, the processes and forms will all be prescribed and their use subjected to internal and external audit. Again, you stand no chance and you need to comply to get anything done.

6.8   Business and Social Etiquette

Business and social etiquette is different in India from the Western world, and not understanding these little subtleties can lead to confusion, embarrassment, and misunderstandings. However, such faux passes seldom undermine personal or

---

[302] [Sankhe 2007, p. 49]

professional relationships and both parties either ignore them or laugh them away, but generally tend to forgive quickly.

While knowing and respecting the dos and don'ts is not a substitute for understanding the values that drive Indian behavior, it can make it easier for the Westerner to navigate in the Indian culture. Figure 6-9 summarizes the most important aspects.

Topic	Etiquette in India
Addressing your counterpart	In India one tends to use the first name with colleagues on peer level, last names are used with superiors. In the IT industry this is changing and usually everybody is on a first-name basis. In South India, people tend to have only one name, sometimes prefixed by one letter, e.g. S Venkataramaiah. A complicated last name like Venkataramaiah would then get abbreviated to Venkat, Venkata, or Ramaiah and be used as a first name. Superiors are sometimes addressed as Sir or Madam and this is even seen in the IT industry today. But never call your driver or the waiter in a restaurant 'Sir'; instead you can call him 'boss', which is a colloquial form of addressing people at a lower level in society whose name one does not know. Titles (e.g. a Ph.D.) and academic credentials are rarely used in conversation or in business correspondence.
Affection	Men and women avoid physical contact in public places; kissing, hugging, and holding hands are inappropriate. But men may walk hand in hand and this does not have a sexual overtone.
Dress code	A suit and tie is always a safe option for men, but not required in India; dark trousers and a light colored formal long-arm shirt are normally sufficient. Shorts are frowned upon even outside offices. Women should cover their shoulders and knees; a dress, long trousers, or a long skirt will do the job.
Eating	Before and after food Indians wash their hands; restaurants provide a separate wash-basin outside the restroom area. Many Indians are vegetarians, beef is not eaten by Hindus, and Muslims avoid pork. Traditionally, Indians eat with their fingers, though in up-market restaurants the Western style of eating with cutlery is predominant. Indian bread (naan, roti, chapati etc.) is not eaten with fork and knife but with the fingers. The left hand is considered as unclean and left underneath the table or in front of the plate; it will never touch your food or your mouth, instead it can be used to pass dishes. Never touch common plates or utensils with your right hand – there may be saliva on it which is considered unhygienic.
Gifts	If invited to an Indian home, a box of chocolates or Indian sweets is an appropriate gift. Never take alcohol to an Indian home unless you know that the host is open to a drink at home. Gifts are usually not opened in the presence of the presenter.
Greetings	The traditional greeting in India is the namaste gesture in which the palms are joined together at chest levels and a slight nod is offered. Today, this is

Topic	Etiquette in India
	only offered at the reception of five-star hotels but hardly seen in the IT industry. Instead, a long and soft handshake is very common with men. Indian women are to be greeted with a slight nod unless the woman offers her hand for a short handshake (see chapter 7.3).
Personal life	Personal questions about being married or about having children can be asked.
Please and thanks	Indians do not have the habit of saying 'please' and 'thanks' for small things; it is assumed that small favors are simply done without acknowledging them. Example: 'Salt!' instead of 'Would you pass me the salt, please?' does not sound rude at all. Also, one would not acknowledge the passing of salt on the table with a 'thank you' – from an Indian point of view this sounds not only exaggerated but also ridiculous and slightly insulting (Who are you that you have to thank me for such a small favor? Didn't you think I would do this for you?)
Shoes	Shoes are never worn inside a temple and usually taken off before entering a home. If one sees the host walking around in his home barefoot, it is a sign of good behavior to take off the shoes even if one is encouraged to leave them on.
Tipping	Some restaurants levy a service charge clearly marked on the bill; and then a separate tip is voluntary and not required. Do not exaggerate on tips, 5% of the bill value should be the upper limit. 10 INR is a good-enough amount for a luggage boy in the hotel, and 50-100 INR an adequate tip for the driver for an entire day. Please do not spoil expectations!

Figure 6-9. Dos and don'ts in India

7 Conducting Offshore Projects

The organizational structure of an IT project involving offshore capacities is different compared to a traditional one-location project. Failure to address these differences can lead to misunderstandings on process or functional requirements, friction between the onsite and offshore team, and finally budget overruns.

7.1 Managing from a Distance

Intercultural issues are intensified through the lack of direct physical interaction as most communications happens on a pure remote and virtual level. Indians and Westerners who remotely work for project teams in different cultures but physically remain in their home cultures are referred to as *virtual delegates*.[303] There is a cultural separation of private and business life, and a geographical division between the physical and virtual working environment.

Thus information exchange will predominantly happen via electronic media, which has its limits in transporting rich social, emotional, and non-verbal information. High-context cultures like India rely on one's ability to read non-verbal cues, which are mostly missing in electronic media. Hence, emails from India are often enriched through smileys or dots (☺, ☹, …).[304]

Because of the physical distance between virtual delegates and the rest of the project team, they only have a very limited possibility to build up a personal relationship and develop trust. It is impossible to sort out different opinions by having a chat over a cup of coffee.

The Indian project teams cannot experience the social presence of the Western project managers (or vice versa in some cases). The managers do not have the possibility to establish their leadership, remind employees of their presence, and control them; they can only establish presence through telephone and electronic media communication.

There are three options for overcoming the lack of controllability:

- The quantity and quality of work can be directly tracked through a performance monitoring framework, i.e. performance indicators like lines of codes, defects found per 1000 lines of code, requests solved, and working hours are monitored and analyzed. However, an overdose of this kind of performance tracking can negatively affect employee satisfaction and in turn lead to high attrition rates in India.
- Targets can be agreed with the employee (management by objectives), employees are completely free in scheduling their work, and their performance is only measured in relation to the extent to which these targets have been met. Given the typical hierarchical organizational structure of the IT & BPO

---

[303] The term virtual delegation is coined by [Holtbrügge/Schillo 2008, p. 121], who also provide an in-depth analysis of remote managing teams in India.

[304] See chapter 6.5 for email communication from and to India.

industry in India and the relative young age of employees, it is doubtful that this model will work in an India intercultural context.

• Western project managers can have a direct counterpart in India with whom they are directly interacting. This can be either an expatriate from their own culture (see chapter 8.2) or a mature Indian project manager, who will in turn interact with the Indian team and be respected by them as a direct superior.

Intercultural training plays an important role in the preparation of Western virtual delegates for their tasks ahead in cooperation with an Indian project team. Their training needs are different from expatriate assignees in that they mostly lack personal experience with India and exposure to face-2-face communication with Indians. Because of their "… spatial separation of private and business life, there is no need to adjust to the living conditions in [India], [but] only to the specific work context. For example, virtual delegates do not have to learn how to eat rice with their hands, to greet people, or to dress appropriately. In contrast to traditional expatriates, virtual assignees in India will not experience hot summers, power cuts, or crowded buses. As a consequence, work-related content is more important than content related to the private realm."[305] Therefore training should concentrate on a distributed delivery framework, on supportive project management tools, and communication skills.

7.2   Setting up Offshore Projects

The main stakeholders within an offshore project are:[306]

• Project owner represented by the steering committee. Finances the project, defines its overall scope, and takes key decisions during project execution.
• Client. The team at the project owner's company that is appointed to work alongside the service provider.
• Front-office (FO). Part of the project team closest to the client; it acts as a bridge between the client and the back-office. The client and the FO together form the onsite team.
• Back-office (BO). The remote location, e.g. India, where the major part of the development or maintenance work takes place.

Figure 7-1 shows a typical organization for offshore IT development projects and BPO offshoring endeavors.

Representatives from the BO should be included in the project setup as early as the estimation phase to leverage past project experiences (industrialization of software development), generate a commitment from the BO towards effort estimations, and speed up the knowledge transfer to the BO.

---

[305] [Holtbrügge/Schillo 2008, p. 139]
[306] Based on [Samuelsen 2008, p. 145-146] and extended.

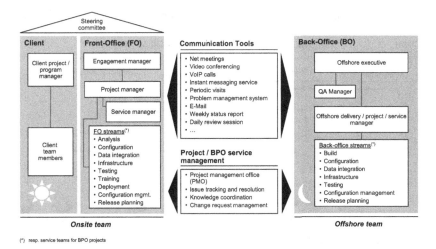

Figure 7-1. Organizational structure for offshore projects[307]

These guidelines also hold true for smaller engagements. While project managers of large offshore projects usually devote some time to drawing up an organizational and communication structure, for smaller engagements this is sometimes neglected. As the following example shows, not considering the requirements of the Indian work culture can lead to devastating effects.

EXAMPLE:[308] A manufacturing company of the German Mittelstand (small and medium sized enterprises, SME) currently runs its ABAP programming unit with six freelancers who interact directly with the business representatives at onsite. It plans to offshore this programming unit in order to realize substantial cost savings. In negotiations with the IT service provider, it insists on an offshore staff augmentation model, i.e. the earlier freelancers are replaced one by one with offshore colleagues and managed by one German FO project manager, who reports to both the client's business unit manager and to a delivery manager in his own organization (Figure 7-2-A). All offshore developers in India were treated as team members and managed directly by the German FO project manager; the staffing originally followed the company's pyramid, i.e. the onsite coordinator was a senior consultant, then there were two associate consultants, two consultants, and one rather junior manager on the team in India. This approach closely resembles the earlier operating model with the freelancers and required hardly any change in the eyes of the manufacturing company. However, within the first three months of operation, the following issues popped up in India: (1) There were quality complaints about all four (associate) consultants in India; in the eyes of the German FO project manager and the client their experience was not comparable to the earlier freelancers. Only the senior consultant's and the manager's technical skills were deemed acceptable. As a result and in order to pacify the client, one by one, all four (associate) consultants had to be replaced with senior consultants. This immediately affected the profitability of the project for the IT service provider, as the higher

---

[307] Adapted from [Acharya et al. 2008, p. 267; Hendel 2008a, p. 72; Samuelsen 2008, p. 146]

[308] This example may sound too simplistic to the reader. However, the tide of events in this project (and similiar incidents in other projects as well) were directly witnessed by the author during his tenure in India.

A) Original project structure as requested by client

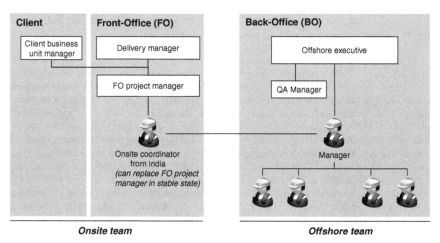

B) Optimized project structure

Figure 7-2. Organizational structures for offshoring a programming unit

cost rates of the senior consultants were not factored into the project calculation. At least, the quality issue was resolved for the moment. (2) While the manager received excellent feedback on his technical skills from the FO and the client, he was still unhappy and had to be forced to stay on this assignment. He did not feel like dirtying his hands with development work; at his level he felt that he should be overseeing the work of others. He was frustrated because he did not have direct control over his subordinates; in fact, he did not really know what they were working on as they were directly managed by the FO project manager. He also got into trouble with the quality assurance (QA) department of his Indian organization because he was unable to provide any defect resolution metrics. (3) Four weeks later an internal issue in India popped up, this time without the client noticing any of the friction at first. All newly on-boarded senior consultants felt de-motivated and requested a project change. What had happened? Given the new skewed hierarchy pyramid, the senior consultants could clearly see that there was no way of getting a promotion while working on this project. According to the Indian career model and in order to move up to the manager level, they were supposed to slowly take up team leadership or at least supervise two or three (associate) consultants on the project. Despite their good technical skills, their performance also continuously dropped because of a lack of motivation. (4) The only one rather happy about his project assignment was the onsite coordinator from India. He did not really take over the responsibility of an onsite coordinator, but he was able to learn about the business processes, gathered experience working abroad, attended German languages classes, and made extra money through his daily allowances which he could send back home to pay back the loan for his newly bought apartment in Bangalore. Finally, the manufacturing company was frustrated with the offshore approach and vouched to go back to their earlier freelancer model despite much higher costs. All the friction would not have been necessary if only the IT service provider would have managed to convince the client to set-up an India-compatible organizational structure for the project. Figure 7-2-B shows a small but important change to the organizational structure: the India offshore team is no longer managed by the FO directly, but all communication, work planning, and quality control of deliverables goes through the manager in India. He communicates on a daily basis with the onsite coordinator, who is his right hand at the client site. After the initial setup phase, even the FO project manager can slowly move out of the project and the onsite coordinator from India can permanently take up his role making the engagement even more cost-effective. This organizational model caters to the following needs of Indian software engineers: (1) The manager has a clearly visible role within the Indian organization; he wheels and deals between the deliverables of his team members and he gets involved into coding only when his team members are struggling. He collects metrics on defects and is thereby compliant with the quality management system of his company. (2) The team members (associate consultants and consultants) are supervised in their deliverables, they sense a new security, and are pushed to good and more work by the manager. They also see a career prospective within the project environment – the best one of them will eventually replace the manager when he moves on to a bigger project, or will become sub-project leader when the engagement with the manufacturing company expands, or will get the chance for a lucrative medium-term onsite assignment when the onsite coordinator returns to India.

7.3 Selecting the Team

Recruitment, selection, and integration are important aspects of assembling a team. While the actual recruitment is usually the job and responsibility of the Indian IT service provider (see chapter 5.1), the Western prime contractor can still influence the composition of the team. The biggest mistake is then to apply the same principles as back home.

Selecting the Project Leader

First, the rule of seniority has to be adhered to. While in the Western world, technical competency or availability is the main selection criteria for the project leader, in India, seniority is much more important than capability and competency. In the end, the project leader needs to be accepted by the team and in India the main criteria is seniority (see chapters 3.2 and 5.2).

Second, the job description of an Indian project manager will also differ from the Western counterpart. A Western manager will still 'get his hands dirty' and look into program code, functional specifications, and so on; Indian managers, however, expect to focus on coordination only. They are managers and not directly involved in delivery. This is an outcome of the strong hierarchy in Indian companies, where delegation is the norm. Promoting someone to a managerial position hence also implies losing a good and trusted expert.

Third, the network and social acceptability of the manager should be considered. A good manager has the ability to move something and in India this relies on individual networks and connections – within the company and outside.

Selecting Team Members

Selecting the team does not stop at the manager level. When looking for team members, it is important to prepare exact task descriptions.[309] Indians want to know exactly what their contribution to the project will be and how this adds value to their own curriculum vitae. For projects of longer duration, and in order to keep employees motivated, a job rotation and career progression path within the project should be planned and communicated to the prospective team members.

Western project leaders have a tendency to look for skilled experts for every project position. In the eyes of an Indian, such a staffing model is not very motivating as it (1) provides limited challenges for the individual, (2) no possibilities to enhance knowledge, (3) no opportunities to train task oversight or management skills, and (4) consequently limits the prospects of promotion.

Instead, the company's pyramid of hierarchy has to be mapped onto the open positions in the project in order to create the right mixture of junior, experienced, and senior colleagues in the project. Then Indian employees can have their eyes firmly fixed on their ultimate goal of career progression and feel an incentive to work hard.

When selecting Indian IT consultants for open job positions in the project, one should look at the following criteria:

- Education. Most Indian IT developers today no longer have graduated from premier colleges and universities in the country, but they are recruited from second and third level institutions outside the big cities. For project positions requiring business analysis or writing functional specifications, candidates with additional degrees should be preferred; this could be an MBA degree from a non-premier local institution.
- Relevant work experience and subject matter expertise. When reading an Indian CV, Westerners need to be extremely careful. Generally, everything is a little exaggerated: the number of years of experience is rounded up, the stated responsibility level is more than the consultant actually had on the project, and an expert-skill on a certain competency might only mean that the consultant has

---

[309] Cf. [Bracken/Carlucci 2008, p. 256]

come across this topic while reading a blueprint document. Therefore, rigorous technical job interviews are necessary before putting anyone onto a project.

- Previous work periods abroad. Extended work periods abroad or even having worked in multi-national environments offshore will almost certainly reduce intercultural communication issues during the project.
- Software certifications. People who are certified business analysts or developers in a certain software package have demonstrated a good deal of initiative in the past; mostly the certification courses and exams are paid for by the company, but the candidates have shown initiative to ask for enrollment and the preparation for it has mostly happened outside normal office hours.
- Level of comfort between manager and subordinate. More than any technical expertise, the manager and the subordinate have to be comfortable working together. Managers have to be able to fully and personally rely on their team; there needs to be a good level of interpersonal trust in order to make the project successful (see chapters 1.2.2 and 5.3).
- English. A good command of English is important but one should not be too swayed by this consideration. It may not be as critical to the role as technical and managerial skills, especially for individuals who are not directly dealing with customers.[310] Whether the English is thickly accented is not so important for most positions in the project and it is very easy to forget this when interviewing Indian colleagues.

An intercultural communication training with a focus on the target culture can work wonders for integrating and motivating the newly assembled team and minimizing friction in the communication process (see chapter 1.6). Further technical and soft-skill trainings have to be identified based on the needs of the project and the proficiency of the team (see chapter 5.1.2).

7.4   Monitoring Progress

Effective distributed work requires stringent project controls. An effective monitoring of offshore work progress in India consists of two factors:

- Project controlling through key performance indicators
- Powerful questions to discover the root causes of deviations

Project Controlling Through Key Performance Indicators

Discipline in project management is key in distributed delivery projects. This especially holds true for the front-office which is the business architect, technical engineer, facilitator, and controller of the overall project budget.

Work progress must be made quantifiable by calculating changes in key performance indicators (KPIs) on a regular basis. Figure 7-3 illustrates a week-by-week

---

[310] Cf. [Bloch/Whiteley 2008, p. 90]

reporting of the status of development objects in a project during the realization phase. Each bar shows the number of development objects with a certain status. With this tool, project management is able to check the overall status of the project, ensure that the work progress is sufficient to meet a deadline, identify responsibilities for bottlenecks, and control the scope of the project. However, this graph does not show how many development objects have changed their status during the last weeks, average throughput times, overruns by individual development objects, number of iterations between development and testing, number of change requests, and number of defects per development object.[311] These KPIs need to be controlled through additional reports and drill-downs.

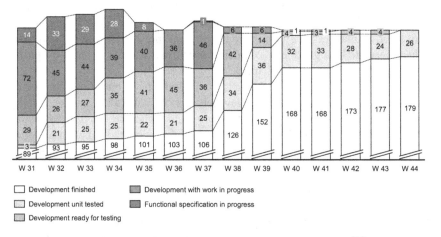

Figure 7-3. KPI-driven development report (example)[312]

Stringent reporting provides the Western project manager with a status overview similar to a health-check up; only symptoms are shown but the root causes of deviations need to be found through personal interaction.

Powerful Questions to Discover the Root Causes of Deviations

Investigating root causes for abnormalities in KPI reports is difficult in an Indian intercultural context. This is a situation requiring great care, as it is loaded with implications for maintaining face (see chapter 6.5.4). Nevertheless, Western project managers need to find a way to drill down to the root causes of an abnormality and get the information from their Indian offshore counterparts.

First, the alignment of the project's KPIs from a Western with the Indian perspective has to be looked at. It may well be that the Indian project managers do not see their needs reflected in the KPIs. Try asking a question like: 'How do you

---

[311] Cf. [Thun 2008c, p. 92-93]
[312] Adapted from [Hendel 2008b, p. 237; Thun 2008c, p. 93]

measure your success', i.e. basically asking for a redefinition of the KPIs from an Indian perspective and then comparing the answer with the project's KPIs.

Powerful positive questions about the project can play the trick for the Westerner to get an honest overview of the project's health:

- 'What has been delivered successfully? What achievements have been made?'
- 'What have your priorities been during the last reporting cycle?'

These questions can be followed up by future-oriented inquiries that in fact try to analyze the past:

- 'How can we achieve a better defect rate? What needs to be done in your opinion?'
- 'How does your new approach affect the number of development objects delivered?'
- 'How can the front-office support you better?'
- 'What are your priorities for the next reporting cycle?'

Such questions generally work well in an Indian intercultural context as they prevent a loss of face and stimulate a critical thinking.

7.5   Transition from IT Development to Maintenance

The transition from the development to the maintenance phase in IT projects can be critical in terms of employee motivation and retention. Typically in India, maintenance projects are less attractive to good employees than development projects. Salaries for employees on maintenance projects tend to be lower. Some IT companies in India even have separate units for development and maintenance work. This is not necessarily because the work on maintenance projects is in reality always less challenging, but there is a pre-conception about it in the Indian IT industry.

Employees fear to 'get stuck' in maintenance work and lose out on their career development. Hence, there is a reluctance of employees to stay with the project after the development phase is over.

This fact has to be built into the project design. For instance, it is a good idea to phase in employees from the maintenance business unit early in the project in order to enable a smooth hand-over.

8 Use of Expatriates

An expatriate is a person temporarily or permanently residing in a country and culture other than that of the person's upbringing or legal residence. The word comes from the Latin ex (out of) and patria (country, fatherland). It is sometimes shortened to expat. The term is mostly used in the context of Westerners living in non-Western countries, although it may also reasonably refer to a non-Westerner residing in a Western country. The key determinants for naming someone an expatriate should be cultural and socioeconomic coupled with causation.

The number of expatriates working in India has swelled to some 40,000 thanks to India's booming economy.[313] That is only a fraction of the number of expatriates in China, Hong Kong, and Singapore, but India is experiencing the fastest growth.[314] On the other side, there are more than 20 million people of Indian origin worldwide living and working outside India. They tend to cluster in the English speaking countries, i.e. USA, UK, and Australia.[315]

This chapter describes how Western companies can successfully tap into this resource pool with their specific skills to bridge intercultural gaps.

8.1 Expatriate Requirements

Expatriates are experienced in dealing with other cultures, have a command of the language, and are competent partners for the business and technological aspects of a project. This 'multicultural fluency' cannot be acquired through seminars or brief project assignments abroad. Companies should hence consider several criteria in selecting expatriates:[316]

- To what degree have candidates acquired cultural sensitivity and adaptability through their stays abroad?
- Are they fluent in the host language? A European expatriate in India should at least have a business proficiency in English. In turn, an Indian expatriate in France or Germany should, in addition to English, also have at least a basic command of French or German.
- Is the candidate able to work independently and without close contact to superiors and colleagues?
- Does the candidate understand the corporate culture?
- Is the candidate willing to travel and move home? How does the candidate's family view the foreign assignment?

These questions can be grouped into affective, cognitive, and behavioral factors (see Figure 8-1).

---

[313] Cf. [Singh 2008]; note that [Lifs 2008] estimates the number of expatriates in India at 30,000.
[314] Cf. [Lifs 2008]
[315] Cf. [Bittinger/Iyengar 2003]
[316] Cf. [Bittinger 2003, p. 3-4]

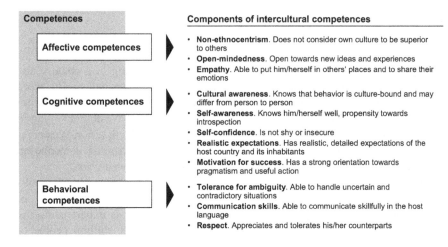

Figure 8-1. Intercultural competences of expatriates[317]

8.2   Western Expatriates in India

8.2.1   Costs of Expatriate Assignments

Using Western expatriates is a costly affair for the dispatching company. A European employee working in India costs three to four times more than at home. After the one-time relocation costs, the following components are usually added to the payslip of an expatriate:

- Hardship allowance is supposed to compensate for social and economic hardships faced by expatriates, e.g. health, safety, threat of violent crime, climate, environment, education, culture, infrastructure, and corruption. According to the Economist Intelligence Unit (EIU), the business information arm of the Economist group, Mumbai is the seventh and Delhi the tenth worst city on earth to live in. Both cities fall under the bandwidth of 'extreme hardship' and a 20% additional salary allowance is recommended as compensation.[318]
- The provision of car and driver is necessary in Indian cities due to an almost complete absence of signage and basic road rules, making it virtually impossible for most foreigners to find their way around.
- Housing costs or cost-of-living allowance is to cover expenses for housing at a standard close to Western levels. Such houses are still very scarce and in a very high demand by the expatriate population and Indians returning from long-term foreign assignments. This creates an artificial niche market in which the rates have gone up beyond control. But even if these houses look gorgeous from the

---

[317] Cf. [Gelbrich 2004, p. 263, 266]
[318] Cf. [Balaram 2002]

outside, there is still a lack of attention to detail in the bathrooms, the kitchen, or the electrical wiring.

- Home leave once a year is granted for the expatriate family to stay in touch with their friends and colleagues back home.
- As living in Indian cities falls under the category of 'extreme hardship', some companies[319] provide generous recreational trips to holiday destinations world-wide.
- Tuition for the education of children to receive a Western style schooling or for a boarding school back home.
- Tax reimbursement payments for any additional taxes payable by the assignee as a result of living abroad.

8.2.2 Expatriate Lifestyle in India

Many expatriates live in segregated compounds rather than integrate with the local population. As a result, a lively community of newsgroups and blogs on the Internet has evolved that links them. There are also social groups run by expatriates to help newcomers adjust and socialize. The idea is to get to know the country better and, in the process, network and thereby create a community of professionals. Examples

Prejudices about expatriates	Putting the myths into perspective
Everything is so cheap in India – you must be saving a lot of money!	Simple merchandise and Indian food is really cheap. However, Western food (olives, parmesan cheese, bacon, etc.) as well as electronic items (TVs, computer, etc.) cost a lot more. Imported products are subject to very high import taxes.
You are living in luxury – just look at the swimming pool and tennis court in your complex!	Going for an evening walk in the neighborhood or a cycling tour over the weekend is not only impossible in India but potentially dangerous. The club house with swimming pool and fitness studio helps to compensate.
Anything you have to do yourself at all? – One maid, a cook, and a driver for one household!	A house in India requires much more cleaning than in the Western world; there is a lot of dust in the air and windows cannot be closed properly. On top of this, India is a multi-layer society with household personnel easily available at inexpensive rates. Many well-earning Indians detest manual and dirty work and prefer to 'get it done'.
You have no direct boss at work? – Great, you can leave office early.	Due to time-differences with the West, most telephone conferences happen late at night in India; private life is pretty much scattered.

Figure 8-2. Putting perceptions about expatriate lifestyle into perspective

---

[319] According to a study by ORC recreational leave is provided by less than 50% of companies, cf. [ORC 2006, p. 4]

are The Bangalore Expat Club (BEC) and the Overseas Women's Club (OWC). While OWC works on social causes and frequently ties up with non-government organizations (NGOs), the BEC focuses on socializing.

The perceived expatriate lifestyle sometimes irritates colleagues at home as well as Indian colleagues who are on local salaries and do not receive these benefits. Figure 8-2 puts these perceptions and prejudices into perspective.

8.2.3   Returning to the Home Country

There are many cases where returning expatriates from India are offered a severance package and asked to leave 'voluntarily'. No doubt these are sad cases of international HR management, but why do they occur so frequently?

When returning to their home country after a long-term assignment abroad, the former expatriates are sometimes viewed by their fellow citizens as foreigners. A nickname in the UK for a former expatriate is the 'when Is' and 'when wes' as they are accused of starting every social conversation by saying 'when I was in India'. Particularly the children face problems back at home; their accent with a lot of foreign influence may sound strange to their classmates. These children often hold multiple passports and speak several different languages fluently; they have a hard timing defining what home is, and are therefore considered as Third Culture Kids (TCKs) .

Returning expatriates are also foreigners in their own companies; after two or five years abroad, the company may have experienced significant changes, such as changes in personnel, politics, policies, and projects that may lead to discrepancies between expectations and actual return experiences. Also, they would have held fairly responsible positions abroad and the parent company has difficulties to match this level of responsibility back home. With increasing time abroad, a greater loss of personal contacts and background information facilitating the re-entry is expected.

Even when a re-entry into the organizational unit back home is guaranteed, the right position for the returnee may not always be available at the end of the India assignment. However, if the assignee cannot be provided with a meaningful position within a short time frame after repatriation, chances of attrition are very high.

8.2.4   Failure Rate of Expatriate Assignments

In addition to the high costs of expatriate assignments, the success rate is rather disappointing. Failed India assignments may cause damage to the company's reputation and result in lost business opportunities.

Soft and often underestimated risk factors are the underlying reason for failure. Inadequate cultural skills and insufficient recognition by the foreign company often cause stress and burden the partnership with the Indian offshoring partner.

Around 15% of expatriates are in top-leadership positions in India;[320] they are messiahs of innovation in global workplaces. However, not everybody welcomes expatriates, and some Indians consider them as a threat to their own career opportunities: "… the superior competencies of a rapidly multiplying expat workforce in the Indian corporate sector are posing a disturbing challenge to desi [Indian] talent, especially in key leadership roles".[321] Some argue that this reflects a poor understanding of the Indian market and talent pool.

Any company placing Westerners in India has to take pre-emptive measures to reduce the likelihood of failure, including a stringent expatriate strategy.

8.2.5 Expatriate Strategy for Westerners

There are three principal objectives of sending expatriates to India:

- To generate knowledge for the India organization by transferring expertise from headquarters to the subsidiary, as well as learning from the subsidiary.
- To develop global leaders. In order for an executive to develop a global perspective on business, it is an imperative to have spent a few years abroad.
- To fill a burning business need.

There is no universally applicable expatriate strategy, as the individual companies and India projects differ significantly. Nonetheless, there are some general practices that facilitate successful expatriate assignments:

- Although immediate needs cannot be ignored, expatriate management is more effective when viewed with an eye on the long-term, i.e. on knowledge creation and global leadership development.[322] Indian employees should feel knowledge enrichment at the workplace through the presence of a foreigner.[323]
- During the assignment, clear frameworks and processes should be developed. The objectives of the assignment need to be clearly defined and aligned with the company and/or project goals.[324] Relationships and the processes of communication between expatriates and other key managers must be absolutely clear and unambiguous.[325]
- People should be carefully selected for expatriate assignments, with their intercultural competencies exceeding their technical skills. However, many companies only raise the question of who wants to go or whose technical profile would fit best. Key elements of 'fitting in' are for example an understanding of local customs, social networks, and integration in the host country.[326] An expatriate who is socially isolated in India would be conceived as displaying Western

---

[320] Cf. [Singh 2008]

[321] [Singh 2008]

[322] Cf. [Black/Gregersen 1999]

[323] Cf. [Vermeer/Neumann 2008, p. 127]

[324] Cf. [Gelbrich 2004, p. 264]

[325] Cf. [Bittinger 2003, p. 1]

[326] Cf. [Knotts 1989, p. 33]

arrogance and enjoy no trust, which means the mission would be a failure right from the start. Those failing to recognize the many social and religious facets of everyday life in India will always remain outsiders.

- Nobody should be persuaded to take up an expatriate assignment – and least persuaded through an attractive financial offer; this is a proven road to dissatisfaction with the host environment and finally a recipe for disaster on the job.
- Establish a network of former, current, and future expatriates that should also include the assignee's dependents. Such a forum can help to discuss and share experiences .
- The repatriation process should be planned well in advance together with the assignee. This can keep the expatriate motivated up to the last day of the assignment and avoid frustration through uncertainty. Further attrition can be avoided through good planning.

Looking at the peculiarities of India, a company can establish some additional measures to make the assignment on the subcontinent successful:

- A thorough health check before the assignment and during the assignment should be conducted. There are different levels of pollution and food poisoning, and hence India is not the country of choice for people with an allergy, asthma, or neurodermatitis.
- Intercultural training should not stop with the assignment to India but be an ongoing coaching process. Professional assistance helps to derive correct judgments of the Indian culture. This training should also include the family. Family visits to the host country should be arranged prior to the start of the assignment to decrease children's reluctance to relocate.
- Men who tend to show a special interest in their female colleagues are not the perfect choice for an expatriate in India. While Western women can mostly handle such colleagues – or even take them to court, an Indian lady will likely be irritated, shocked, or morally offended.
- Employees of Indian origin[327] or Westerners married to an Indian might aggressively push for an India expatriate assignment in their companies. While their cultural pre-exposure can be a real asset, it will not be roses all the way. If employees of Indian origin have lived abroad for too long, they may find it difficult to readjust. India is developing quickly and they may remember a work culture that is no longer there. Finding the right salary for assignees of Indian origin is difficult. An expatriate salary will definitely lead to friction with the Indian colleagues and a local Indian salary will not motivate them to take up the expatriate assignment in the first place. It is hence necessary for the company to establish firm processes and rules for expatriate salaries worldwide. As a golden rule, the home country defines the local payroll. However, for persons of Indian origins there are many factors defining the home country,

---

[327] Employees of Indian origin are either called NRIs (non-resident Indians) if they still have their Indian passport or PIOs (person of Indian origin) if they have taken up a foreign citizenship.

e.g. the country of birth, upbringing, education, and residence over the last 5 or 10 years; country in which individual has invested in real estate and contributed to the pension fund (i.e. proof of retirement planning); country of origin of spouse; country where the commitment for education of children lies.

- The company should not try to save money on expatriates but instead provide sufficient financial benefits[328] and try to enable them to lead a comfortable life abroad. The standard of living in a third-world country is completely different from the homeland and spending a little more towards upmarket housing and relocation support can drastically change the comfort level of the Western employee in India. It is not possible to go for an evening walk in the neighborhood, for a cycling tour over the weekend; hence a house in a gated complex with a community swimming pool and a fitness studio does wonders for the adaptation of the expatriate to the new environment.
- Direct team leadership should be avoided, as it would be difficult for expatriates on their first assignment to India to understand the subtle undercurrents and needs of their Indian team members. Instead, only very few selected India managers should report directly to the expatriates and the people management should be done by these managers. An additional advantage is that the assignees can thus better concentrate on tasks where they can deliver real added value to the Indian enterprise; people management in India can much better be done by Indians.
- India being a hierarchical society, job titles matter a lot. Often there is a proliferation of job titles in the Indian IT industry, i.e. an Indian senior consultant has a completely different skill profile and also years of experience than a Western senior consultant. In order to be heard by the Indian management, the expatriate needs to be at least a Director or Vice President. If an adjustment of the expatriate's corporate title has to be made, this should be done well before they are presented to the Indian subsidiary. On the other hand, if the expatriate is supposed to disseminate technical expertise and have very limited management interaction, the job title will not matter as much.

Different types of assignments serve different purposes catering both to the needs of the company, the expatriates, and their families (see Figure 8-3):

- Long-term. The expatriates move to the host country together with their families. Usual long-term durations are three to five years, which enables expatriates to settle down, concentrate on work without a having to pack suitcases again.
- Short-term. Typical short-term assignment last less than a year and may or may not involve family accompaniment.
- International commuter. The employee takes up a serviced apartment in India and commutes on a frequent basis, while the family remains in the home country.
- Frequent flyer. The employee takes frequent trips to India but does not relocate.

---

[328] Cf. [Vermeer/Neumann 2008, p. 127-128]

These types of assignments are chosen for different reasons. Managerial control is a significant factor for decisions to use long-term and frequent flyer assignments. From a one-year cost perspective, there is usually not much of a difference between these assignment types. The long-term assignment becomes less expensive if there is a requirement for the expatriate to stay in India for more than two years.

Factors for choosing assignment type	Assignment type			
	Long-term	Short-term	Commuter	Frequent flyer
Managerial control	●	○	◑	●
Knowledge transfer	●	●	●	◑
Management development	●	●	○	○
Develop international experience	○	●	◑	◑
Costs	○	○	○	○
Inability to long-term planning, volatility	○	●	◑	●
Family	◑	○	●	◑

Importance of factors
● High
◑ Medium
○ Low

Figure 8-3. Different purposes of expatriate assignments to India

Expatriate involvement is important whenever change is a factor, but it becomes less important in a steady state, i.e. when offshored functions are operating at an acceptable quality and service level. However, in offshore application development the style of communication and interaction is usually more complex and this may call for a more permanent expatriate involvement.[329]

Regarding the number of expatriates involved in a project, there is also no 'right' number. However, usually one or two cross-culturally experienced expatriates are all that is needed to manage communication issues and ensure more effective outcomes.

8.3   Indian Expatriates in the West

Although much ado is created in businesses about sending Westerners on expatriate assignments to India, exchange in the opposite direction is also happening and actually at a much greater rate.

---

[329] Cf. [Bittinger 2003, p. 3]

8.3.1 Onsite Assignments of an Indian

The expatriate assignment of an Indian to the Western world generally receives much less attention with respect to intercultural preparation, assignment benefits, and planning of job responsibilities on re-entry into India. Therefore, they are simply referred to as onsite assignments in this book. Many reasons contribute to this difference.

Onsite assignments for Indians are seldom planned as part of the career progression of an individual, but they almost always follow a business need. Thus, assignments are mostly not long-term and more likely to be in the range of a few weeks to one year. Assignments lasting a few weeks up to three months are mostly about knowledge transfer, understanding business requirements, bug fixing, testing, and software roll-out. Longer assignments are needed for the role of onsite coordinator in large projects; however, these rarely pass the 6 months to 12 months threshold. All other motives for sending Indians abroad are generally considered second to the business need.

Many Indian offshore companies rotate the colleagues working onsite, aiming for Indian staff to gain at least a fundamental affinity to the Western culture, though the structure of onsite teams is thus frequently disrupted.[330] Onsite assignments are hence considered a part of the training process.

This rotation principle is also often used as a means to motivate Indian employees; especially for junior colleagues, international assignments still hold a special attraction. In addition, this approach represents a potential workaround if long-term work permits for Indians are difficult to attain.

Similar to the requirements for Western expatriates, Indian assignees should also have a cultural openness, and it has to be expected that they would culturally adapt to the Western culture – even if this is in stark contrast to their own cultural values.

The last and probably major reason for the foreign assignments of Westerners and Indians being so different is costs. At the end of the day, offshoring is about cost arbitrage, and 'pampering' an Indian IT engineer with assignment benefits would eat heavily into this margin and thus the business case owners do not care a great deal for it. This line of thought is aggravated by the fact that the budget owners and decision makers are mostly Westerners, and some of them (still) have a preconception of a two-class worldwide society in their minds. From a humane point of view, this is really appalling. However, it may be more understandable from a business and cost perspective. One only needs to consider the absolute minimum costs incurred by an onsite assignment to see that the costs to the company are almost as high as for utilizing a Westerner with similar qualifications for the same job. These additional costs are:

- Costs for air ticket, local transportation, and apartment
- Additional insurances, such as health and liability insurance

---

[330] Cf. [Sinha/Terdiman 2002, p. 8]

- Daily allowances for food and to cover the difference in cost of living
- Meeting minimum salary requirements and paying local taxes.

On assignments with duration of more than 4 or 6 months, employees are usually permitted to take their immediate family with them. However, costs for admitting the children to English speaking kindergartens and schools are seldom reimbursed.

8.3.2   Tapping into the NRI Resource Pool

Rather than delegating Indians from India to the Western world, companies can also tap into the pool of more than 20 million people of Indian origin living outside India worldwide. One distinguishes

- PIOs (persons of Indian origin) who were born abroad or have adopted a foreign citizenship but whose parents or grandparents are from India;
- NRIs (non-resident Indians) who still have an Indian passport but live abroad.

They particularly tend to cluster in the English speaking countries and have experiences with the Indian and Western cultures.[331] However, personnel have to be selected carefully. Some Indians have been living abroad long enough to be out of touch with the current business practices in India. This could potentially cause havoc in intercultural teams, as the Indian business culture has developed rapidly in the last 20 years and these employees would be neither recognized by the Indian nor the Western parties. Other Indians have distanced themselves from their original culture and are no longer interested in interacting with Indian colleagues.

8.3.3   Onsite Assignment Strategy for Indians

Again, there is no universally applicable expatriate strategy. Given the business needs and cost constraints discussed above, there is some general advice for how to achieve more successful assignments:

- Although immediate project requirements cannot be ignored, there should be some kind of long-term planning from a human resource perspective. Promising individuals should be tagged for future onsite assignments and tried to be placed proactively by the Indian management.
- Westerners should feel knowledge enrichment in their projects through the presence of an Indian. Sending a greenhorn without deep technical expertise to an onsite assignment will only aggravate misconceptions about working together with offshore developers and their quality. Instead, only the best people should be sent abroad.
- Clear frameworks, processes, and expectation settings should govern the onsite assignment. Especially the communication process is a key factor; the Indian IT engineers need to know whom to contact onsite in case of health problems,

---

[331] Cf. [Bittinger/Iyengar 2003]

job dissatisfaction, and any other personal issues. In other words, the Indian engineers are taken out of their comfort zones and placed in a new and unfamiliar environment. Their Indian superiors are geographically far away, and they require a new onsite hierarchy and people to guide them.

- People should be carefully prepared for onsite assignments. This includes inter-cultural communication training about the target culture and things expected in this culture – both in professional and private life.
- The process of returning should be well planned. This keeps employees happy and motivated up to the last day of their onsite assignment and helps to bring attrition rates down.
- The assignment benefits should be well balanced to cover the additional costs of living, provide some room for travel over the weekend, and have the potential for some savings. Especially the savings part needs to be carefully adjusted for the onsite assignment to be an incentive for the employee but not the only goal in their professional life. In some companies software developers only demand onsite projects because of high daily allowances, which in turn enable them to pay back their housing loans in India faster.
- Last but not least, a thorough health check is required. Going from a warm and tropical climate to the freezing winters of Switzerland requires as much adaptation as traveling from a moderate continental climate to India.

EXAMPLE: An Indian software developer is employed by the Indian subsidiary of an MNC IT Company in Bangalore; he has worked for a few years as a SAP® ABAP developer. Recently he has undergone a four week training program in the area of SAP® BIW. A few weeks after that he is sent on an onsite assignment to Germany where he is asked to do mainly ABAP programming work. He is unhappy about this situation and fears to lose his newly acquired BIW skills. During a lunch break he complains to the customer that he is not motivated and unhappy about the ABAP development job he has to do. Of course the customer is surprised about this rather unprofessional behavior and protests against the Indian developer with the multinational IT company. What went wrong? There was no established communication process or at least the Indian software developer was not aware of it; he should have first gone to his front-office project manager of the MNC IT Company and discussed his concerns with him. He was further unaware about the possible fragile relationship between the customer and the MNC IT Company.

Different types of assignments serve different business purposes.

- Business traveler. Employees take a one-time trip to the onsite project location and typically stay there for two to six weeks in a hotel or serviced apartment; their families remain at home in India. For most countries this can be covered by a business visa and the work content is most likely to be knowledge transfer, training, project set-up, architecture planning, functional design, testing, and roll-out support.
- Work permit. A typical work permit assignment lasts from three months to one year. Employees take up a fully furnished or a serviced apartment and their families are likely to accompany them. On the work front, they will be fully integrated into the onsite project team and most likely work either as a technical experts or onsite coordinators for the offshore team in India.

- Foreign payroll. If the assignment is planned to exceed one year, there is an option to take the Indian employee on the payroll in the host country. This allows for a deeper integration into the Western company and its corporate culture.
- PIO / NRI. This is not quite an onsite assignment as PIOs and NRIs already live and work in the host country; they are connected to India through ancestry and various levels of emotional bonds.

These types of assignments are chosen for different reasons (see Figure 8-4). The extent of project control and knowledge transfer is the most important deciding factor.

Factors for choosing assignment type	Assignment type			
	Business traveler	Work permit	Foreign payroll	PIO / NRI
Project control	◑	●	◑	●
Knowledge transfer (West to India)	●	○	○	◑
Knowledge transfer (India to West)	●	●	○	○
Develop international experience	○	◑	○	○
Costs	◑	◑	○	○
Flexibility	●	◑	○	○

Importance of factors
● High
◑ Medium
○ Low

Figure 8-4. Different purposes of onsite assignments

Regarding the number of Indian onsite assignees involved in a project, there is no 'right' number and a lot depends on the specific project requirements. Compared to Western expatriates in India, there will be more Indians on onsite assignments and tasked with more hands-on project jobs and less managerial oversight activities.

9 Recommendations for Effective Collaboration

Cultural differences and problems are real and have to be addressed to run successful India offshore projects. However, this does not mean that offshore projects will automatically become more successful. Instead, they will only thrive and deliver benefits faster if an adequate basis in form of a government structure has been established.

In a nutshell, Westerners should consider five important adaptations to their own behavior when working with Indians. When reading them, please consider that effectiveness in intercultural collaboration is not about being right or wrong, but about getting a job done effectively, that is with as less friction as possible.

- *Accept differences.* Forget any thoughts of cultural superiority, don't try to impose your thoughts and values on India, and simply 'say yes' to the differences. "To do so, however, we must stop ranking both people and talents and accept the fact that there are many roads to truth and no culture has a corner on the path or is better equipped than others to search for it."[332]
- *Put relationships before tasks.* Try to get to know your Indian counterparts as people, establish a personal relationship, and they will reward you with unprecedented loyalty. At the end, this will get the task done successfully.
- *Be friendly in your communication.* Allow your Indian counterparts to save their face in all your communication, don't be too direct, and find a more friendly way in bringing your message across.
- *Use powerful questions.* Never make Indians believe that they know what it is you want to hear; they will try to please you. Instead, ask openly for their opinion through powerful questions. Don't assume that you have been understood; ask cleverly for reconfirmation.
- *Accept hierarchy.* Don't try to change the organizational structure of the Indian IT and BPO industry, India does not work without its steep hierarchy.

As the world is becoming more and more 'flat', there are great opportunities for exciting and fascinating new work experiences. The ability to work together seamlessly and free of conflict across cultures is going to distinguish people at the workplace; employees caught in their own universe of thoughts and values will be left behind. In the future, colleagues who master the art of intercultural communication are going to be in high demand at a global level. India is a developing economic powerhouse, not only in the IT and BPO sector but also as a customer for the world's consumer goods. Experimenting and learning to collaborate with Indians will pay dividend to individuals and their professional careers alike.

---

[332] [Hall 1976, p. 7]

List of Abbreviations

AD	Anno domino
BC	Before Christ
BEC	Bangalore Expat Club
BJP	Bhartiya Janata Party
BO	Back office
BOSS	Burn-out stress syndrome
BPO	Business Process Outsourcing
CA	Copyright Act
CAGR	Compound annual growth rate
CBD	Central business district
CCM	Captive critical mass
CEO	Chief Executive Officer
CIO	Chief Information Officer
CMM	Capability maturity model
COR	Charge-out-rate
CPI	Communist party of India/Consumer price index
CPM	Communist party of India (Marxist)
CV	Curriculum vitae
EIU	Economist Intelligence Unit
EUR	Euro currency (€)
FIO	Firm of Indian origin
FO	Front office
GLOBE	Global Leadership and Organizational Behavior Effectiveness Research Project
HR	Human Resources
IIM	Indian Institute of Management
IIT	Indian Institute of Technology
IMF	International Monetary Fund
INC	Indian National Congress
INR	Indian Rupee currency
IOR	Indian Ocean Region
IP	Internet protocol
IPC	Indian Penal Code
ISB	Indian School of Business Hyderabad
ISDN	Integrated Services Digital Network
ISO	International Organization for Standardization
IT	Information Technology
ITA	Information Technology Act
ITES	IT enabled services
KPI	Key-performance indicator
LeT	Lashkar-e-Tayyaba

LPI	Leadership practices inventory
MBA	Master of Business Administration
MNC	Multinational Corporation
NASSCOM	National Association of Software and Services Companies
NCR	National capital region
NGO	Non-government organization
NRI	Non-resident Indian
ORC	Offshore resource center
ODC	Offshore development center
OWC	Overseas Women's Club
PGSEM	Postgraduate degree in software enterprise management
PIO	Person of Indian origin
PMP®	Project management professional
RBI	Reserve Bank of India
R&D	Research and development
SEI	Carnegie Mellon Software Engineering Institute
SEZ	Special economic zone
SIETAR	Society for Intercultural Education and Research
SIMI	Students Islamic Movement of India
SME	Small and medium sized enterprises
SPI	Software process improvement
SRA	Special Relief Act
STP	Software technology park
TCKs	Third culture kids
TCS	Tata Consultancy Services
UK	United Kingdom
US, USA	United States of America
USD	USD currency ($)
USSR	Union of Soviet Socialist Republics
Y2K	Year 2000

Throughout the book conversion from amounts in INR to USD is based on an exchange rate of 0.0238 as of May 2008; for converted amounts both the INR and USD amount is provided.

Any opinions expressed in this book are those of the author and not necessarily a view held by Capgemini as well.

References

Acharya P, Chintada V, Garg N, Jha J (2008) Case Study: Management Learning for Distributed Delivery from a Major Engagement in the CPR Industry. In: Hendel A, Messner W, Thun F (eds) Rightshore! Successfully Industrialize SAP Projects Offshore. Springer, Heidelberg

Agarwal H, Aggarwal V, Garg M, et al. (2007) Ragging in India. A Summary Report on Incidents, Social Perceptions and Psychological Perspectives. Coalition to Uproot Ragging from Education (CURE). http://www.noragging.com/analysis/CR2007_05-16_RaggingInIndiaSummary.pdf (accessed 23 Mar 2008)

Apte S, McCarthy JC, Ross CF, Bartolomey F, Thresher A (2007) Shattering the Offshore Captive Center Myth. Trends, Forrester Research

Arya AS (2000) Recent Developments toward Earthquake Risk Reduction in India. Current Science, Special Section Seismology 2000, Vol. 79 No 9, 10 Nov 2000. http://www.ias.ac.in/currsci/nov102000/1270.pdf (accessed 27 Aug 2008)

Ashkanasy NM (2007) The Australian Enigma. In: Chhokar JS, Brodbeck FC, House RJ (eds) Culture and Leadership Across the World. The GLOBE Book of In-Depth Studies of 25 Societies. Lawrence Erlbaum Associates, Mahwah (NJ)

Ashkanasy NM, Gupta V, Mayfield MS, Trevor-Roberts E (2004) Future Orientation. In: House RJ, Hanges PJ, Javidan M, Dorfman PW, Gupta V (eds) Culture, Leadership, and Organizations. The GLOBE Study of 62 Societies. Sage Publications, Thousand Oaks (CA)

Bagchi I, Mohan V (2007) Qauida Video Says Delhi on Hit List. The Times of India, 07 Aug 2007

Balaram G (2002) Mumbai's Spirit Largely Outweighs its Inconveniences, Say Expats. Times of India, 20 Oct 2002, http://timesofindia.indiatimes.com/cms.dll/articleshow? artid= 25702509 (accessed 18 Feb 2008)

Bartels R (1967) A Model for Ethics in Marketing. Journal of Marketing. Vol. 31 No 1, pp. 20-26

Basu K (2004) India's Emerging Economy: Performance and Prospects in the 1990s and beyond. The MIT Press

BBC 160502 (2002) Pakistan 'Prepared Nuclear Strike'. BBC News World South Asia. http://news.bbc.co.uk/1/hi/world/south_asia/1989886.stm (accessed: 10 May 2008)

BBC 110505 (2005) Gujara Riot Death Toll Revealed. BBC News World South Asia. http://news.bbc.co.uk/2/hi/south_asia/4536199.stm (accessed: 24 Aug 2008)

BCG Wharton (2007) What's Next for India: Beyond the Back Office. Special Report, The Boston Consulting Group and Wharton University of Pennsylvania

Bittinger S (2003) Expatriates Help Reduce Risk in Offshore Outsourcing. Gartner Group Research Note, TU-21-2151

Bittinger S, Iyengar P (2003) Indian Expatriates Help Bridge Cultural Gap in Offshore AD. Gartner Group Research Note, M-15-5318

Black JS, Gregersen HB (1999) The Right Way to Manage Expats. Harvard Business Review, Vol. 77 (2)

Bloch S, Whiteley P (2008) How to Manage in a Flat World. Get Connected to your Team – Wherever they are, FT Prentice Hall, New Delhi

Booth S (2007) Inspirational Variations? Culture and Leadership in England. In: Chhokar JS, Brodbeck FC, House RJ (eds) Culture and Leadership Across the World. The GLOBE Book of In-Depth Studies of 25 Societies. Lawrence Erlbaum Associates, Mahwah (NJ)

Bracken K, Carlucci J (2008) Case Study: Distributed Delivery of an SAP Solution at a US Life Science Company. In: Hendel A, Messner W, Thun F (eds) Rightshore! Successfully Industrialize SAP Projects Offshore. Springer, Heidelberg

Brass PR (2005) The Production of Hindu-Muslim Violence in Contemporary India. University of Washington Press

Brodbeck FC, Chhokar JS, House RJ (2007) Culture and Leadership in 25 Societies: Integration, Conclusions, and Future Directions. In: Chhokar JS, Brodbeck FC, House RJ (eds) Culture and Leadership Across the World. The GLOBE Book of In-Depth Studies of 25 Societies. Lawrence Erlbaum Associates, Mahwah (NJ)

Brodbeck FC, Frese M (2007) Societal Culture and Leadership in Germany. In: Chhokar JS, Brodbeck FC, House RJ (eds) Culture and Leadership Across the World. The GLOBE Book of In-Depth Studies of 25 Societies. Lawrence Erlbaum Associates, Mahwah (NJ)

Budhwar P, Luthar H, Bhatnagar J (2006) The Dynamics of HRM Systems in Indian BPO Firms. Journal of Labor Research, Vol. XXVII, No. 3, Summer 2006

Budhwar P, Varma A, Singh V, Dhar R (2006) HRM Systems of Indian Call Centres: an Exploratory Study. International Journal of Human Resource Management, Vol. 17 No 5, May 2006

Business Line 300408(2008) Tax waiver for STPI units to continue till March 2010. Business Line & The Hindu, 30 Apr 2008

Business Week 150208 (2008) Capgemini: 'Building a Global Powerhouse'. Business Week Newsmaker Q&A, 15 Feb 2008

Carl D, Gupta V, Javidan M (2004) Power Distance. In: House RJ, Hanges PJ, Javidan M, Dorfman PW, Gupta V (eds) Culture, Leadership, and Organizations. The GLOBE Study of 62 Societies. Sage, Thousand Oaks (CA)

Carmel E, Tjia P (2005) Offshoring Information Technology. Sourcing and Outsourcing to a Global Workforce. Cambridge University Press, Cambridge

Castel P, Deneire M, Kurc A, Lacassagne M-F, Leeds CA (2007) Universalism and Exceptionalism: French Business Leadership. In: Chhokar JS, Brodbeck FC, House RJ (eds) Culture and Leadership Across the World. The GLOBE Book of In-Depth Studies of 25 Societies. Lawrence Erlbaum Associates, Mahwah (NJ)

Chandra A, Rau P, Ryans JK (2002) India Business: Finding Opportunities in this Big Emerging Market. Paramound Market Publishing, Ithaca

Chhokar JS (2007) India: Diversity and Complexity in Action. In: Chhokar JS, Brodbeck FC, House RJ (eds) Culture and Leadership Across the World. The GLOBE Book of In-Depth Studies of 25 Societies. Lawrence Erlbaum Associates, Mahwah (NJ)

Chhokar JS, Brodbeck FC, House RJ (eds) (2007) Culture and Leadership Across the World. The GLOBE Book of In-Depth Studies of 25 Societies. Lawrence Erlbaum Associates, Mahwah (NJ)

CIA Worldbook (---) The World Factbook. http://www.cia.gov/library/publications/the-world-factbook (accessed 21 Mar 2008)

CNN 011006 (2006) India Police: Pakistan Spy Agency Behind Mumbai Bombings. CNN, 01 Oct 2006, http://edition.cnn.com/2006/WORLD/asiapcf/09/30/India.bombs/index.html?section=cnn_world (accessed 01 Aug 2007)

Coppa A, Bondioli L, Cucina A, Frayer DW, Jarrige C, Jarrige JW, Quivron G, Rossi M, Vidale M, Macchiarelli R (2006) Palaeontology: Early Neolithic Tradition of Dentistry. Nature, Vol. 440, April

Crystal D (2003) The Cambridge Encyclopedia of the English Language. Cambridge University Press, 2nd ed, Cambridge

Das G (2000) India Unbound. From Independence to the Global Information Age. Penguin Books, New Delhi

Davies P (2004) What's This India Business? Offshoring, Outsourcing and the Global Services Revolution. Nicholas Brealey International, London

De Luque MS, Javidan M (2004) Uncertainty Avoidance. In: House RJ, Hanges PJ, Javidan M, Dorfman PW, Gupta V (eds) Culture, Leadership, and Organizations. The GLOBE Study of 62 Societies. Sage, Thousand Oaks (CA)

DivorceRate (---) Divorce Rate in India. http://www.divorcerate.org/divorce-rate-in-india.html (accessed 22 Mar 2008)

Emrich CG, Denmark FL, den Hartog DN (2004) Cross-Cultural Differences in Gender Egalitarianism. In: House RJ, Hanges PJ, Javidan M, Dorfman PW, Gupta V (eds) Culture, Leadership, and Organizations. The GLOBE Study of 62 Societies. Sage Publications, Thousand Oaks (CA)

Farrell D, Laboissière M., Rosenfeld, J (2005) Sizing the Emerging Global Labor Market. The McKinsey Quarterly, No 3, pp. 93-103

Farrell D, Laboissière M, Rosenfeld J, Stürze S, Umezawa F (2005) The Emerging Global Labor Market: Part II – The Supply of Offshore Talent in Services. McKinsey Global Institute

Friedman T (2005) The World is Flat. A Brief History of the Globalized World in the Twenty-first Century. Allen Lane & Penguin Books, London

Gartner (2007) Dataquest Insight: India-Centric Service Providers Continue to Impact the IT Services Market, ID G00150179

Gelbrich K (2004) The Relationship between Intercultural Competence and Expatriate Success: A Structural Equation Model. Die Unternehmung, Vol 3/4 (58)

Gelfand MJ, Bhawuk DPS, Nishii LH, Bechtold DJ (2004) Individualism and Collectivism. In: House RJ, Hanges PJ, Javidan M, Dorfman PW, Gupta V (eds) Culture, Leadership, and Organizations. The GLOBE Study of 62 Societies. Sage, Thousand Oaks (CA)

Gereffi G, Wadhwa V, Rissing B, Kalakuntla K, Cheong S, Weng Q, Lingamneni N (2007) Framing the Engineering Outsourcing Debate: Placing the United States on a Level Playing Field with China and India. Duke School of Engineering. http://memp.pratt.duke.edu/downloads/duke_outsourcing_2005.pdf (accessed 03 Jan 08)

GlobalTalentMetrics (2008) Attrition in India. India's First and Most Comprehensive Research. Global Talent Metrics Executive Research Series, Global Talent Metrics in association with Summit, Alignmark, and IIM-B. Not yet published

Guha R (2007) India after Gandhi. Macmillan, London

Gupta RK (2005) India's Economic Agenda: An Interview with Manmohan Singh. McKinsey Quarterly, 2005 Special Edition Fulfilling India's promise

Hale K, de Souza R, Brown R, Potter K, Morikawa C (2008) Forecast: Outsourcing, Worldwide, 2000-2012. Gartner Dataquest Market Statistics, ID ITST-WW-DB-DA03, 25 Jun 2008

Hall E (1976) Beyond Culture. Anchor Books, New York

Hamm S (2007) India's Currency Problem. Business Week, http://www.businessweek.com/globalbiz/blog/globespotting/archives/2007/07/indias_currency.html (accessed 14 Jul 2008)

Hartog DND (2004) Assertiveness. In: House RJ, Hanges PJ, Javidan M, Dorfman PW, Gupta V (eds) Culture, Leadership, and Organizations. The GLOBE Study of 62 Societies. Sage, Thousand Oaks (CA)

HeadlinesIndia (2007) Over 3 Million Cases Pending in Courts. Headlines India, Vol. VII/151, 23 May 2007. http://www.headlinesindia.com/main.jsp?news_code=41562 (accessed 10 Aug 2007)

Hendel A (2008a) Offshore ERP Services. In: Hendel A, Messner W, Thun F (eds) Rightshore! Successfully Industrialize SAP Projects Offshore. Springer, Heidelberg

Hendel A (2008b) Case Study: Software Development for a Global Manufacturing Company. In: Hendel A, Messner W, Thun F (eds) Rightshore! Successfully Industrialize SAP Projects Offshore. Springer, Heidelberg

Hindu 160808 (2008) Ahmedabad Serial Blasts Mastermind among 10 Arrested. The Hindu, http://www.hindu.com/thehindu/holnus/000200808162171.htm (accessed 20 Aug 2008)

Hofstede G, Hofstede GJ (2005) Cultures and Organizations. Software of the Mind. McGraw Hill, New York

Hofstede G (---) Hofstede™ Cultural Dimensions. www.geert-hofstede.com (accessed 26 Jan 07)

Holmberg I, Åkerblom S (2007) Primus Inter Pares: Leadership and Culture in Sweden. In: Chhokar JS, Brodbeck FC, House RJ (eds) Culture and Leadership Across the World. The GLOBE Book of In-Depth Studies of 25 Societies. Lawrence Erlbaum Associates, Mahwah (NJ)

Holtbrügge D, Schillo K (2008) Managing from a Distance: Virtual Delegation to India. In: Hendel A, Messner W, Thun F (eds) Rightshore! Successfully Industrialize SAP Projects Offshore. Springer, Heidelberg

Hoppe MH, Bhagat RS (2007) Leadership in the United States of America: The Leader a Cultural Hero. In: Chhokar JS, Brodbeck FC, House RJ (eds) Culture and Leadership Across the World. The GLOBE Book of In-Depth Studies of 25 Societies. Lawrence Erlbaum Associates, Mahwah (NJ)

House RJ, Hanges PJ, Javidan M, Dorfman PW, Gupta V (eds) (2004) Culture, Leadership, and Organizations. The GLOBE Study of 62 Societies. Sage Publications, Thousand Oaks (CA)

House RJ, Javidan M (2004) Overview of GLOBE. In: House RJ, Hanges PJ, Javidan M, Dorfman PW, Gupta V (eds) Culture, Leadership, and Organizations. The GLOBE Study of 62 Societies. Sage Publications, Thousand Oaks (CA)

Howard S (2002) India and Pakistan Camped on Brink of War over Kashmir. Disarmament Policy, Vol. 65, Jul-Aug 2002, http://www.acronym.org.uk/dd/dd65/65nr01.htm (accessed 11 May 2008)

HSBC Global Research (2007) Rethinking the European Competitive Landscape

Huntley H (2005) Management Update: Five Reasons Why Offshore Deals Fail. Gartner Group Research, ID G00129077, 8 Jun 2005

Iyengar P (2006) Critical Mass is Necessary for Captive Centers to Succeed. Gartner Group Research, ID G00138230, 14 Mar 2006

Jalote P (2001) The Success of the SPI Efforts in India. Software Quality Professional, Mar 2001, http://www.cse.iitk.ac.in/users/jalote/papers/IndiaSPI.pdf (accessed 16 Jun 2008)

Javidan M (2004) Performance Orientation. In: House RJ, Hanges PJ, Javidan M, Dorfman PW, Gupta V (eds) Culture, Leadership, and Organizations. The GLOBE Study of 62 Societies. Sage Publications, Thousand Oaks (CA)

Javidan M, House RJ, Dorfman PW, Hanges, PJ, Sully de Luque M (2006) Conceptualizing and Measuring Cultures and their Consequences: a Comparative Review of GLOBE's and Hofstede's Approaches. Journal of International Business Studies, Vol. 37 No 6, Nov, pp. 897-914

Johnson G (1995) Cultural Atlas of India, Andromeda Oxford

Johnson J (2007) India's Steely Drive is Overcoming Jaded Colonial Attitudes. Financial Times, 03-04 Feb 2007, p. 8

Jones ML (2007) Hofstede – Culturally Questionable? Oxford Business & Economics Conference, Oxford (UK), 24-26 Jun 2007. http://ro.uow.edu.au/commpapers/370 (accessed 05 May 2008)

Kabasakal H, Bodur M (2004) Humane Orientation in Societies, Organizations, and Leader Attributes. In: House RJ, Hanges PJ, Javidan M, Dorfman PW, Gupta V (eds) Culture, Leadership, and Organizations. The GLOBE Study of 62 Societies. Sage Publications, Thousand Oaks (CA)

Kakar S, Kets de Vries M, Kakar S, Vrignaud P (2002) Leadership in Indian Organizations from a Comparative Perspective. IJCCM International Journal of Cross Cultural Management, Vol. 2(2) 239-50

Kapoor A (2007) An Economic Overview of India. In: Millar R (ed) Doing Business with India. GMB Publishing

Knotts R (1989) Cross-Cultural Management: Transformations and Adaptations. Business Horizons, Jan-Feb:29-33

Lambsdorff JG (2007) Corruption Perception Index. In: Transparency International (eds) Global Corruption Report 2007. Corruption in Judicial Systems. Cambridge University Press, Cambridge

Lawler J (---) http://www-personal.umich.edu/~jlawler/aue/indian.html (accessed 25 Feb 08)

Lifs (2008) Expats Swell in India. Little India. http://www.littleindia.com/news/128/ARTICLE/1976/2007-12-03.html (accessed 17.02.08)

Lindell M, Sigfrids C (2007) Culture and Leadership in Finland. In: Chhokar JS, Brodbeck FC, House RJ (eds) Culture and Leadership Across the World. The GLOBE Book of In-Depth Studies of 25 Societies. Lawrence Erlbaum Associates, Mahwah (NJ)

Luce E (2007) In Spite of the Gods: The Strange Rise of Modern India. Abacus

Mak D (2007) Bribe Payers Index (BPI) 2006. In Transparency International (eds) Global Corruption Report 2007. Corruption in Judicial Systems. Cambridge University Press, Cambridge

Manghan A, Wugmeister M, Titus D (2007) Outsourcing to India. Dealing with Data Theft and Misuse. Computerworld, 06 Jul 2007

Mehra P, Fitter PM, Rajendran M (2008) Inflation. Paying the Price. Business World, 07 Jul 2008

Messner (2008a) Offshoring in India: Opportunities in Risks. In: Hendel A, Messner W, Thun F (eds) Rightshore! Successfully Industrialize SAP Projects Offshore. Springer, Heidelberg

Messner (2008b) Economic and Business Effects of IT Offshoring. In: Hendel A, Messner W, Thun F (eds) Rightshore! Successfully Industrialize SAP Projects Offshore. Springer, Heidelberg

Messner (2008c) Intercultural Aspects of Project Management in India. In: Hendel A, Messner W, Thun F (eds) Rightshore! Successfully Industrialize SAP Projects Offshore. Springer, Heidelberg

Mukherji A (2008) We don't Need no Education... only Tuitions. Sunday Times of India, p. 17, 27 Apr 2008

Müller O (2006) Wirtschaftsmacht Indien. Chance und Herausforderung für uns. Carl Hanser, Munich

Nasscom (2007) Indian IT Industry: NASSCOM Analysis. http://www.nasscom.in/upload/5216/IT Industry Factsheet - Sep 07.pdf (accessed 30 Nov 07), Sep 2007

Nasscom (2008) Indian IT-BPO Industry: NASSCOM Analysis. http://www.nasscom.in/upload/5216/IT Industry Factsheet-Aug 2008.pdf (accessed 04 Sep 2008), Aug 2008

Naukrihub (2007) Training in IT / Software Industry.http://traininganddevelopment.naukrihub.com/training-scenario/it/ and related pages (accessed: 19 May 2008)

Negandhi AR, Palia AP (1988) Changing Multinational Corporation – Nation State Relationship. The Case of IBM in India. APJM Vol. 6 No 1, p. 15-38

ORC (2006) What are Companies Currently Doing for their Assignees in Bangalore and Mumbai, India? ORC Global Workforce, Quarterly Newsletter, Issue 37, http://timesofindia.indiatimes.com/Business/India_Business/Expat_managers_practice_what_they_preach_Study/articleshow/2753662.cms (accessed 18 Feb 2008)

NYT (1991) Company News. IBM in India. The New York Times, 29 Aug 1991

Pandit R (2008) China's Deep-sea Plans Alarm India. Times of India, 04 May 2008, p. 14

PTI (2008) Hefty Pay May Eat into Margins of Indian IT Cos. The Economic Times, p. 7, 26 May 2008

Rajeevan M, Subramanian M, Beligere P, Williams R (2007) Research Study of Captives in India and China: A Majority of Parent Organizations also Rely on Third-Party Relationships! Infosys Research, http://www.infosys.com/global-sourcing/white-papers/captives-research-study.pdf (accessed: 13 Jun 2008)

Ramachandran S (2004) India: The Crime of Politics. Asia Times, 28 Feb 2004, http://www.atimes.com/atimes/South_Asia/FB28Df04.html (accessed 24 Mar 2008)

Reber G, Szabo E (2007) Culture and Leadership in Austria. In: Chhokar JS, Brodbeck FC, House RJ (eds) Culture and Leadership Across the World. The GLOBE Book of In-Depth Studies of 25 Societies. Lawrence Erlbaum Associates, Mahwah (NJ)

Sahay A (2007) Political Background and Overview. In: Millar R (ed) Doing Business with India. GMB Publishing

Sako M (2006) Infosys Technologies: Challenges of Becoming a Truly Global Company. Case study, Saïd Business School, University of Oxford

Samuelsen (2008) How to Start a Rightshore® Project. In: Hendel A, Messner W, Thun F (eds) Rightshore! Successfully Industrialize SAP Projects Offshore. Springer, Heidelberg

Sankhe S (2007) Creating a Modern Indian city: An Interview with India's Chief Minister. The McKinsey Quarterly. Special edition: Building a better India

Sharma B (2004) Vistas for the Young in Foreign Tongue. The Tribune, Jobs & Careers, 12 Oct 2004, http://www.tribuneindia.com/2004/20041012/jobs/main1.htm (accessed 22 Mar 2008)

Singh S, Bindloss J, Clammer P, Eberle J, Harding P, Hole A, Horton P, Karafin A, Phillips M, Richmond S, Robinson M (2005) India. Lonely Planet, Victoria

Singh S (2008) Expat Managers Practice what they Preach, Times of India, 4 Feb 2008, http://timesofindia.indiatimes.com/Business/India_Business/Expat_managers_practice_what_they_preach_Study/articleshow/2753662.cms (accessed 18 Feb 2008)

Sinha D, Terdiman R (2002) Potential Risks in Offshore Sourcing. Gartner Group Market Analysis, ITSV-WW-DP-0360

Sinha JBP (1997) A Cultural Perspective on Organizational Behaviour in India. In: Earley CP, Erez M (eds) New Perspective on International Industrial/Organizational Psychology. New Lexington Press, San Francisco

Sivan J (2008) Chennai Set to Pip Bangalore, Hyderabad. Times of India, 09 May 2008

Storti C (2007) Speaking of India. Bridging the Communication Gap when Working with Indians. Intercultural Press/Nicholas Brealey Publishing, Boston (MA)

Subramanian M, Atri B (2006) Captives in India: A Research Study. Infosys Research, http://www.infosys.com/global-sourcing/white-papers/captives-research-v2.pdf (accessed 13 Jun 2008)

Thierry H, den Hartog DN, Koopman PL, Wilderom CPM (2007) Culture and Leadership in a Flat Country: The Case of the Netherlands. In: Chhokar JS, Brodbeck FC, House RJ (eds) Culture and Leadership Across the World. The GLOBE Book of In-Depth Studies of 25 Societies. Lawrence Erlbaum Associates, Mahwah (NJ)

Thun F (2008a) The Rightshore® Model. In: Hendel A, Messner W, Thun F (eds) Rightshore! Successfully Industrialize SAP Projects Offshore. Springer, Heidelberg

Thun F (2008b) Industrialization of Application Implementation. In: Hendel A, Messner W, Thun F (eds) Rightshore! Successfully Industrialize SAP Projects Offshore. Springer, Heidelberg

Thun F (2008c) Transforming the Front-office. In: Hendel A, Messner W, Thun F (eds) Rightshore! Successfully Industrialize SAP Projects Offshore. Springer, Heidelberg

Time (1947) The Trial of Kali. Time, Vol. L No 17, 27 Oct 1947

Times (2006) World University Rankings. The Times Higher Education Supplement, 06 Oct 2006. http://www.thes.co.uk/downloads/rankings/worldrankings2006.pdf (accessed 03 Aug 2007)

TOI 150906 (2006) Government Shuts over 600 Bangalore Schools. Times of India, 15 Sep 2006

TOI 060707 (2007) Kafeel was only Engineer in Family of Docs. Times of India, 06 Jul 2007

TOI 020607 (2007) It's Caste War: 5 Killed as Meenas, Gujjars Clash. Times of India, 02 Jun 2007

TOI 110208 (2008) Two Years on, Cops Name IISc Shooter. Times of India, 11 Feb 2008

TOI 140208 (2008) Maha Exodus: 10,000 North Indians Flee in Fear. Times of India, 14 Feb 2008

TOI 240208 (2008) 25,000 North Indians Leave Pune; Realty Projects Hit. Times of India, 24 Feb 2008

TOI 040508 (2008) Parties Unite to Slam Bush Food Remark. Times of India, 04 May 2008. http://timesofindia.indiatimes.com/India/Parties_unite_to_slam_Bush_food_remark/articleshow/3008540.cms (accessed: 11 May 2008)

TOI 250708 (2008) 8 Blasts Rock Bangalore. Times of India, 25 Jul 2008. http://timesofindia.indiatimes.com/articleshow/3279730.cms (accessed: 20 Aug 2008)

Umamaheswari R, Momaya K (2008) Role of Creative Marketing in 10X Journey: Case of IT Firms from India. IMR Indian Management Review, Vol 20 No 1, Mar 2008, pp. 113-130

Vermeer M, Neumann C (2008) Praxishandbuch Indien. Wie Sie Ihr Indiengeschäft erfolgreich managen. Kultur verstehen, Mitarbeiter führen, Verhandlungen gestalten. Gabler, Wiesbaden

Weibler J, Wunderer R (2007) Leadership and Culture in Switzerland – Theoretical and Empirical Findings. In: Chhokar JS, Brodbeck FC, House RJ (eds) Culture and Leadership Across the World. The GLOBE Book of In-Depth Studies of 25 Societies. Lawrence Erlbaum Associates, Mahwah (NJ)

Wharton (2007) Will Growth Slow Corruption in India? Knowledge @ Wharton, Forbes.com, http://www.forbes.com/2007/08/15/wipro-tata-corruption-ent-law-cx_kw_0814whartonindia_print.html (accessed 24 Mar 2008)

About the Author

Wolfgang Messner started his career in 1995 as a business analyst and international project manager for Deutsche Bank AG. Already in 1998, he was delegated to Deutsche Bank's Indian subsidiary Deutsche Software (India) Pvt. Ltd. as expatriate project manager, and his team in Bangalore was instrumental in making the core banking system compliant to the new Euro currency. Between 1999 and 2006, he consulted major European companies on business transformation projects with a focus on customer relationship management (CRM). In 2005, he accepted an invitation from the Indian Institute of Management Bangalore (IIM-B) and conducted a postgraduate MBA/PGSEM course on customer relationship management. After joining Capgemini in Germany in 2006, he again moved to India in early 2007. He is now on an assignment in Bangalore as director with Capgemini India responsible for offshore delivery for clients in Central Europe.

Wolfgang Messner holds a doctorate in marketing from the University of Kassel (Germany), an MBA from the University of Wales (UK), and an advanced degree in computing science (Dipl.-Inform.) from the Technical University Munich (Germany). He is author, co-author, resp. co-editor of four books, and has more than 25 papers in international journals and magazines to his credit.

Wolfgang Messner is married to Pratibha, an Indian national, and lives in Bangalore, India.

Index